GERMAN HUNTING GUNS OF THE GOLDEN ERA

1840–1940

HANS E. PFINGSTEN
(1937–2004)

GERMAN HUNTING GUNS OF THE GOLDEN ERA
1840–1940

BY

HANS E. PFINGSTEN

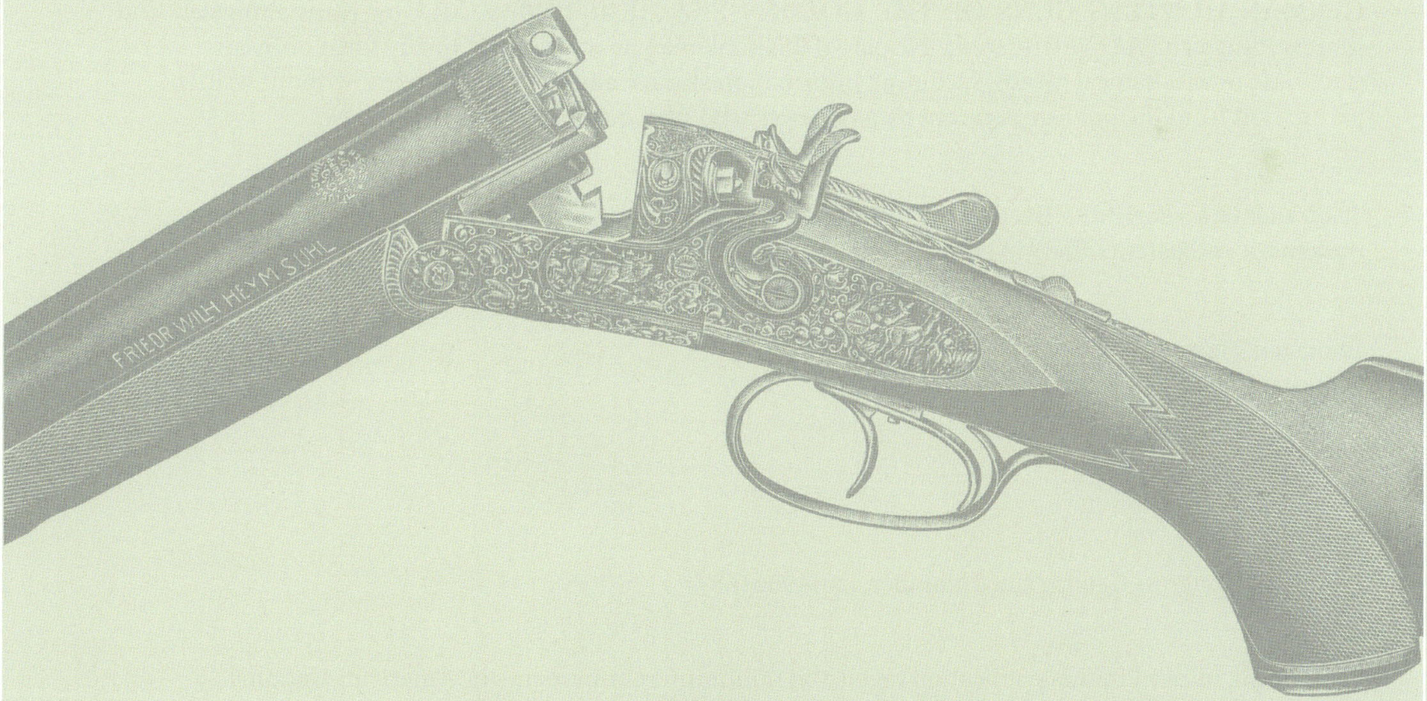

SAFARI PRESS INC.
Essex, Connecticut

SAFARI PRESS INC.

An imprint of Globe Pequot, the trade division of
The Rowman & Littlefield Publishing Group, Inc.
4501 Forbes Boulevard, Suite 200
Lanham, Maryland 20706

Distributed by NATIONAL BOOK NETWORK

Pfingsten, Hans
Pfingsten, Marcia

ISBN 978-1-57157-443-5

Library of Congress Catalog Card Number: 2014936168

∞™ The paper used in this publication meets the minimum requirements of American National Standard for Information Sciences—Permanence of Paper for Printed Library Materials, ANSI/NISO Z39.48-1992.

TABLE OF CONTENTS

PREFACE

This volume was written to acknowledge the work of craftsmen and artisans from an era that will never be seen again. German guns built before 1939 exhibited a high level of quality and finish. Collectors marvel at the subtle lines and superb craftsmanship of a Rasch or a Springer. Others find satisfaction using a beautiful Sauer shotgun made well before World War I and wonder at the history that gun has witnessed in its century of existence. Many people have had the thrill of picking up a fine old gun from Germany or Austria and are in awe of the level of engraving, fit, and finish. Hunters have delighted in carrying a drilling while walking through fields and in woods, for they knew that they were ready to take any game that presented itself. They, too, marveled at the geniuses of a bygone day that invented and built such a gun, and they offered up a sincere "thank you" for the quality of the firearm they carried in their endeavors in field and woods.

The severe restrictions that were placed on Germany after World War I brought hard years for all the gun makers. In the devastation following World War II, Germany was divided and two of the most prominent gunmaking centers were occupied by Russian troops. Many companies, large and small, closed their doors forever, and all their records, including the origins and the production of fine German sporting arms, were mostly lost. Consequently, it is a further purpose of this book to document, as much as possible, the existing knowledge of these guns; that said, fragments of the history will still remain. Collectors, hunters, artisans, and students of firearms history should all find features of interest within these pages.

The origins of these guns for those of us in North America lie far off in a land and culture very different from ours. For German natives, it is a story of home and a look at a unique part of their history and way of life. If this book can help illuminate that story and answer questions about the origins and cultural heritage of German and Austrian gunmaking, it will have served its purpose. It celebrates beauty and pride in workmanship that we are fortunate to witness.

ACKNOWLEDGMENTS

A book like this cannot be done without help. I would like to thank all those who gave so generously of their valuable time, trusted me with their pricey firearms, and contributed to this project immeasurably with their ideas and knowledge. With their assistance, this work became a reality.

Special thanks go to the following:
Bruce and Claudia Hamilton for their computer expertise.
George Hoyem whose knowledge and skill as editorial consultant contributed greatly to this book.

I would also like to thank:

Josef Ahammer
Peter Arfmann
Norman R. Blank
Peter Bezan
Hans Benders
Dieter Blum
Victor Brandl
Vern Brinkerhoff
George Brockner
Silvio Calabi
Shamus Daly
John Drake
Lars-Yngue Eckstrom,
Axel Eichendorff
Bob Elliot
Fredrik Franzen
Dr. Harald Friedrichs
Hans-Jürgen Fritze
Hendrik Frühauf
Marko Frühauf
Paul Goodwin
John Gangel
Jim Hallam
Allen Hallock
George Hoenig
Heinz-Gerd Hoffmann
Kirby Grahmam Hoyt
Jagen & Fischen
Reimer Johannsen
Rolf Kallmeyer
Knute Kolman
Wayne Koecher
Clair Kofoed
Walter Kolough
Bernhard Knöbel
Peter Koopmann
Michael Krause
Christoph Kuchenreuter
Martin Kuchenreuter
Cliff Labounty
Chuck Lailer
Roger Lake
J. P. Lamont
Christian Madsen
Alfred A. Mathes
David Moses
Thomas Müller
J. C. Munnell
Bill Munson
Ross Munson
John A. Neumann
David Nobel
Peter Oppenhuizen
Jean-Jacques Perodeau
Michael Petrov
Marianne Piacenza
A. J. (Gus) Planchon
Merton Proctor
Ed Reilly
Siegfried Richter
Al Rickli
Randy Rogers
Tom Roles
Ron Romanella
James Russell
Ross Seyfried
Jerry Smith
Eduard Stepanow
Robert Stepanow
Jeff Stephans
August Testa
Fritz Waniek
Hamilton Watkins
Dick Westbrook
Bill Wise
Frank Young

A note from Marcia Pfingsten:

I want to thank Dietrich Apel, Larry Schuknecht, and Dick and Kathy Hummel for their time and effort in proofreading the final manuscript. I would also like to thank Ludo Wurfbain of Safari Press for publishing my late husband's work.

INTRODUCTION

The term "German" as used in this book includes all areas of the former Prussian empire and any lands inhabited by German-speaking people. Likewise, "Austrian" includes regions of the former Austro-Hungarian Empire, ruled by the Habsburg princes. In the past it included Hungary, parts of Poland, Bohemia, Moravia, Serbia, Silesia, and Croatia. This book is a history of break-open shotguns, rifles, drillings, and combination guns produced in these countries during the period of 1840–1940. Information about the great tradition of German and Austrian bolt-action guns has been excluded because they have been documented in detail by other authors.

Research material has been gathered from many sources. These include old catalogs and ads, factory records, books, periodicals, individuals, and, of course, surviving firearms of the period covered in this book. Every effort has been made to be as accurate as possible, but, because of the arbitrary nature of historical research, there may be errors. This is by no means a complete record.

During World War II, the Allies targeted for destruction anything relating to arms and armament in Germany. Under the terms of surrender, the gunmaking center of Suhl was eventually left in the control of Soviet Russia. Any gun found was seized, and many wound up in the hands of the communist party hierarchy. The Soviet Union transported most gunmaking machinery and equipment east for use in the production of its military hardware. At the time of German reunification in 1989 and after nearly five decades of communist rule, scant information on gunmaking or the records of the gunmaking companies in Suhl survived.

Allied occupation troops seized thousands of arms and, unfortunately, destroyed many. Documented stories tell of piles of guns being run over in the streets by tanks. This happened to a collection of about thirty luxury guns owned by Karl Paul Merkel. War weary German civilians surrendered their weapons as ordered, but some hid or destroyed family heirlooms rather than relinquish them. Many of these guns were never recovered or were damaged beyond repair.

The miracle is that we have as many guns as we do to study and enjoy. GIs mailed many fine German and Austrian firearms back to the United States after unit commanders signed the appropriate forms. Fortunately, enterprising American soldiers brought home the so-called "duffel-bag gun" by the thousands. Without these clandestine efforts, many excellent examples of artistry would have undoubtedly been destroyed. These war souvenirs joined many other superb guns that had been imported from larger German firms, especially Sauer, before World War II.

Waffen tips

The reader will find Waffen tip boxes containing little-known and interesting facts distributed throughout the book.

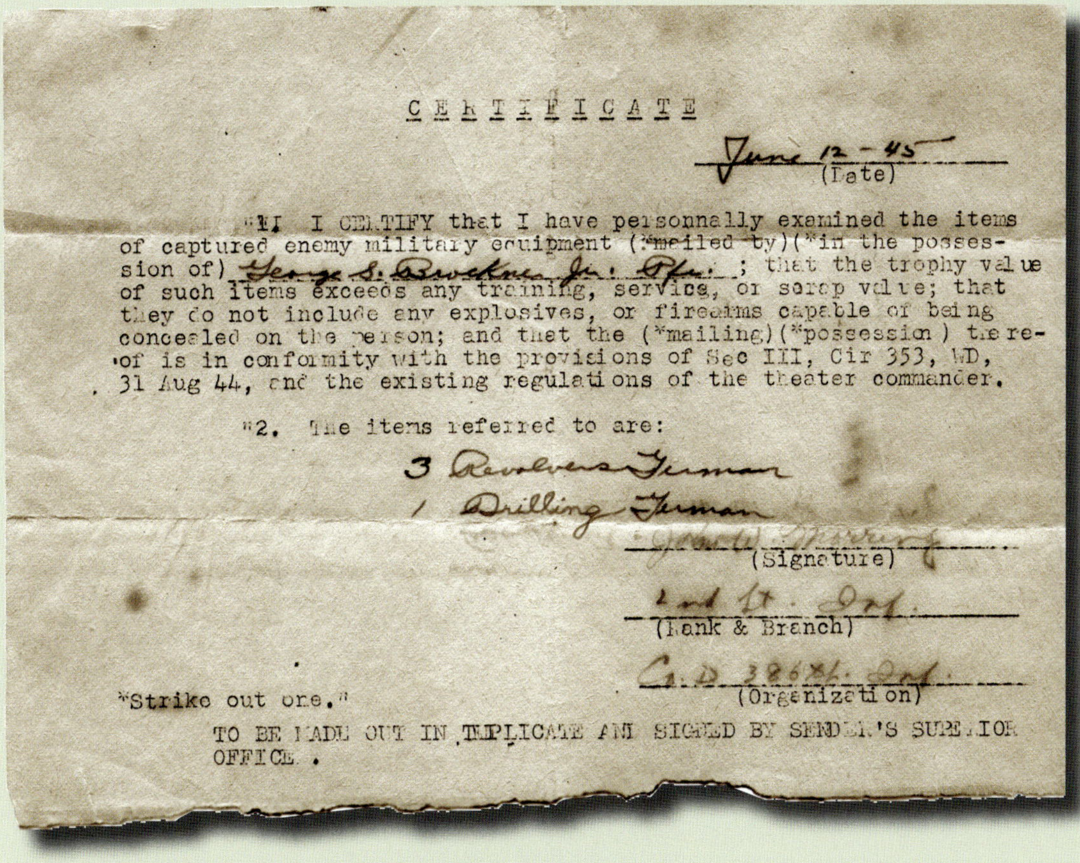

CERTIFICATE

June 12 - 45
(Date)

*1. I CERTIFY that I have personally examined the items of captured enemy military equipment (*mailed by)(*in the possession of) George S. Brockner Jr. Pfc. ; that the trophy value of such items exceeds any training, service, or scrap value; that they do not include any explosives, or firearms capable of being concealed on the person; and that the (*mailing)(*possession) thereof is in conformity with the provisions of Sec III, Cir 353, WD, 31 Aug 44, and the existing regulations of the theater commander.

*2. The items referred to are:

3 Revolvers German

1 Drilling German

(Signature)

2nd Lt. Inf.
(Rank & Branch)

Co. D 386th Inf.
(Organization)

Strike out one.

TO BE MADE OUT IN TRIPLICATE AND SIGNED BY SENDER'S SUPERIOR OFFICER.

U.S. Government certificates for bringing back firearms.

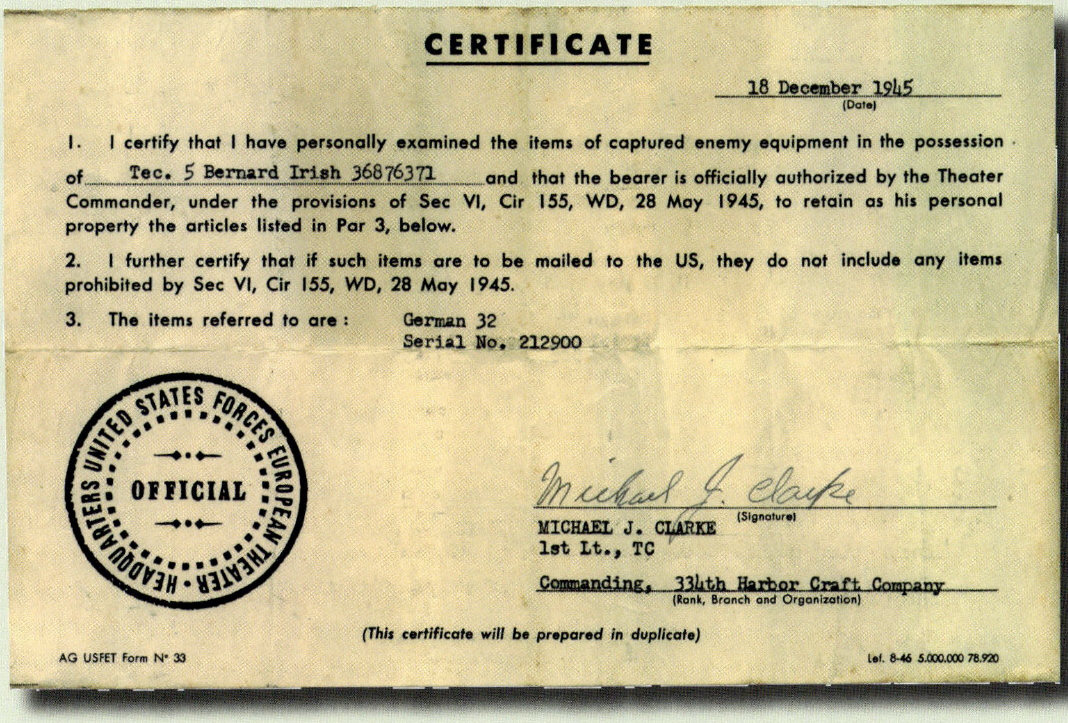

CERTIFICATE

18 December 1945
(Date)

1. I certify that I have personally examined the items of captured enemy equipment in the possession of Tec. 5 Bernard Irish 36876371 and that the bearer is officially authorized by the Theater Commander, under the provisions of Sec VI, Cir 155, WD, 28 May 1945, to retain as his personal property the articles listed in Par 3, below.

2. I further certify that if such items are to be mailed to the US, they do not include any items prohibited by Sec VI, Cir 155, WD, 28 May 1945.

3. The items referred to are: German 32
Serial No. 212900

HEADQUARTERS UNITED STATES FORCES EUROPEAN THEATER
OFFICIAL

Michael J. Clarke
(Signature)
MICHAEL J. CLARKE
1st Lt., TC

Commanding, 334th Harbor Craft Company
(Rank, Branch and Organization)

(This certificate will be prepared in duplicate)

AG USFET Form N° 33

Inf. 8-46 5.000.000 78.920

Part 1
Hunting

Introduction to Hunting

Hunting played an important role in food gathering in all early societies, and that included the Germanic tribes as well. Marksmanship and the ability to handle arms were necessary to defend a town or city anywhere, and citizens were called upon to prepare and train with weapons. These skills became the foundation for a long hunting tradition on the Continent.*

Noble families established vast estates for the primary purpose of hunting. In the Germanic culture, from the royal monarch to the gamekeeper, the pursuit of game and the associated rituals were held in the highest esteem. Rules of sportsmanship and a strict code dictated every aspect of the hunt: from the clean kill and the clothing of the hunter to the salute to the fallen prey at the end of the hunt. The great halls of the hunting lodges were lined with the trophies taken and honored in this manner. Even the language used by the hunting fraternity separated them from nonhunters. Because of the rules decreeing that animals would only be hunted using weapons and techniques worthy of the quarry and because quality was paramount in Teutonic societies, much cultural pride went into the production of fine hunting guns.

Game on the vast land holdings of the ruling classes had been managed for centuries by foresters and gamekeepers in the employ of the aristocracy. Kings and the nobility believed that hunting was their God-given right, and violators who infringed on it were punished severely. Large-scale social hunts were arranged regularly by nobles on their hunting estates. In many regions, local farmers and their servants were forced to work without compensation on these hunts.

Even though the middle of the nineteenth century brought reforms, state and government lands remained closed to the public for hunting. Wealthy landowners were able to stalk game on their own estates, and less affluent citizens were able to hunt only on leased parcels of land. Likewise, while members of the privileged nobility and the upper class stocked their gun rooms with a multitude of stalking rifles, double-rifles, and shotguns, the majority of the hunting fraternity could afford only one gun for game. This often meant the acquisition of one shotgun or cape gun, or, at a later time, a drilling. It also required that the owner of a combination gun become completely familiar with the firearm in order to master the safeties and varied features of the gun. There was an advantage to the hunter in this. If one sporting arm is always used in a number of different hunting situations, the owner will become expert in its handling.

Combination guns—a break-action hunting firearm that has at least two barrels—had several advantages. One was their versatility. Although they were often thought to be inaccurate, too heavy, or too complicated by some, gunmakers were constantly making improvements on the models and designs. These improvements were distinctly advantageous to the gunmaking industry. Because of these advances, over time combination guns increasingly became more popular. Not only was their

*It was also the start of target clubs and associations. In target shooting, members competed for prizes, and high honors were awarded to the best shots. The popularity of target shooting was later transferred to shooting games *(Schützenfeste)*, and this in turn further stimulated interest in sporting arms among a wider section of the populace.

Three German hunters about to leave on a morning duck hunt.

versatility valued by the hunter, but their workmanship and beauty attracted collectors.

As with anything inherently collectible, guns with certain barrel configurations were more in demand than others as hunting habits and conditions shifted. We can see this is still true today. Game, diminished in some areas, flourishes in others because of environmental changes, and any change in the choice of prey will be reflected in the selection of the firearm to be used in its pursuit.

Today, Europe remains the source of the combination gun because of tradition but also because a great number of species can still be hunted in the same area during the same time frame. Thus Europeans, especially those in the German-speaking countries as well as in Scandinavia and Eastern Europe, remain loyal to the combination gun.

Court hunts in the seventeenth century were elaborately staged.

Return from a mountain hunt.

Prince Carl Friedrich (left) was heir to the principality of Wied-Neuwied, an area near Koblenz on the Rhine River. His brother, Prince Maximilan (right), was a noted naturalist who explored the Missouri River in 1832. They are posed here in their hunting gear, circa 1840.

Hunting party in the Rhine Palatinate about 1890.

This vintage photo shows a small hunting party of local businessmen and farmers near the village of Lockstedt in northern Germany at the turn of the twentieth century. This photograph was taken in the fall. On the far left the local pub owner poses with bottle and glass, trademark of his occupation. Undoubtedly, the members of this group had fortified themselves against the inclement weather by warming themselves with a traditional shot or two of "target" water to improve their aim!

The guns shown are all double-barrel hammer shotguns with the exception of the hammer drilling held by the seated gentleman in the center. His gun is a 16/16 gauge with an 11mm rifle barrel, a popular caliber at that time. One or two guns appear to be pinfire (Lefaucheux) shotguns, probably of Belgian manufacture. They show the characteristic hinged-steel fore-ends, underlevers, and ornate trigger guards. Slugs or possible buckshot (Rehposten) were used to bring down the roebuck deer.

Game

Moose, male
Moose, female and calves
Red deer, male
Fallow & sika deer, male
Red, fallow & sika deer, female & calves
Mouflon, male
Mouflon, female & lambs
Roe deer, male
Roe deer, female mouflon
Chamois
Alpine marmots
Brown hares & mountain hares
Seals
Badgers
Pine marten & stone marten
Capercaillie, black grouse, & crossbreeds
Hazel grouse, ptarmigan, & rock ptarmigan
Partridges
Pheasants
Wood pigeons
Woodcocks
Snipes & curlew
Greater busters
Geese
Ducks
Buzzards, fish-eating ducks, & seagulls

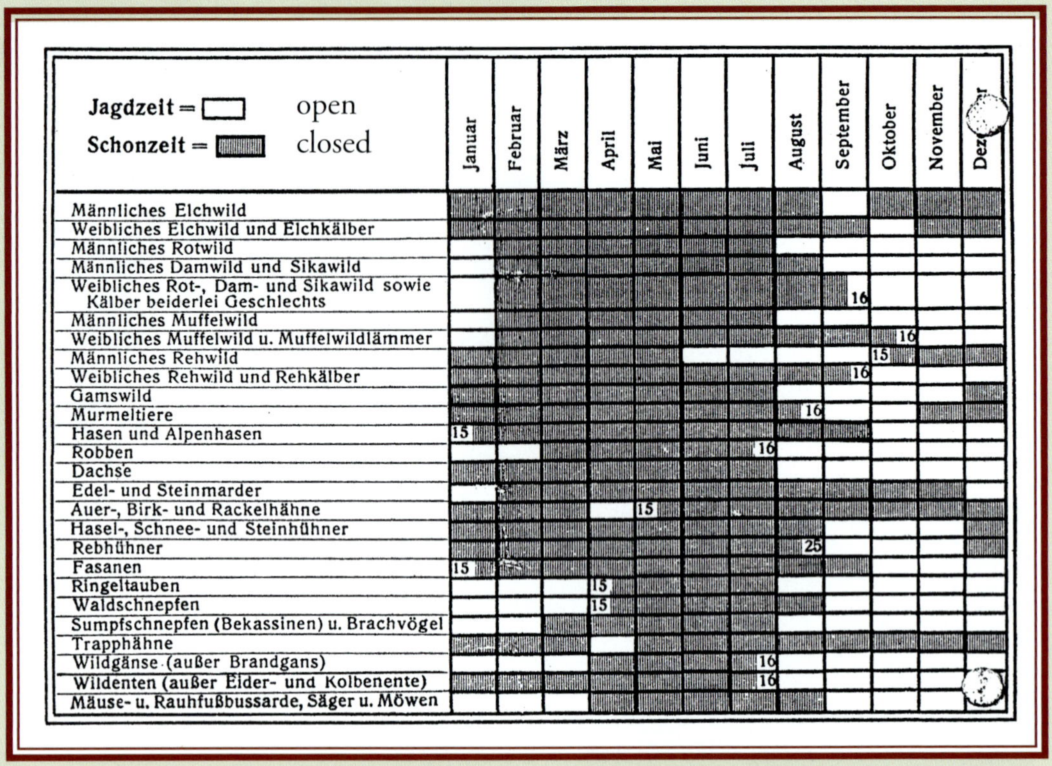

This list, part of a 1937 German hunting license, shows clearly the overlapping hunting seasons of different game. A hunter, therefore, could stalk seals—if his hunting area included the coastline—as well as deer and ducks on the same day at the same location. A combination gun such as a drilling was the preferred hunting firearm of the day.

Waffen tips

Using buckshot to hunt deer was once permitted in Europe but is now prohibited.

Hunting Mansions and Lodges

Throughout the past centuries, the nobility viewed hunting as their privilege, and it was an important part of their elite position. They built and maintained hunting lodges where they and their guests hunted for pleasure. All over Europe these mansions ranged from simple manor houses to hunting palaces and every kind of chalet, chateau, and castle in between. Often they were staffed by an army of servants, foresters, carriage drivers, and gun handlers who were kept busy preparing elaborate social hunting and shooting events. Large rooms, halls, and corridors displayed record trophies, firearm collections, and paintings and tapestries of the hunt. These were designed to show off the nobles' wealth to visiting monarchs and dignitaries. Yet there were aristocrats who chose to seek the solitude of a simple hunting lodge high in the mountains or deep in an untouched part of the country where they could temporarily return to a simpler way of life.

The Prussian kings maintained one of their hunting mansions at a lake just outside Berlin in the Grunewald (Green Forest). Built in the Baroque architectural style, it was the center of activity during the annual fall hunt. Today it houses an extensive collection of sporting arms and accoutrements.

Archduke Johann of Austria dressed in simple green attire. He favored a single-shot stalking rifle, which he loaded and cleaned himself. (This was customarily done by a servant.) His respect for game and its preservation was well known.

Waffen tips

Stalking rifles used in the mountains were stocked to the muzzle to reduce damage to the barrel when climbing.

In 1885, Crown Prince Rudolf joined his father, Emperor Franz Joseph of Austria, on a hunt in the Austrian mountains. Consumed by hunting fever, Prince Rudolf shot at a stag that was running in the direction of the sovereign's stand. The bullet went wide and seriously wounded a gunbearer in the arm, missing Franz Joseph by inches. The emperor paid the wounded man on the spot for his suffering and told him never to talk about the incident to anyone.

Crown Prince Rudolf of Austria.

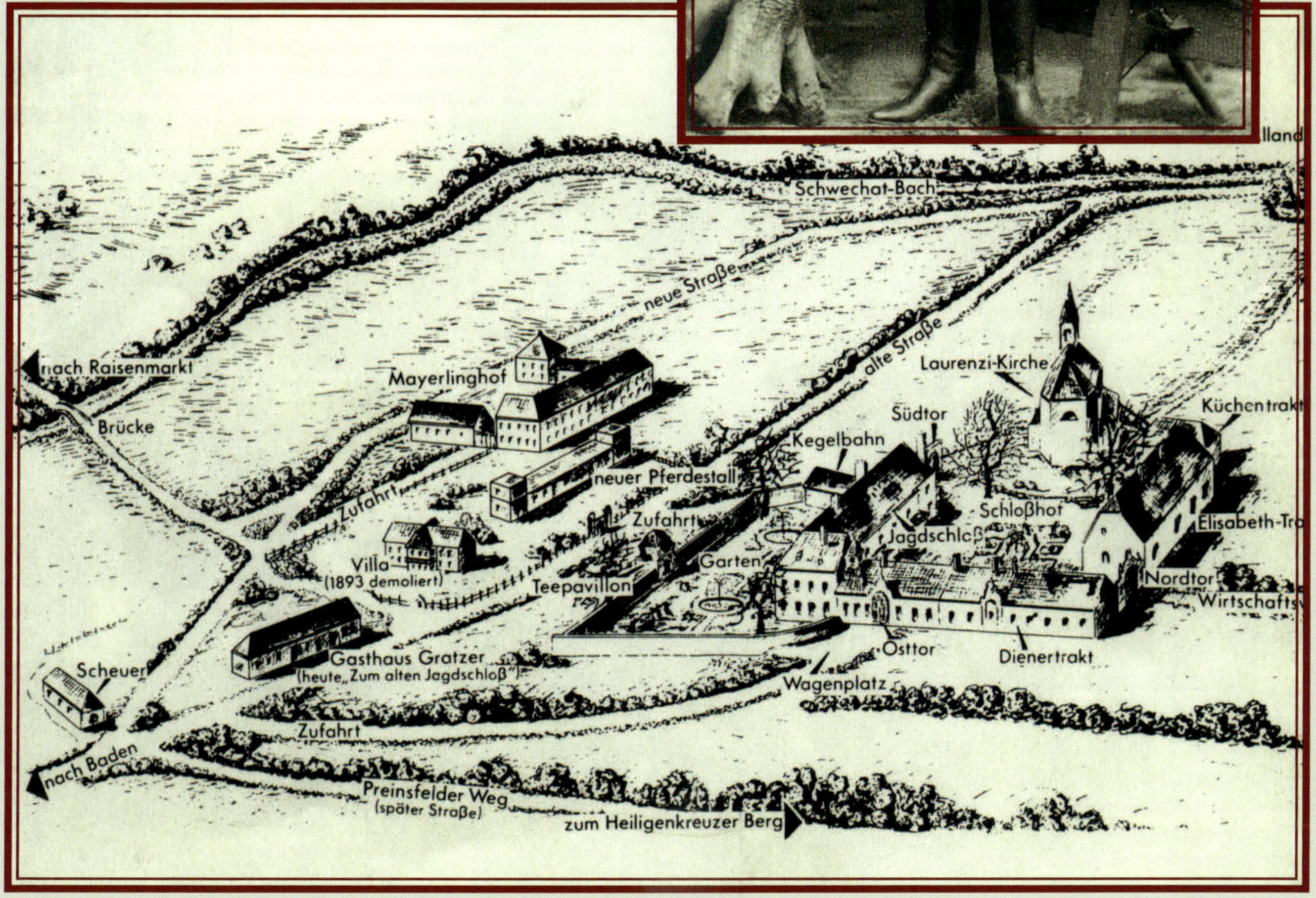

Mayerling, the hunting palace of Crown Prince Rudolf, was the scene of many social hunting events. It was also the place where Rudolf and his lover, Baroness Mary Vetsera, committed suicide in January 1889.

Annual hunts were a social event attended by emperors and kings. Baron de Rothschild conducted an annual hunt until well into the twentieth century. The opulence of the estate of this wealthy financier outside Paris, France, contrasts greatly with the mountain hunting cabin of Prince Regent Luitpold seen in the picture below.

Prince Regent Luitpold (1821–1912) of Bavaria (center with beard) in front of his hunting chalet after a hunt for European red deer (Rothirsch).

Royal Hunts

"Hunting is His Majesty's passion," was certainly an apt phrase for quite a few continental rulers. The German Emperor Kaiser Wilhelm II, for one, was obsessed with hunting. Although handicapped because of a congenital deformity of his left arm, he was an excellent marksman who tirelessly pursued record trophies of game that roamed his vast forests and hunting grounds.

The Kaiser shot with his right arm only, often using the rail of a blind or the branch of a tree to steady his aim. At times, the Kaiser used his gamekeeper's shoulder to support his gun, and it was reported that this forester, on occasion, had to clamp his hand over the rear sight of the wildly swinging gun barrel until His Majesty had mastered his hunting fever and calmed down enough to pull the trigger.

The Kaiser preferred light, break-open double rifles, side-by-side shotguns, and Mauser bolt-action rifles in calibers 16mm and 8mm. His hammerless bird guns in 20-gauge, fitted with ejectors and stocked without

The German emperor (right) hunting with his uncle King Edward VII of England (left). On the Continent, the Kaiser liked to hunt in the Alps and in Hungary with the Austrian Emperor Franz Joseph, his son Crown Prince Rudolf, and his nephew Archduke Ferdinand. In Russia, he stalked elk, bear, stag, and wolf with his cousin Czar Nicholas II. As the grandson of Queen Victoria, the Kaiser hunted wild fowl and foxes in England.

This group of foresters is getting ready to signal the conclusion of the hunt. They will now honor the kill, a centuries-old tradition still practiced today. Note the small flags (Lappen) emblazoned with the Prussian eagle, which is noticeable on the left behind the line of uniformed foresters. These flags were employed to cordon off stretches of the forest to drive game along predetermined routes.

a cheekpiece, were special orders from the shop of Wilhelm Förster, court gunsmith *(Hofbüchsenmacher)* in Berlin, and gunmaker Johann Jakob Reeb in Bonn. For hunting hare, he used 16-gauge shotguns that were more solidly built to withstand heavy use. Kaiser Wilhelm, at times, expended up to 1,000 rounds a day in firing four shotguns. The double barrels of some of his guns were not soldered together but connected with flexible steel rings, which was a method pioneered by the Fluid Steel Division of Krupp, in Essen. This system never caught on in the English-speaking world.

King Edward VII of England.

In this picture, the Kaiser (center in uniform) socializes at his hunting lodge in the Grunewald, a forest outside Berlin. An invitation to attend a royal court hunt was a high honor.

Kaiser Wilhelm (background, far left) waiting for the drive to begin and talking to his head forester (second from left), while a gamekeeper readies the rifles (third from left).

Note the hunting sword worn by the aide in the foreground. It was worn on the left side, underneath the coat on a belted hanger, with the grip extending through an opening in the tunic.

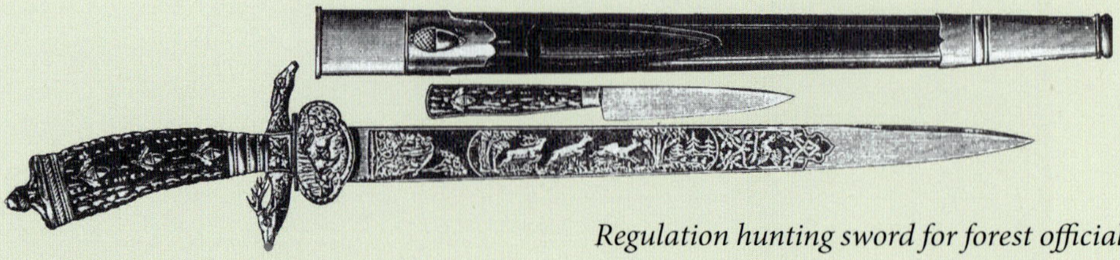

Regulation hunting sword for forest officials.

Belt for carrying hunting sword.

These deer and wild pigs were the result of a day's hunt. The animal population on the Kaiser's estates was well managed by an army of foresters and gamekeepers for his pleasure and that of his court. Royal hunts were highly organized affairs, planned to the last detail and resulting in a high number of kills. Kaiser Wilhelm, normally very affable, became unhappy when the preparation and execution of a hunt did not go as planned. When he did not shoot enough game, he became infuriated, and the forester in charge took the brunt of his displeasure. Members of his hunting party were mindful not to shoot more game than His Majesty.

The Kaiser (third from the right above) and the person on the far right (above) carry fur muffs suspended from a leather sling around their necks. This was a fashionable hunting accessory for a gentleman hunter, and it was used to keep his hands warm.

This soft-lined hunting muff was made from fox fur and has a pocket for cartridges.

A regulation ivory-handle hunting sword and knife for middle and upper forestry personnel.

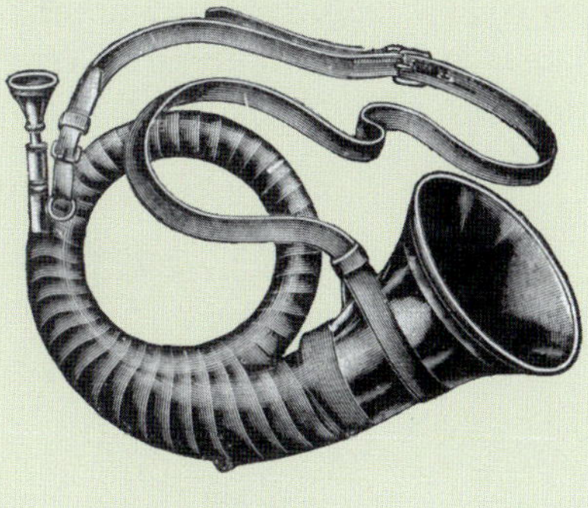

Hunting horn.

Archduke Franz Ferdinand and his wife, the Countess of Hohenberg, are surrounded by foresters and beaters in the Austrian Alps. Franz Ferdinand, heir to the throne of the Austro-Hungarian Empire, was an excellent marksman. Their assassination sparked World War I.

After weeks of preparations by his foresters, the Archduke went on shooting binges with two gun loaders handing him loaded double rifles and a forester calling the shots. Wooden staffs to aid in climbing and steady rifles were used extensively by hunters and drivers alike. After a hunt, the Archduke inspected all downed animals and compared his count to the records kept by his forester during that hunt. If he was satisfied with the accuracy, he signed the list. Through meticulously kept records of his kills, we know that he shot an unbelievable 272,571 game animals during his lifetime.

Dignitaries and guests arrive at a meeting place for refreshments after the hunt. Every guest was encouraged to wear green hunting attire. It consisted of a hunter's hat or cap, a double-breasted tunic, dark green breeches, and knee-high boots. A hunting sword (Hirschfänger) with an ivory or stag handle completed the habit. Imperial foresters (Förster) *wore a similar uniform with braided green shoulder boards and silver acorns, which designated their ranks in the forest service.*

Waffen tips

Kaiser Wilhelm's preferred caliber was the 6mm because of its slight recoil.

THE LEGEND OF SAINT HUBERTUS

Saint Hubertus, circa 656–727 AD, was the first Bishop of Liège. He was a Christian saint—paganism still existed at the time—and the patron saint of hunters, mathematicians, opticians, and metalworkers. He was also known as the Apostle of the Ardennes. For centuries Saint Hubertus has been called upon to give protection to the hunter against attacks from wild beasts, accidents in handling weapons, and the ravages caused by rabies.*

There are several sagas going back centuries surrounding Saint Hubertus and Hubertus fraternities. The following is the generally accepted version of how he became the patron saint of hunters: From a very early age, Hubertus, like many nobles of his time, was addicted to the chase. Hubertus was the eldest son and heir apparent to the Duke of Aquitaine, and he lived at court, partaking in hunts frequently. After his wife died giving birth to their son, Hubertus retreated from the court, withdrew into the forested Ardennes, and gave himself up entirely to hunting.

One Good Friday morning when the faithful were crowding into churches, Hubert was again out hunting. As he pursued a magnificent stag, the animal turned, and, as the legend states, Hubertus was astounded when he saw a crucifix perched between its antlers. Suddenly, he heard a voice saying, "Hubertus, unless thou turnest to the Lord and leadest a holy life, thou shalt quickly go down into hell."

*Rabies was carried by game animals, and there was no antidote for the dreaded disease until Pasteur and Roux developed the first rabies vaccination in 1885. A Saint Hubert's Key was used in Europe until the early twentieth century as a traditional cure for rabies and was named for Saint Hubertus, the patron saint of hunters. The key was a metal nail or bar that had a decorative head. The key was heated, and the head pressed to the area where a person had been bitten by an animal believed to have rabies. If performed immediately after having been bitten, the victim was sometimes saved. The heat would cauterize and sterilize the wound, killing the rabies virus. The practice was endorsed by the Catholic Church, and keys were used by priests at places where Saint Hubertus was associated.

Hubertus motifs are engraved on many drillings and combination guns and found on various hunting accessories.

This is a deeply chiseled receiver plate.

Hubert dismounted, prostrated himself, and said, "Lord, what wouldst Thou have me do?"

He received the answer, "Go and seek Lambertus, and he will instruct you."

Profoundly affected by the vision, the count became a disciple of Bishop Lambertus of the town of Liège and, after a pilgrimage to Rome, was himself ordained bishop by the Pope. Hubertus is credited with the Christianization of the Ardenne region of Germany.

Sankt Hubertus (German) is honored among sport hunters as the originator of ethical hunting behavior. During Hubert's religious vision, the stag is said to have lectured Hubertus about holding animals in high regard and having compassion for them as God's creatures with a value in their own right. Certain ethical principles of hunting are said to have come from this lecture: The hunter ought to shoot only when a humane, clean, and quick kill is assured. He ought to shoot only old stags past their prime breeding years and to relinquish a much-anticipated shot on a trophy to instead euthanize a sick or injured animal that might appear on the scene. Further, one ought never shoot a female with young in tow so as to assure the young will have a mother to guide them to food during the winter. Such is the legacy of Hubert who still today is taught and held in high regard in the extensive and rigorous German and Austrian hunter-education courses. To this day, 3 November is celebrated in his honor as Saint Hubertus Day.

Facing page: The fountain of the Weaponsmith (Waffenschmiedebrunen), located in the Suhl town square.

PART 2
GUNMAKERS

Suhl, the City of Weapons *(Waffenstadt)*

Soft, malleable iron ore, found in abundance in the hills surrounding a valley in the Thuringian Forest, first attracted miners around 800 AD. Initially raw ore was shipped and traded to other regions, but eventually ironsmiths settled in the valley and the tiny village of Suhl was established. There the early settlers found plentiful wood for charcoal to smelt ore and water to power hammers, making this area advantageous for local craftsmen. They forged, traded, and sold farming implements like shovels, scythes, and plows. They also produced military hardware at competitive prices: iron points for arrows and bolts for crossbows. These endeavors resulted in steady growth for the settlement.

This painting by German artist Erich Buchholz (1891–1972) shows the city of Suhl around the turn of the twentieth century.

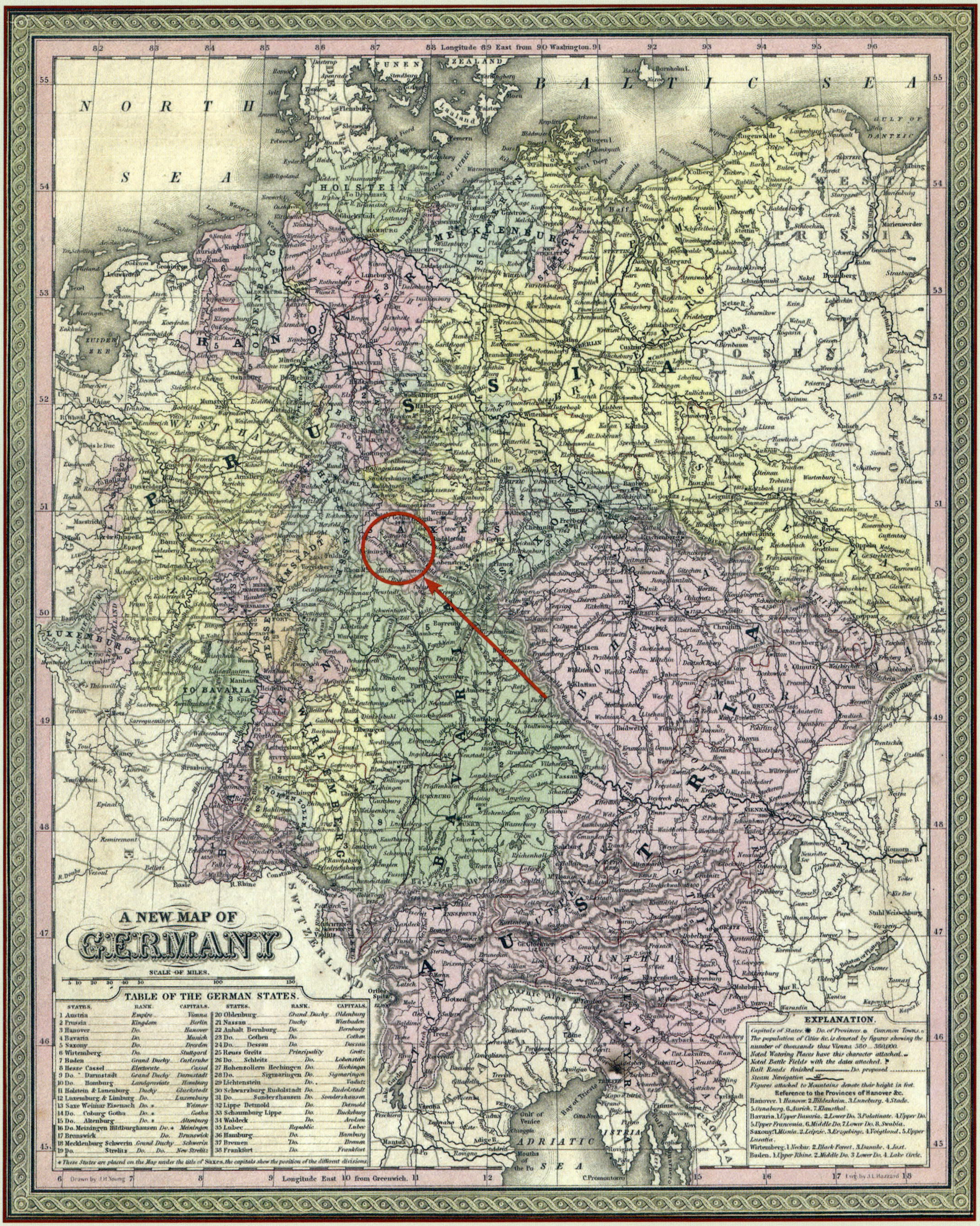

Map of Germany in 1850.

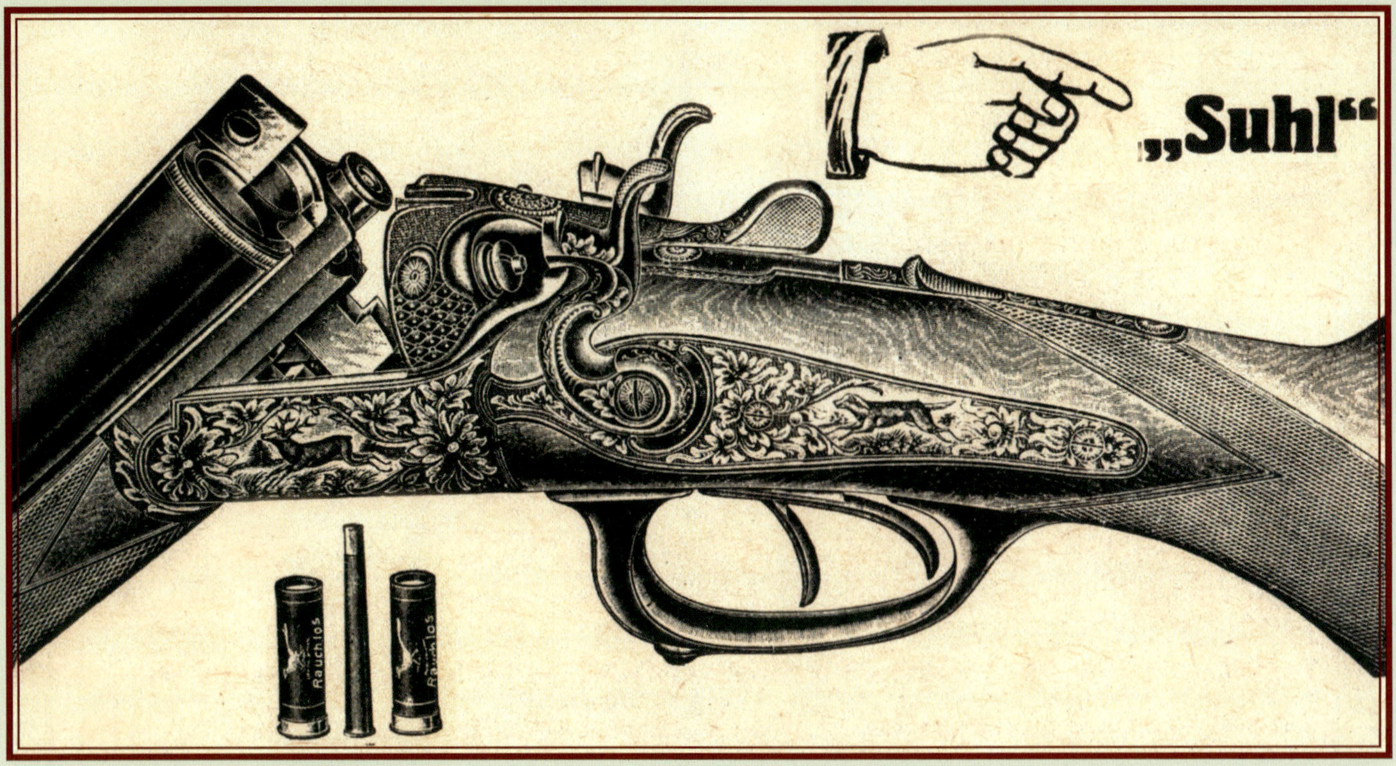

Advertisement for a hammer drilling, handmade in Suhl. Firearms from Suhl became known throughout the world for their quality and performance. Sporting firearms excelled because of the care and attention given to the detail of the mechanisms, the fit of gun parts, and their harmonious form.

Around 1000 AD, craftsmen and artisans in Suhl were producing a multitude of weapons and armor. Helmets, breastplates, shields, and sword blades were forged for knights and noblemen. By 1470, eight-hundred people worked in the iron mines in the area. In the early 1500s, Suhl gun-barrel smiths produced barrels for firearms that could penetrate the armor of knights. Gun, lock, and stockmakers were in demand. The gunmakers of the town produced matchlock, wheellock, flintlock, and percussion weapons. Princes and rulers were quick to order these inexpensive, functional military weapons by the thousands. Once it was established as a center for gunmaking, Suhl began to attract talented artisans from France, England, Austria, Belgium, and other countries. These artisans brought with them ideas and techniques practiced in gunmaking elsewhere.

During times of war, guns were sold to any fighting faction. If a gunmaker received a large order for military muskets that exceeded his capacity, he would contract other local firms for the production of subassemblies. Sometimes he would form an alliance or partnership with other manufacturers to fulfill a contract. During peacetime, Suhl gunmakers crafted firearms for the hunter, developed defensive weapons, and produced luxury arms for kings and noblemen.

Wilhelm Brenneke

The name "W. Brenneke" is found on headstamps, in caliber descriptions, and on shotgun ammunition the world over. Wilhelm Brenneke was born the second oldest of eight children in Hannover, Germany, in 1865. Early in life he showed an ability to draw and to understand technical concepts. As a small boy, he wandered about the countryside with a bow and arrow. He developed an unbounded enthusiasm for hunting and for all kinds of sporting arms and their performance.

It came as no surprise to his family that he wanted to learn the gunmaking trade. At the age of fourteen, he tried to become an apprentice to the well-known gunmaker Scherping of Hannover. To his great disappointment, he was turned down. Scherping advised him against learning the gun trade because he did not see a future in it. Wilhelm Brenneke went to work for a locksmith instead and finished his apprenticeship building safes. Interested in many technical fields, he found employment as a journeyman boilermaker, and, after moving to Hamburg in 1883, he worked for a lock and safe company.

After finishing his military service in the Imperial German Navy, where he was a machinist on a torpedo boat, Wilhelm moved to the city of Leipzig. There he started selling books by traveling from village to village on a bicycle. This venture proved a financial success, and soon his mail-order business had twenty employees. Financially secure, he married at the age of twenty-seven and three years later founded the Wilhelm Brenneke Gewehr und Geschossfabrik in Leipzig. It was his passion to develop highly accurate and extremely powerful hunting projectiles. The company remains in the hands of his descendants today.

In this family photo, Wilhelm Brenneke poses in the center, fourth from the left.

DEUTSCHES REICH

Zeugniss
über die Befähigung
zum
Maschinisten dritter Klasse
auf Deutschen Seedampfschiffen.

Machinist certificate.

Wilhelm Brenneke was an ardent hunter, committed to clean "kills" in order to spare the game unnecessary pain. He tested, developed, and improved his own bullets while hunting on his estate by keeping precise records of his shots and their effect on the game. Brenneke poses in this photo with a trophy stag.

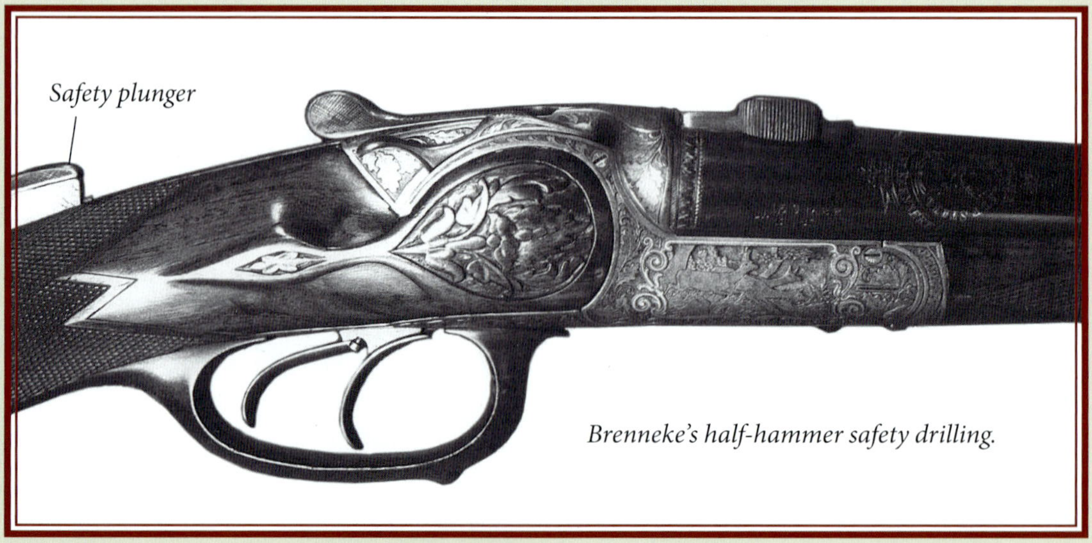

Brenneke's half-hammer safety drilling.

Having experimented with guns and ammunition, Brenneke bought Reichert's gun shop in Leipzig and opened the Wilhelm Brenneke Rifle and Bullet Factory (Wilhelm Brenneke Gewehr und Geschossfabrik). *He soon opened a branch in the town of Suhl under the management of Konrad Heym, and it was there he developed and patented his new safety drilling. The self-cocking, half-hammer drilling with four safeties was not a financial success. The cost of making this handfitted, hand-engraved gun remained too expensive. After seven years, Brenneke halted the production of this now rare sporting firearm.*

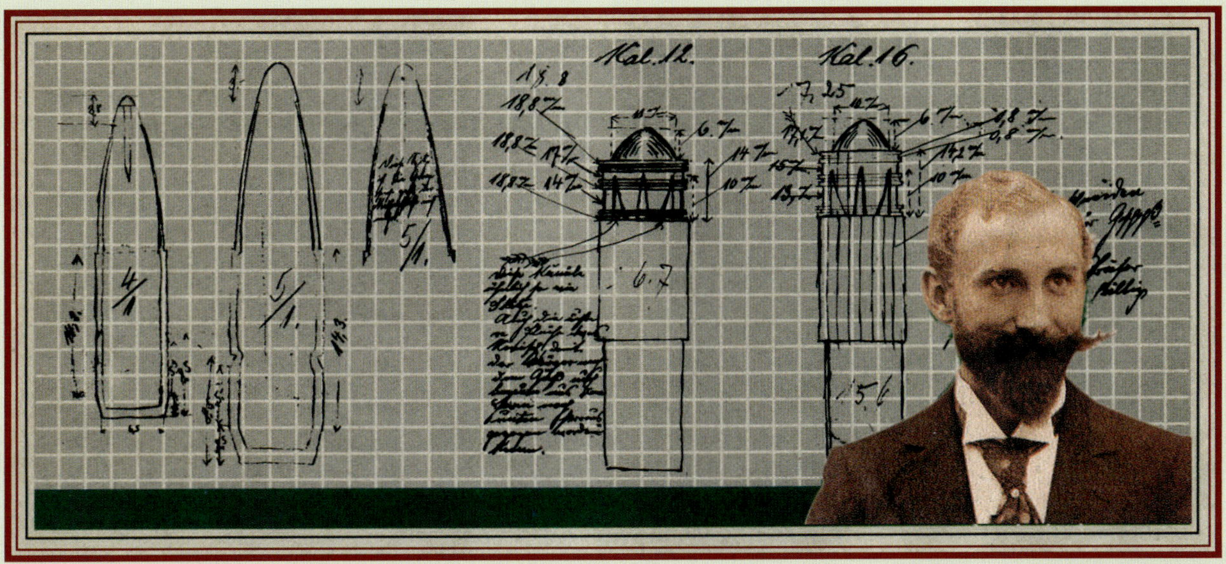

In 1897 Brenneke introduced his new lead-alloy bullets, followed in 1898 by the production of his first shotgun slugs.

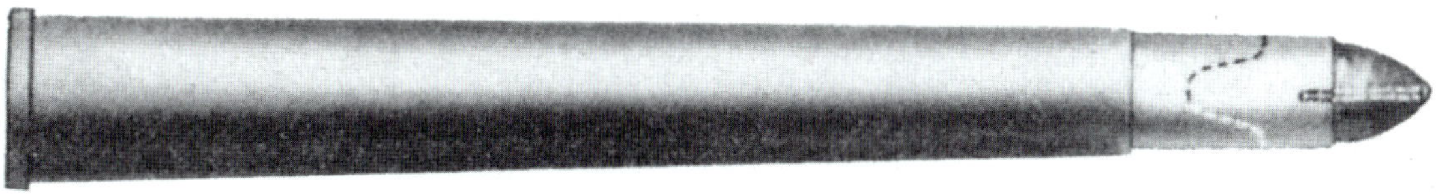

Steel tipped later model

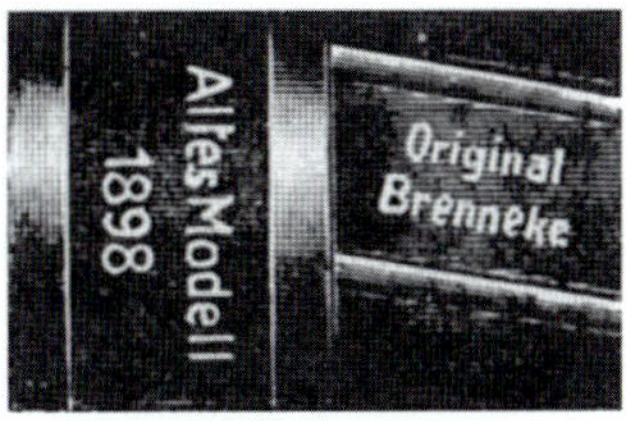

Original model 98

One of several cartridges Wilhelm Brenneke developed in 1898 was the 8x72R with a "Torpedo-Ideal-Bullet" and the 16-gauge shotgun slug. The success of Brenneke slugs (Flintenlaufgeschosse) *was due to their well-balanced design. Their accuracy offered the farmer and hunter an alternative to buckshot.*

As a passionate automobile enthusiast who participated in numerous rallies, Wilhelm Brenneke branched out into the automobile trade. Between 1900 and 1930, the Brenneke company represented French firms Dion-Bouton, Clément-Bayard, Renault, and the German Horch, Dixi, and Essex automobiles.

At the industrial hunting show and exhibition in Berlin in 1937.

Brenneke standing at the left during a 1925 rally.

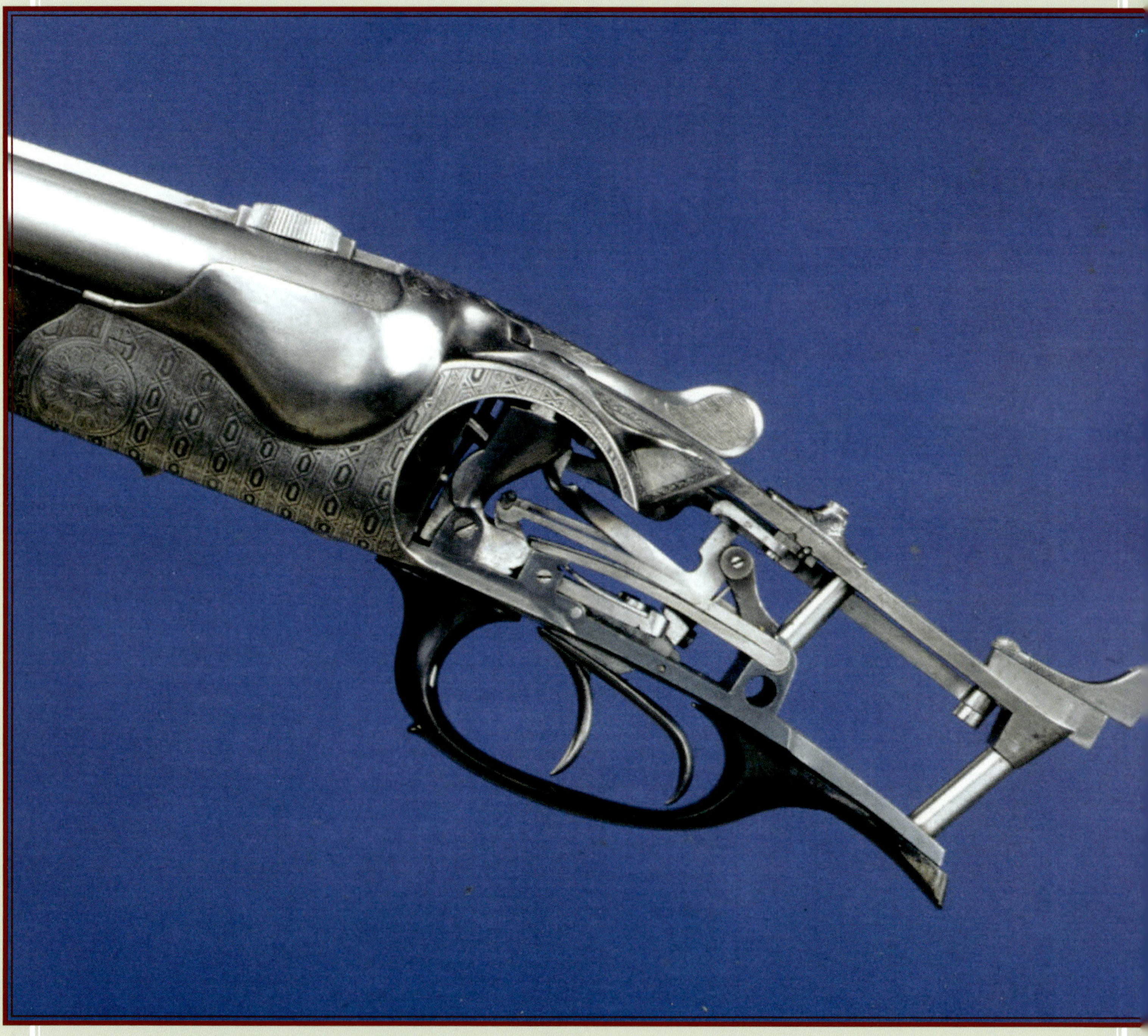

Brenneke safety drilling with exposed hammers.

The caption reads: "Hunters throughout the world value Brenneke rifles and ammunition."

At the end of World War II, the eighty-year-old Wilhelm Brenneke started over in West Berlin. He saw the beginning of the rebuilding of his company before dying on 4 November 1951 at the age of eighty-seven.

Brenneke slugs are today produced in a factory near Hannover under the leadership of Brenneke's great-grandson, Peter Mank. Brenneke cartridges are produced by the German firm Dynamit Nobel A.G.

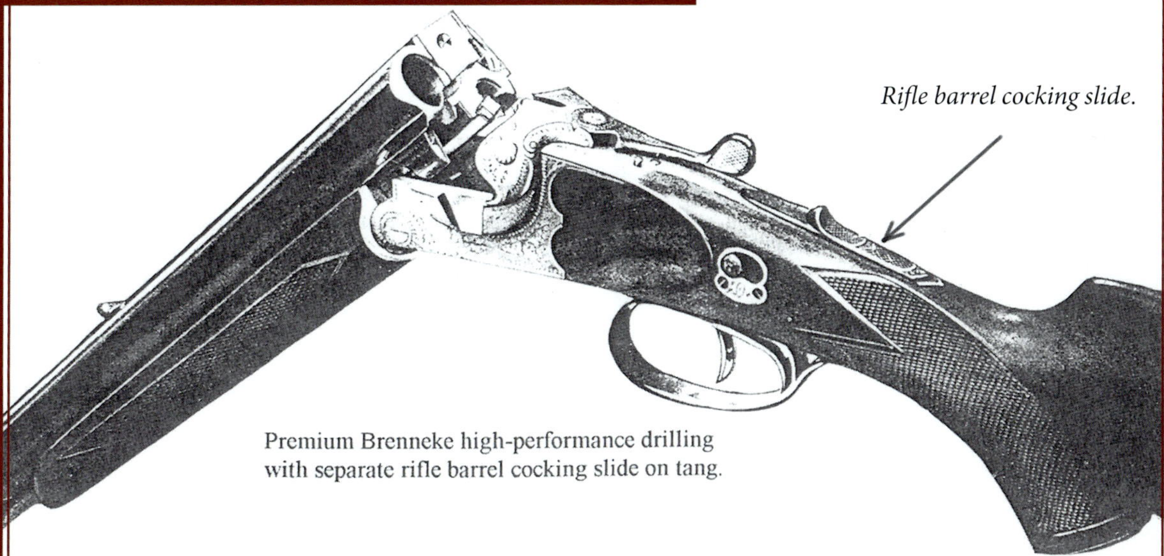

Rifle barrel cocking slide.

Premium Brenneke high-performance drilling with separate rifle barrel cocking slide on tang.

Waffen tips

Wilhelm Brenneke developed the widely used 7mm metric calibers 7x64 and 7x65R.

Hermann Burgsmüller

Gunmaker Hermann Burgsmüller established his first gun shop in 1876 in Kreiensen, a small town in the Harz Mountains southeast of Hannover. The business consisted of a modest building with attached living quarters. As a master gunmaker, Burgsmüller became a member of the gunmakers' guild in Kreiensen. Because his reputation for superior workmanship spread among hunters, he was able to expand his enterprise. He counted as his customers many aristocrats that included Prince Heinrich of Prussia, King Ferdinand of Bulgaria, and the Archduke of Luxembourg.

The rapid expansion of the Burgsmüller business continued over the next decades. Together with his son, Karl, who was also a trained gunsmith and managed the growing company, Burgsmüller patented several improvements on hunting and sporting guns. They included scope mounts and barrel inserts, which the Burgsmüllers sold under the trade name "Columbus." Another innovation, the popular Burgsmüller vierling,

Hermann Burgsmüller (left) was the founder of the company and a guild master gunsmith (Innungs-Büchsenmachermeister). *Karl Burgsmüller, Hermann's son, was the manager of the company and a guild member gunsmith* (Büchsenmacher).

This Burgsmüller & Söhne advertisement says, "Our program includes vierlings with three locks, drillings, scopes, and barrel inserts. We also deliver to accredited gunsmiths."

featured a new barrel configuration. The location of the .22-caliber barrel on this gun allowed the placement of an automatic rear sight.

A substantial catalog, which contained hundreds of firearms, accessories, furnishings, and loading equipment, was published yearly. Also included in the catalog was equipment for camping and the outdoors. The company maintained an extensive mail-order business that processed a thousand orders a day in 1909, according to the company's catalog. H. Burgsmüller & Söhne was also a dealer in new, used, and obsolete military arms and equipment.

Notice the fine engraving on this Burgsmüller drilling with a separate cocking for the rifle barrel.

Note the barrel arrangement on this Burgsmüller vierling.

Above, the Burgsmüller gun shop in 1876.

At left, the Burgsmüller gun factory in 1898. Repairs as well as scope installations and custom orders on luxury sporting arms were completed by skillful craftsmen in the gun shop.

The Burgsmüller factory in 1909.

Friedrich Wilhelm Heym

Friedrich Wilhelm Heym founded his own gun factory in Suhl in July of 1865. He manufactured and sold a variety of sporting firearms that included target rifles, shotguns, combination guns, double rifles, and double-rifle drillings, for which he was particularly well known. When the company was issued a patent for the first hammerless drilling (three-barrel) in 1891, the name Heym became known throughout Europe. As a result the firm experienced rapid growth in the succeeding years.

After World War II, the company moved from Suhl, which became part of East Germany, to Münnerstadt, a town in lower Franconia, West Germany. The firm introduced and patented a number of innovations in sporting firearms and, in cooperation with the Mauser Company, developed a new bolt-action rifle known as

Friedrich Wilhelm Heym and family.

A view of the interior of the machine shop.

Model 3000. Today the company still builds sporting firearms and customizes them to any specification required by the buyer.

It's interesting to note that there were other Heyms who worked in the gunmaking trade in Suhl: Martin and Johan Heym worked in Suhl between 1763 and 1769 and were possibly related to Caspar Heym (1702–1756) and his son, Johan Christian Heym, from Stockholm, Sweden. At one time or another the following gunmakers were active in Suhl: Heym Brothers (gun factory, 1865), Conrad Heym (1876, and Franz Heym (weapons factory). A Herman Heym apparently worked in the London, England, factory branch of Friedrich Wilhelm Heym of Suhl between 1889 and 1893.

Early Heym factory in Suhl.

FRIEDR. WILH. HEYM
GEWEHR-FABRIK
SUHL

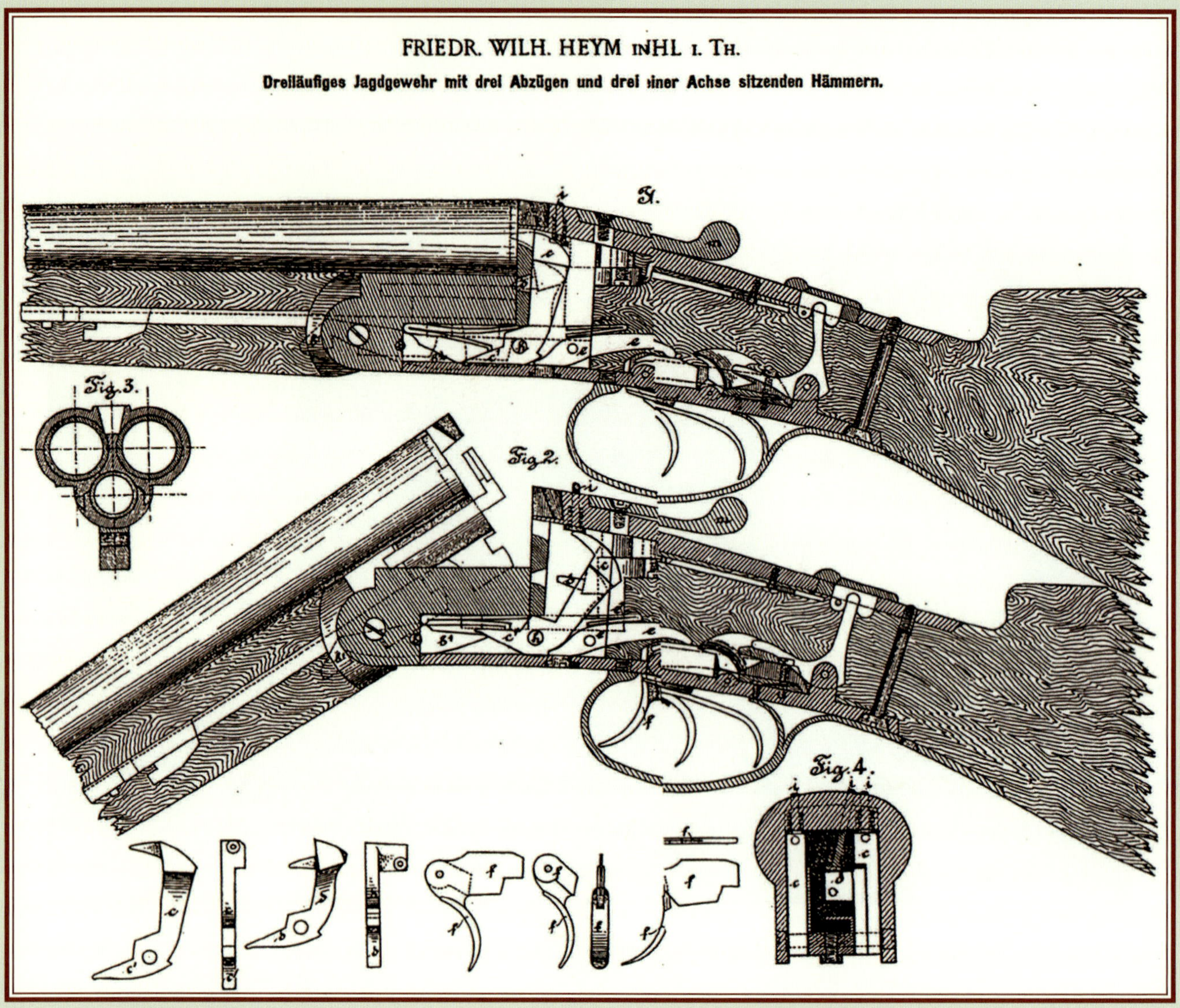

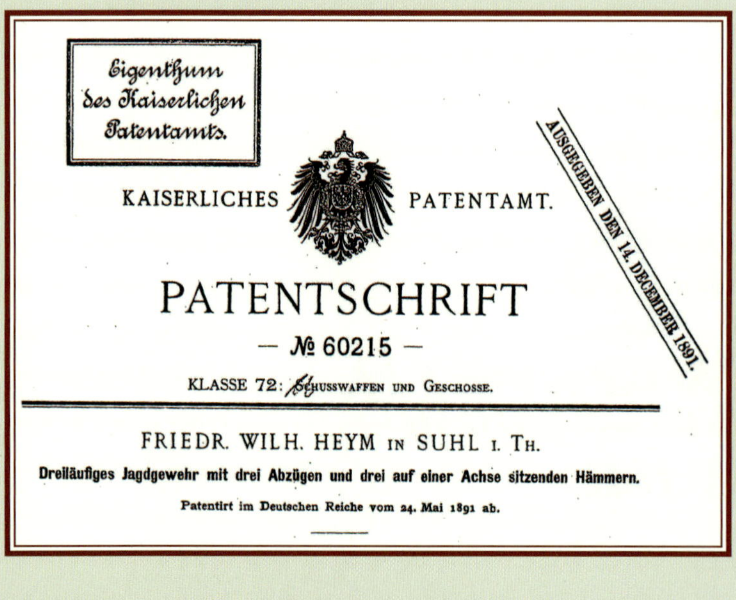
Eigenthum des Kaiserlichen Patentamts.

KAISERLICHES PATENTAMT.

AUSGEGEBEN DEN 14. DECEMBER 1891.

PATENTSCHRIFT

— № 60215 —

KLASSE 72: SCHUSSWAFFEN UND GESCHOSSE.

FRIEDR. WILH. HEYM IN SUHL I. TH.

Dreiläufiges Jagdgewehr mit drei Abzügen und drei auf einer Achse sitzenden Hämmern.

Patentirt im Deutschen Reiche vom 24. Mai 1891 ab.

Above, the patent for the first hammerless drilling with three triggers and strikers issued to Friedrich Wilhelm Heym. On 24 May 1891, Heym was issued Patent No. 60215 for a three-barrel hunting rifle with three triggers and three hammers on the same axis. This was the birth of the first hammerless drilling. The company expanded its production of drillings, shotguns, and over-and-under rifle/shotgun combinations. Russia was the company's most important export market until 1914.

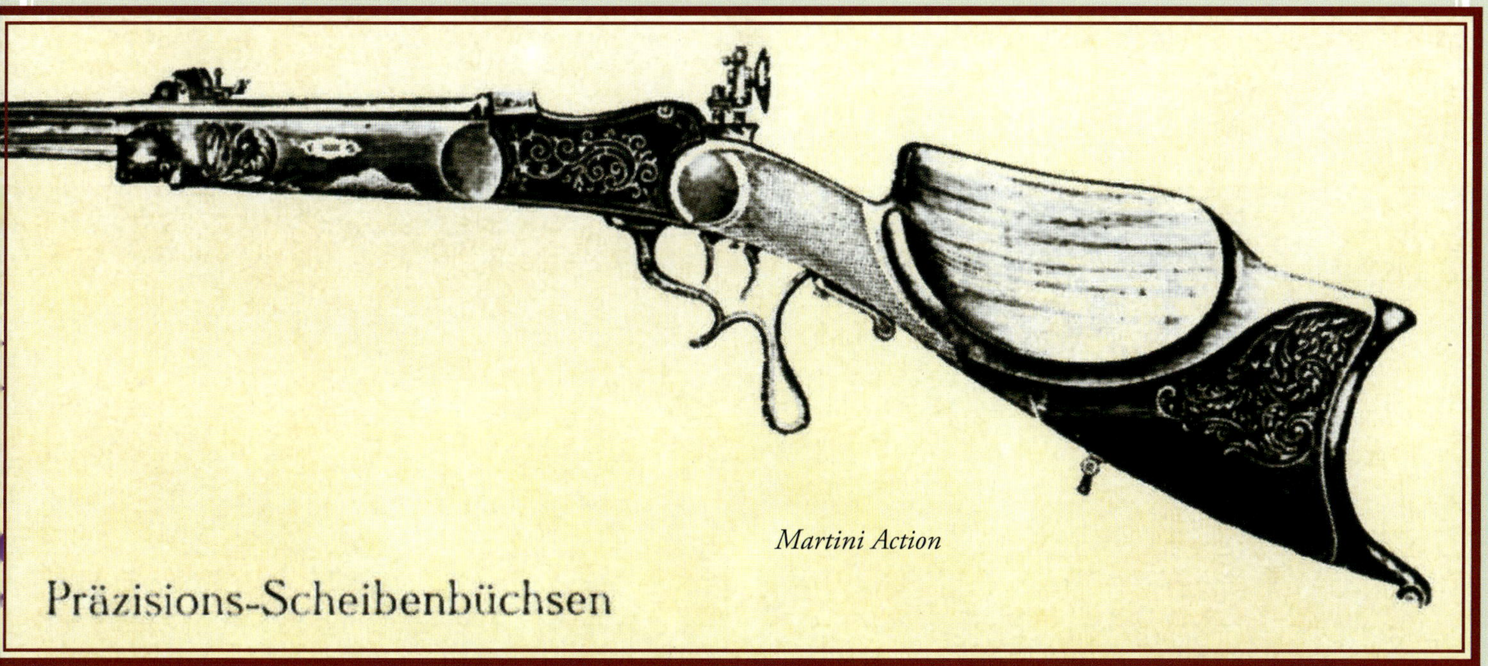

Heym precision target rifle, caliber 8.15x46R.

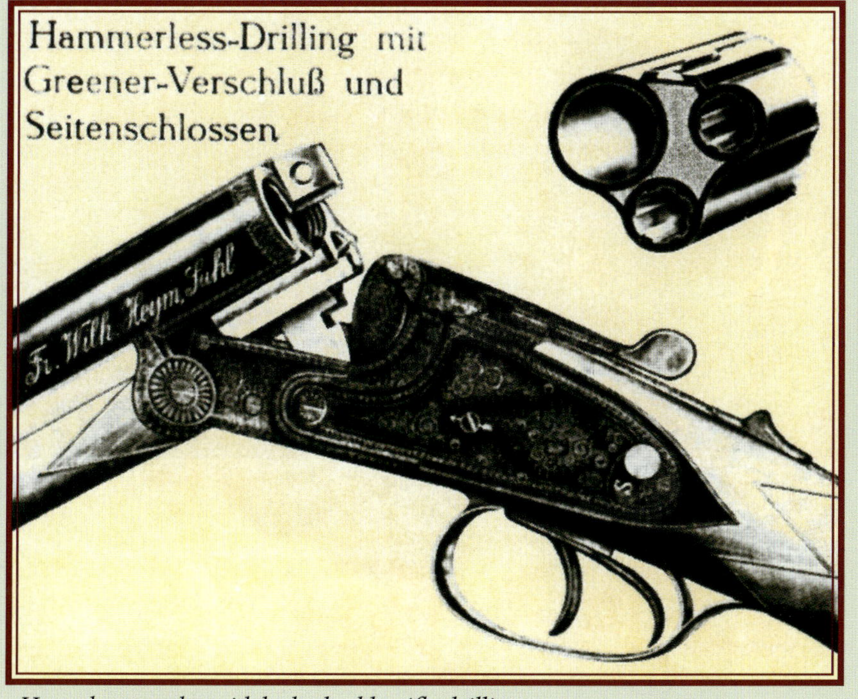

Heym hammerless sidelock, double-rifle drilling.

This Friedrich Wilhelm Heym shotgun has beautiful engraving.

FRANZ JÄGER

One of the most innovative gunmakers of his time was the Suhl gunsmith Franz Jäger. Born in Saxony in 1876, he finished his apprenticeship in Zella-Mehlis before immigrating to the United States in 1898. Returning to Europe after six years, he initially worked in Liege, Belgium, before moving to Suhl where he started his own gun business. His company equipped sporting firearms of many Suhl gunmakers with single triggers, which Franz Jäger had designed and perfected during his stay in the United States. Jäger's single-trigger units were also installed in Charles Daly's "Prussia" shotguns—a name synonymous with quality worldwide. By 1906, the firm Franz Jäger & Company employed forty-eight workers, gunsmiths, and journeymen.

Franz Jäger served in the German Imperial Army during the first year of World War I. When the Kaiser decided that skilled gunmakers could make more important contributions by building weapons, Jäger was exempted from further military service and sent home. The company's production during World War I, consequently, underwent a change from

Jäger gun factory in Suhl.

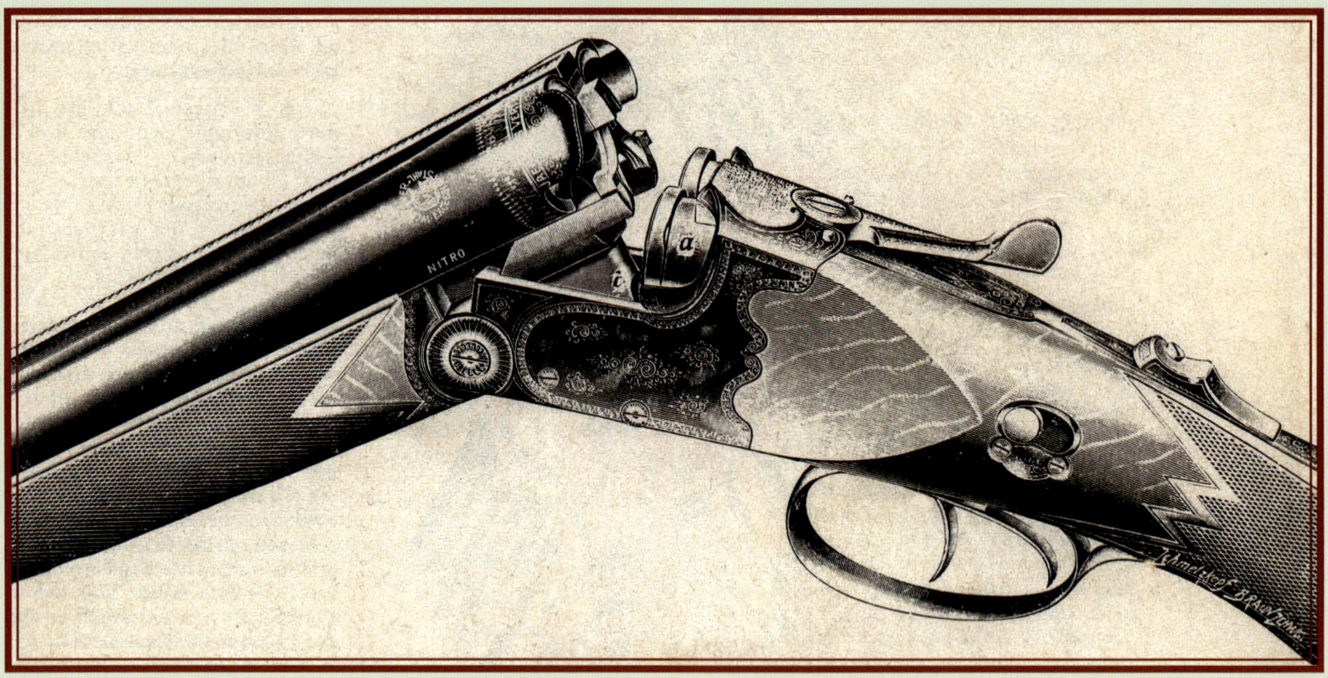

The pivot-block action was a revolutionary design by Franz Jäger, whose design was ahead of its time. The barrel extensions enclosed the pivoting breechblock on all sides when the action was closed.

sporting firearms to weapons of war. At the end of hostilities of World War I, the company returned to the manufacturing of firearms for the hunting public.

During the time between the war, Jäger worked on a new pistol design and became known as a reliable gunsmith and a talented inventor. In gearing up for World War II, the company again switched from the manufacture of sporting firearms to that of weapons of war. Because Franz Jäger's wife was Jewish, however, his career as a gun designer came to an end before the Second World War.

Franz Jäger's son, Paul, studied engineering and worked in his father's business. He moved to the United States in 1929 when the Depression threatened the existence of the company in Suhl and many employees had to be dismissed. After working for gun firms in New York and Philadelphia, he opened his own business, Paul Jaeger, Inc., in Jenkintown, Pennsylvania. Another son, Kurt, owned a gun shop, which he called Waffen-Jäger, in the city of Mainz, Germany. He worked in this business for many years before his retirement. Gunmaker Dietrich Apel, grandson of Franz Jäger, arrived on the East Coast of the United States in 1952. He worked for many years for his uncle Paul Jäger and continued the business when Paul Jäger retired. In 1987, he established his own company in New Hampshire under the name New England Custom Gun Service. Dietrich Apel is also the founder of the present-day German Gun Collectors Association.

This is an advertisement for hunting guns: "Doppelflinten *(side-by-side shotguns),* Drillinge *(drillings),* Büchsflinten *(cape guns*),* Büchsen *(single-shot rifles),* Doppelbüchsen *(double rifles), and scopes."*

*A cape gun is a side-by-side version of a combination gun and is typically European. German and Austrian cape guns have the rifle barrel on the right side and are fired by the front trigger.

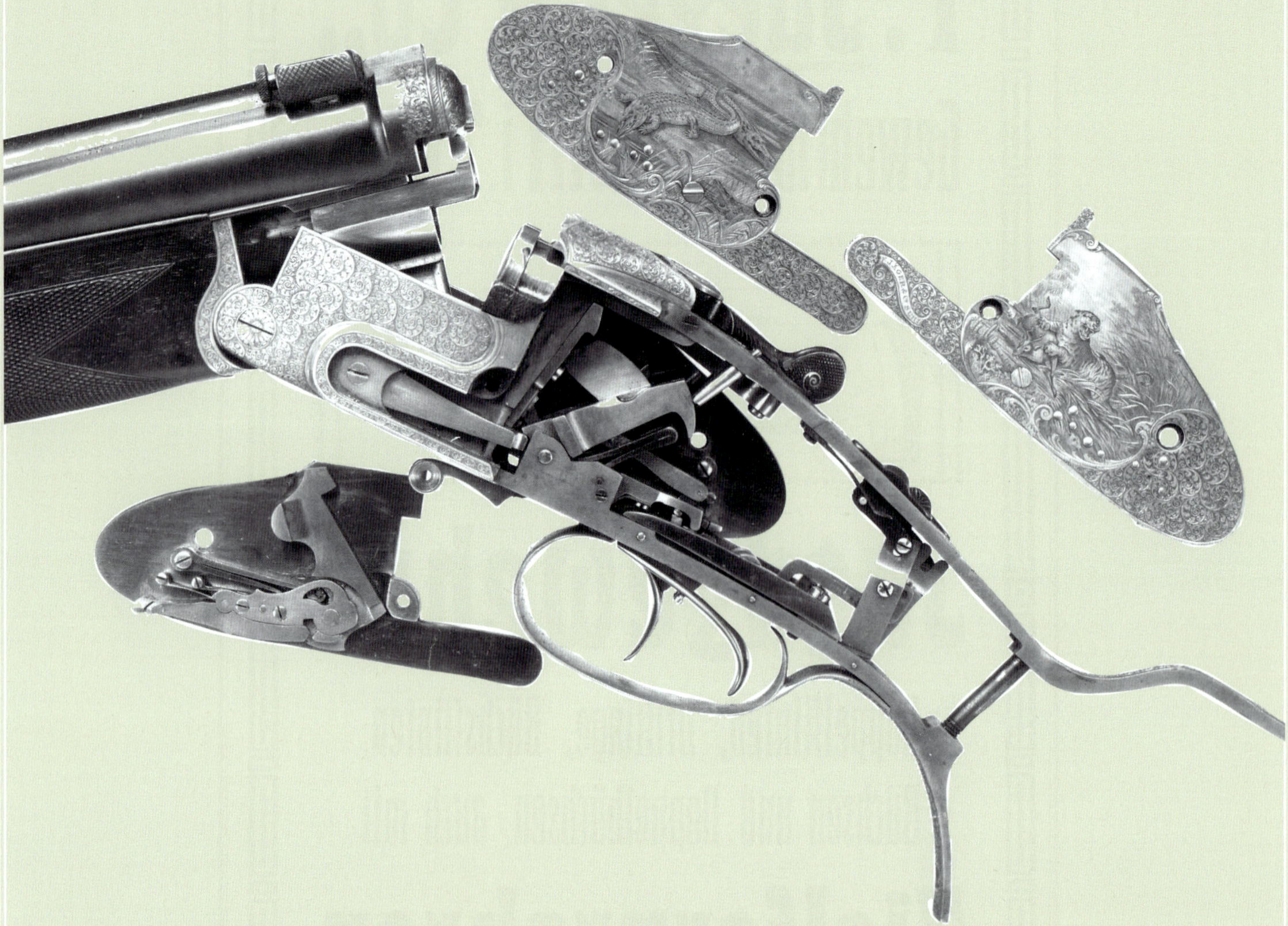

This Franz Jäger Vertikal-Block Drilling, also called the tilting block, is to this day considered to be one of the strongest actions for heavy calibers. It has interchangable sidelocks and engraving that ranks with the finest gun engraving in the world. This can be seen in the fine detail of the two crocodiles and the tiger.

SEMPERT & KRIEGHOFF

Sempert and Krieghoff had its beginning in Suhl in 1886. The firm was founded by Ludwig Krieghoff and a friend by the name of Sempert. (His first name is not known.) Sempert had worked as an engineer for Edison in the United States, and after a promising start in this gunmaking venture, Sempert decided to return to the United States. He obviously was more interested in the development of the new field of electricity than in pursuing a career in gunmaking.

After Sempert left, Ludwig Krieghoff and a few employees continued to build sporting arms on a custom-made basis. By the turn of the century, the sales program also included loading accessories, powder measures, and safeties for hammerless guns. Under the slogan "The Barrel Shoots, the Stock Scores," Ludwig Krieghoff also developed and patented a stock-fitting gun (Reichs Patent No. 123902).

Son Heinrich Krieghoff learned the gunmaking business and engraving trade in his father's factory. As was often done, gunmakers sent their sons to their colleagues in other countries to gain experience. Heinrich Krieghoff traveled to Sheffield, England, and to the large gunmaking center at Liege, Belgium, to become familiar with different manufacturing methods. Upon his return, he worked for his father until the outbreak of World War I. In 1916, he founded a company to supply parts to other gunmakers in Suhl.

GEWEHRFABRIK SEMPERT & KRIEGHOFF SUHL IN THÜR.

GEGRÜNDET IM JAHRE 1886

Suhl plant, turn of the twentieth century.

This "Neptun" sidelock drilling in caliber 9.3x72R with 16/16-gauge barrels.

After World War I and during the following depression, many arms manufacturers went out of business, but during this time Heinrich Krieghoff was fortunate to acquire the machinery of Valentin Christian Schilling, a well-known Suhl gunmaker. He also bought the firm of Sempert & Krieghoff when his father retired.

When Ludwig Jr. joined his brother, Heinrich, they began to fabricate parts and barrels for other gunsmiths; they also made finished hammer and hammerless combination guns, cape guns, and double rifles. The firm also developed the Sempert barrel insert for shotgun tubes. The company's specialty became the drilling, which was built in a number of models: Waldschütz, Sempert, Sempert-Anson, Sempert Privat, Sempert Luxes, Trumpf, and Neptun. These self-cocking or hand-cocking (hand spanner) versions with steel or aluminum actions were available in literally hundreds of variations, engraving styles, and special features.

By the late 1930s, the work force in Suhl had grown to 3,000 when Krieghoff started to supply the military in the months leading up to World War II. The manufacture of sporting arms ceased, and the entire output of the main plant and several newly opened factories, with 6,000 workers, began producing firearms for the armed forces. In 1945, the family and several dozen gunsmiths and employees were evacuated to the town of Heidenheim by the American army on its withdrawal from Suhl. The Soviet army moved in and occupied Thuringia, the area around Suhl, which later became part of East Germany. The Soviets subsequently transported all machinery and the remaining gun experts to the Soviet Union. The factories and facilities of Suhl were destroyed.

Heinz-Ulrich Krieghoff, the son of Heinrich, returned from a P.O.W. camp in 1946, and with his father, opened a small gun shop in Heidenheim. Relocating again in 1950 to the town of Ulm in Bavaria, they founded the new firm of Heinrich Krieghoff, K. G. [*Kommandit gesellschaft* or partnership in English]. With a dozen workers, they were able to build their first air guns, the only type of gun permitted at that time. By 1954, drillings were again in production. The firm has expanded steadily to this day.

Barrel straightening and system work was and still is done by hand.

Here craftsmen are fitting action parts and quick detachable scope mounts.

This Krieghoff drilling has a separate cocking for the rifle lock.

Krieghoff's "Neptun" model has a hand-detachable trigger mechanism. Note the fine engraving on this Krieghoff "best" drilling.

The Mystery of H. A. Lindner

Ghost or Gunmaker*

For centuries the German city of Suhl in Thuringia was renowned for its superbly crafted tools and armor. Its skilled gunsmiths and artists also supplied domestic and foreign markets with sporting and military arms. The manufacture of firearms in this famous gunmaking center was highly specialized and differed distinctly from gun developments here in the United States.

At the turn of the twentieth century, hundreds of skilled craftsmen, journeymen, apprentices, fitters, engravers, goldsmiths, metal workers, stockmakers, and lock, action, and system makers worked in and around Suhl and neighboring Zella-Mehlis. Water- and steam-powered iron works supplied bayonets, barrels, and gun actions. Local suppliers imported barrel blanks, ivory from Africa, and walnut from France and Italy. Buffalo horn from Asia was shaped into trigger guards, inlays, caps, and butt plates. Factories furnished steel, hand tools, machinery, measuring instruments, and forges. A separate industry emerged to service the hundreds of machines used in the manufacturing of firearms.

Gun dealer Heinrich Anschütz, who traveled extensively throughout Europe for many years, was the author of a book entitled *The Gun Factory in Suhl*

View of Suhl's city square in 1811.

Oscar Will, dealer and manufacturer, owned Venus Gun Works, and he featured this shotgun in his 1902–1903 catalog. It appears to be a Lindner double except that it has a round crossbolt, a pistol grip, and a horn trigger guard.

(Die Gewehrfabrik in Suhl). His work, published in 1811, described in detail the handcrafting of military and sporting arms at the time. Although the title and text of his book suggest a large gunmaking facility, the gun industry in Suhl was, in fact, fragmented into hundreds of independent shops and enterprises. A few larger gun manufacturers like J. P. Sauer & Son, Simson & Company, Gebrüder Merkel, and Sempert & Krieghoff were the exceptions.

As a consequence of this fragmentation, the German armed forces, which had contracted with Suhl firms for decades, finally tired of dealing with numerous separate establishments and individuals, so the military built new centralized manufacturing plants and arsenals in Berlin and Erfurt. These facilities allowed for better quality control and increased production of military arms.

The lack of military contracts, especially during peacetime, forced Suhl gunmakers to concentrate on the production of sporting arms for domestic as well as overseas customers. These included American dealers such as E. C. Schmidt, T. L. Golcher, Daniel M. Lefever, William R. Schaefer, and several others. Skilled German workers built most of the shotguns marketed by well-known New York importer Schoverling & Daly. Its successors included Schoverling, Daly & Gales, and Charles Daly, Inc. Many of these outstanding Suhl craftsmen worked for and supplied parts and assemblies to H. A. Lindner, maker of refined shotguns.

The history of the Lindner firm is shrouded in obscurity. Although Suhl was not bombed during WWII, business records did not survive the ravages of time and paper collection drives during both world wars. Lindner's name is largely unknown in Germany. The author could find no living family member to provide information on the Lindner firearms company. Unfortunately, with the prevalent antigun and antihunting climate in Europe today, the lives and accomplishments of nineteenth-century gunmakers

*"Ghost or Gunmaker, The Mystery of H. A. Lindner—Part I." *The Double Gun Journal,* Vol. 16, Issue 2, Summer 2005, pp. 83–91

"Ghost or Gunmaker, The Mystery of H. A. Lindner—Part II." *The Double Gun Journal,* Vol. 16, Issue 4, Winter 2005, pp. 115–125

This Lindner shotgun was made for Charles Daly in New York.

This early Lindner advertisement reads: "H. A. Lindner, Suhl, Rüssenstrasse 6. H. A. Lindner Sporting Gun Factory Specialty: Charles Daly shotguns for export to North America." The company recommends its double- and single-barrel shotguns in all calibers and varied price ranges. Meticulously crafted in the English style and equal in every aspect to English shotguns.

H. A. Lindner, Gewehrfabrikant,
Suhl, Rüssenstr. No. 6.
Anfertigung **feinerer Doppelflinten.**
Specialität: **Daly Guns** zum Export für Nord-Amerika.

This advertisement targeted the German hunter and sportsman, indicating that H. A. Lindner at times actively attempted to increase domestic sales. The "export to North America" reference served the same purpose, implying that since his doubles were highly regarded by Daly clients in the U.S., they should also be favored by his German customers.

H.A. LINDER - SUHL
Founded 1874
Berlin Salesrooms
P. HELBIG WILHELMSTRASSE 53
SPECIALTY
CHARLES DALY GUNS
FOR
EXPORT TO NORTH AMERICA

are often ignored and relevant facts and any surviving material disregarded. However, the Lindner name lives on through the creations that carry his mark.

Daly shotguns were associated with the name Linder. The spelling of the name, without the second "n" was probably caused by a misprint of an advertisement in a German trade publication or an error in its translation. The author is indebted to fellow collectors for providing an image of a sidelock shotgun engraved on the barrel rib: H. A. Linder Suhl. The owner of the gun suspected that it was a forgery. The author concurs. The engraved letters are crudely incised and ill-fitting the designated space on the matted rib.

While there are hundreds, if not thousands, of persons who answer to the name Lindner or Linder, only one gunmaker with his name spelled "Lindner" can be placed in Suhl at the time Daly shotguns were made. The mysterious Linder chap and the elusive H. A. Lindner are one and the same person.

The spelling error has resurfaced in publications and on Web sites, ad nauseam, whenever Lindner guns are discussed. Regrettably, the "Linder" spelling is still with us. The author suspects that this is partially caused by the absence of factual information or simply because it rolls off the tongue more easily than the name "Lindner." Texas gun dealer Bob Jones, who has handled Lindner doubles for several years, thinks that it doesn't make much difference one way or the other, and he might have a point. On the other hand, we know that a gunsmith by the name Linder did not exist in Suhl and the surrounding area at the turn of the twentieth century, so for the sake of historic accuracy, the author believes that the name "Linder" should be put to rest once and for all. It is akin to calling a Winchester rifle a Wichester.

Heinrich August Lindner (H A L) was born to Georg Lindner and his wife Dorothea in 1848. As an accomplished gunsmith, he assisted his father until 1874; he then established his own firm in Suhl at Rüssenstrasse 6, with a shop located at Judithstrasse. Later (the exact date is not known), the business relocated to Schleusinger Strasse 28. On 21 April 1877, when he was 29 years old and his livelihood secure, he married Hedwig Auguste Triebel. He continued to export shotguns to the New York sporting goods firm of Schoverling, Daly & Gales and several other firearms dealers in the United States.

Successful and respected, the gunmaker retired sometime between 1913 and 1918. In the 1920s, he still lived at Schleusinger Strasse as a pensioner; he remained there until his death on 10 November 1933, at the age of 85. His widow died during WWII on 5 May 1941. A Gertrud Lindner—maiden name Schorr who might have been a sister-in-law—still lived at the above address until 1948.

We can assume that Heinrich August Lindner learned the gunmaking trade in his father's shop at the age of fourteen or fifteen, as was the custom of that time. There is no reliable record of his private life and not much is known of his day-to-day activities. We know he began as a working gunmaker, mastered technical challenges, and became a gifted craftsman. With an artist's eye, he designed magnificently appointed, elegantly shaped

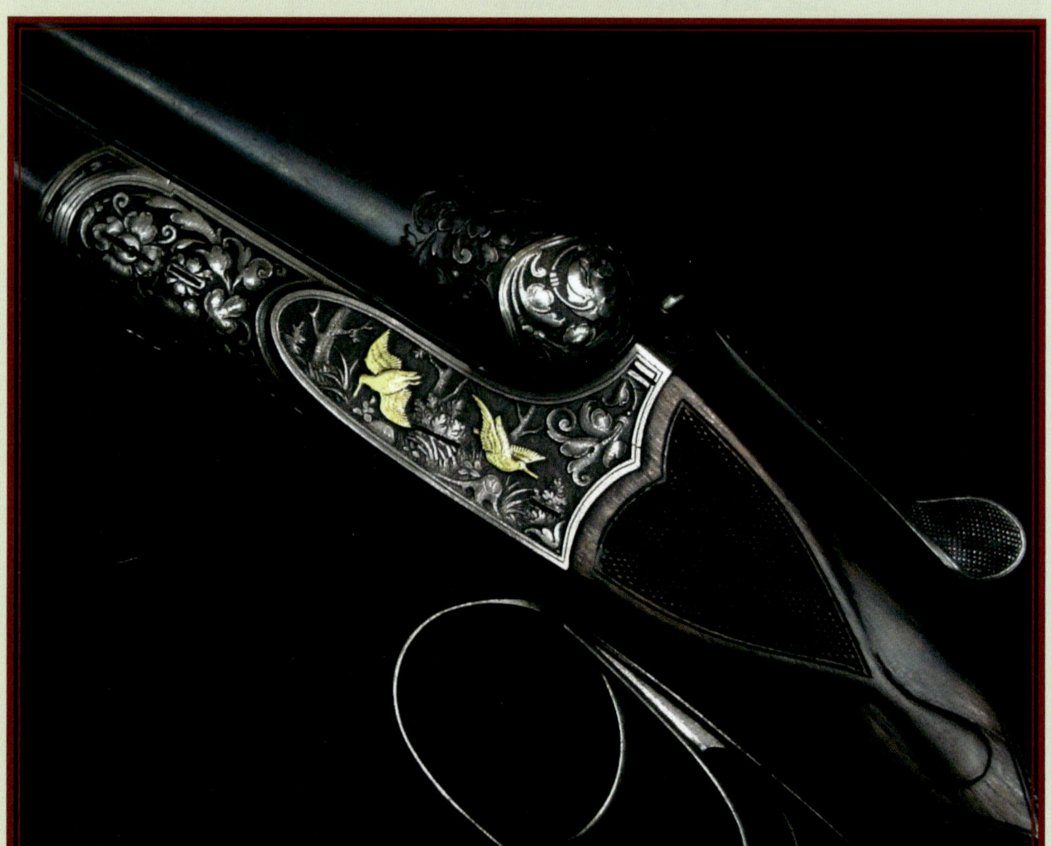

Another example of a Lindner shotgun made for Charles Daly in New York.

This recent photo shows the renovated property at Rüssenstrasse 8. This house was adjacent to the Lindner house at Rüssenstrasse 6, which was torn down years ago to make room for apartment buildings. Sided with locally mined gray slate, the house in the photo is representative of what No. 6 must have looked like at the turn of the twentieth century.

The Lindner house in Suhl as it appears today. The upper floors contained offices and living quarters; the workshop was in the basement (souterrain).

Anson & Deeley boxlocks. It is also apparent that he was an entrepreneur, and as a dealer in the gun trade, he devoted considerable time to a thriving wholesale export business.

Subsequently, we are faced with an equally enigmatic Mr. H. A. Lindner. Probing for facts in Germany has been time consuming and difficult. With few exceptions, younger gunmakers do not recognize the name. Who was he?

Why the big interest in a gunmaker who was just one of hundreds of gunsmiths in Suhl? The older generation, now in their eighties or nineties, might recall the name and the fact that he exported shotguns to the New World. A few retired gentlemen in their nineties, reaching deeply into their memory, can add an anecdote here and a fact there.

We have to ask ourselves then, why was his firm not better known? In a world-renowned gun manufacturing center such as Suhl where successive generations of modest gunsmiths became famous, H. A. Lindner remains a mysterious figure. Equally intriguing are the diverse features and the variety of markings and serial numbers found on his shotguns. Appreciative owners, scholars, and collectors need to piece more details together in the future before time erases the last available shreds of information.

The historical record of the city of Suhl, published in 1846, mentioned a Georg Lindner as the owner of a gun

Late hammer gun by H. A. Lindner.

Early hammerless double by H. A. Lindner.

factory. This master gunmaker *(Büchsenmachermeister)* lived and worked in Suhl at 120 Rasen Street. He was known as *Gewehrfabrikant,* a manufacturer of custom-built, side-by-side shotguns. His "factory" in 1850 was actually a small shop supporting a work force of, at the most, four or five journeymen. Guns were essentially hand-built, assisted by a limited number of machine-powered tools, since the output of the shop did not allow for expensive machinery.

The total production of the gun shop was small; the highest serial number known is 2620, not a large number for a firm supplying a major export market. To put this in perspective, at the same time J. P. Sauer exported guns in the 100,000 serial-number range. This implies that the Lindner operation was a small shop, despite being called a factory, which furnished guns of outstanding craftsmanship to a discriminating clientele.

Georg Lindner built hammer guns for retail and wholesale buyers in Germany. Through his connections to firms in the United States, he also supplied shotguns to American clients until his retirement in the early 1870s. Many of these early doubles made by Georg Lindner were not marked or carried only the signatures of German or American dealers on barrel ribs or locks. It is one of the reasons why the Lindner name was not widely known in Germany.

Historically, many Suhl gunsmiths excelled in the manufacture of a variety of firearms. They switched back and forth between the production of shotguns to rifles and from military arms to sporting firearms. This flexibility was born out of the necessity to survive economically. One significant factor set Heinrich August Lindner apart from other Suhl gunmakers. As his father before him, he insisted on exclusively creating superbly crafted shotguns. This single-mindedness is intriguing in view of the fact that the making of top-grade, double-barrel shotguns on the Continent commanded neither the monetary rewards nor the importance it did in England.

At a time of English dominance in the manufacture of superb doubles, sales of choice or "best" German shotguns were lacking. Germans favored the combination gun and stalking rifle in order to harvest a variety of game. Although Continental makers advertised their proficiency in building fine-quality firearms *(Feine Gewehre)* in the English style equal to or surpassing those of their colleagues across the channel, the German aristocracy and wealthy patrons still preferred English guns.

German gunwriters and authors seeking to change this perception about the superiority of English shotguns began to educate the public in the late 1800s and early 1900s. They urged prospective clients to buy German sporting arms of equal or superior quality instead of English ones. Manufacturers increasingly pleaded their cause in their catalogs. Slowly German sportsmen began to appreciate doubles made in their own country. Any connoisseur who has examined guns built in Suhl or elsewhere in Germany can attest to the precision, craftsmanship, graceful beauty, and the flawless finish of firearms made by German master artisans. By the 1930s, expensive English firearms had lost much of the appeal they once held in Germany.

Early Lindner hammer doubles are difficult to identify today since dealers and mail-order houses insisted on affixing their own signatures and logos on the firearms they advertised. Better-known large manufacturers such as J. P. Sauer & Sohn, negotiating from a position of strength, were able to use their own trademarks and names in catalogs of wholesalers. Lindner did offer an *llustrierte Preisliste* (an illustrated price list), but none has surfaced. We do not know whether it was a single sheet or a complete catalog.

Three years ago, gunwriter Clair Kofoed recorded and photographed a Lindner double inscribed "H. A. Lindner Suhl Diamant Qualität" on the top rib. (See photo below.) The spelling of the inscription clearly indicated that this specific shotgun was initially destined for a German customer. A gun for the American trade would have displayed a "Diamond Quality" logo. (See photo on next page.)

Reportedly, Diamant Qualität shotguns were skillfully made and praised as being crafted by artists in their field who lavished utmost attention on every detail of barrels, actions, stocks, and performance. Prices ranged from RM 440 to 550 (at an exchange rate of $1 to 4.20 reichsmarks).

The name Diamant Qualität appeared also in German ads in the 1920s. German wholesaler/dealer Alfred Kind (owner of the Akah catalog) ordered his German firearms exclusively from Suhl, and he offered "Diamant" brand, hammerless shotguns in his 1926 catalog for the domestic market. These doubles were probably produced by the firm of August Schüler. Engraved and inlaid in gold, they were promoted to be of the finest quality and workmanship, featuring modified A & D actions and hidden crossbolts.

Most Lindner shotguns were exported to Daly in New York; others were made for the domestic market. In Suhl, Lindner was occasionally referred to as a "rucksack" gunmaker who used his backpack to deliver and pick up gun parts from skilled workers living within walking distance. Apparently this term was mildly disparaging, and it is attributed to envious competitors who were aware of his profitable association with Schoverling, Daly & Gales.

Employing outworkers (experts working out of their homes or shops) was an efficient system practiced not only in Suhl but also in all large gunmaking centers such as Ferlach in Austria, Birmingham in England, and Liege in Belgium. Today we would call H. A. Lindner a "custom gunmaker" whose job was to supervise the fitting of barrels, actions, and stocks, to commission engravers, and to inspect final assemblies.

For a brief time before World War I, Lindner collaborated with Peter Helbig in Berlin. A master gunmaker, Helbig had located his establishment at prestigious Wilhelmstrasse 53 in the center of Berlin. Since Helbig was well established, this may be seen as another effort by H. A. Lindner to increase the exposure of his finely wrought doubles to diplomats and an international clientele in the German capital.

At the close of the percussion era in 1873, and possibly earlier, Schoverling, Daly & Gales started to sell imported firearms from its New York location. The Charles Daly logo went on his guns in 1875. This coincided with the founding of the H. A. Lindner business a year before in 1874.

In the early 1880s, the New York sporting goods dealer offered the first Lindner hammerless doubles for sale. H. A. Lindner clearly saw the advantages of exporting handmade guns to North America, especially in the face of stiff competition on the domestic market with rival Suhl makers and during often turbulent times. He benefitted from the association his father had formed with Schoverling & Daly and concentrated on an increasingly steady stream of orders from the New York importer and other American dealers.

It is logical that Lindner shotguns changed over time, combining improvements in materials with new innovations by Continental and English gunsmiths. In 1865, Georg Lindner could not have built shotguns for Daly with the same features and refinement as supplied by his son Heinrich in 1910. Gun designs changed from hammer to hammerless and became more complex: A 20-gauge Lindner hammerless double of the 1907 vintage is composed of 96 individual parts. Stronger steel forgings allowed for smaller actions and lighter barrels. Concealed, modified Greener crossbolts eventually replaced Doll's head fasteners. Krupp, Röechling, and Witten Fluid Steel barrels superseded Damascus. The final perfection of the well designed A & D actions allowed the gunmaker to turn his attention to rework and refine the appearance of his doubles.

The New York importer and Lindner agreed on features desired for shotguns made for the American market. Given the close ties with England, it comes as no surprise that they were patterned after English doubles. American customers preferred gently scalloped, scroll-engraved actions instead of deeply chiseled hunting scenes and oak-leaf designs. Trigger guards were shaped from steel instead of from buffalo horn, and sling swivels

An example of a Lindner over-and-under shotgun that was made for Charles Daly in New York.

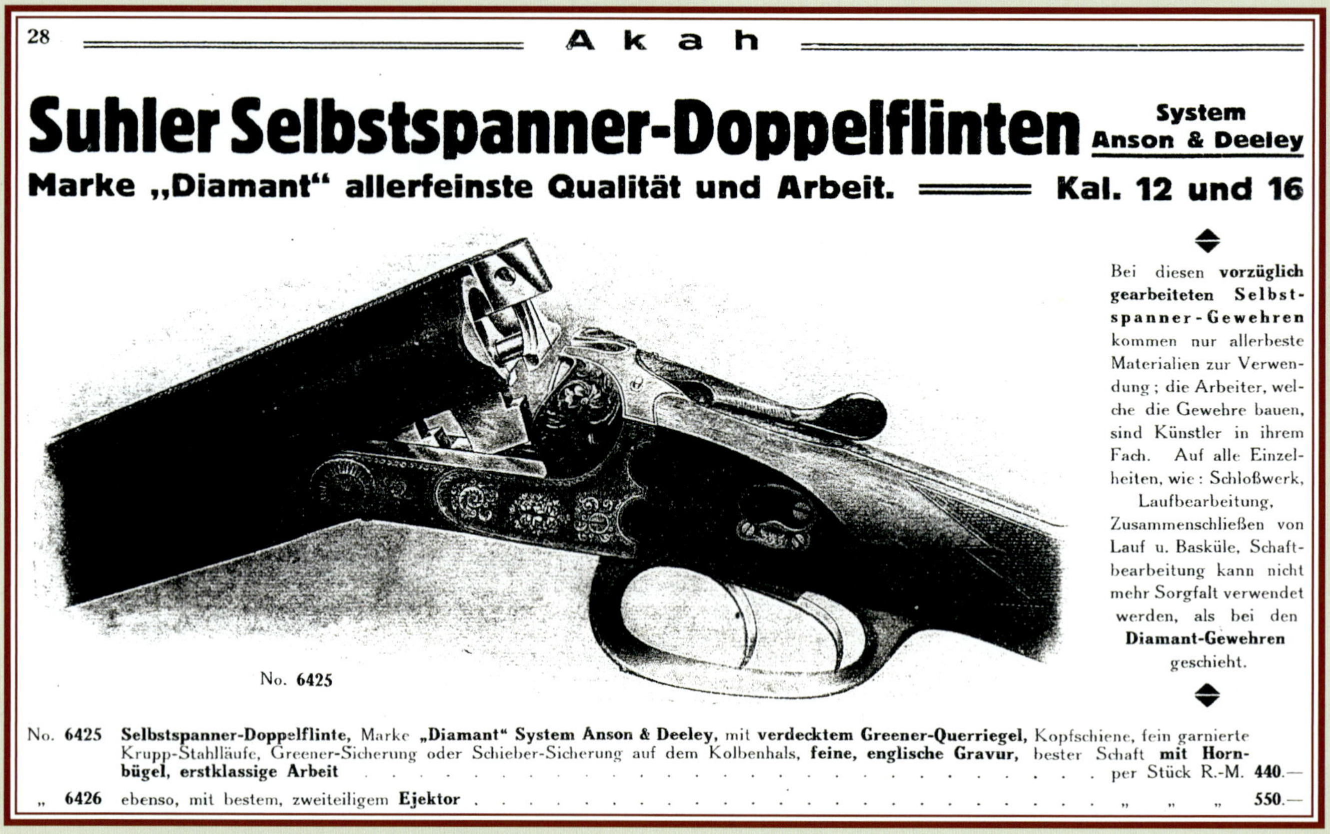

28 — Akah

Suhler Selbstspanner-Doppelflinten System Anson & Deeley

Marke „Diamant“ allerfeinste Qualität und Arbeit. — Kal. 12 und 16

Bei diesen **vorzüglich gearbeiteten Selbstspanner-Gewehren** kommen nur allerbeste Materialien zur Verwendung; die Arbeiter, welche die Gewehre bauen, sind Künstler in ihrem Fach. Auf alle Einzelheiten, wie: Schloßwerk, Laufbearbeitung, Zusammenschließen von Lauf u. Basküle, Schaftbearbeitung kann nicht mehr Sorgfalt verwendet werden, als bei den **Diamant-Gewehren** geschieht.

No. **6425**

No. **6425** **Selbstspanner-Doppelflinte,** Marke **„Diamant“ System Anson & Deeley,** mit **verdecktem Greener-Querriegel,** Kopfschiene, fein garnierte Krupp-Stahlläufe, Greener-Sicherung oder Schieber-Sicherung auf dem Kolbenhals, **feine, englische Gravur,** bester Schaft **mit Hornbügel, erstklassige Arbeit** . . . . . per Stück R.-M. **440.**—

„ **6426** ebenso, mit bestem, zweiteiligem **Ejektor** . . . . . „ „ „ **550.**—

This image was taken from a 1926–1927 Akah catalog..

In a 1907 catalog, gunmaker J. P. Sauer & Sons offered a Lindner look-alike A & D shotgun. This Sauer double featured a round cross-bolt, a top lever with a waist, side indicators, pistol grip, and cheekpiece.

were omitted. As a rule, customers requested straight stocks without cheekpieces or ones with round pistol grips in the Prince of Wales style; they also demanded superior gun performance. We can assume that a grading system was agreed on, eventually culminating in a magnificent top grade known as the Diamond Regent.

Most Lindner guns can be identified by one of two makers' marks: a stylized crown over a set of crossed pistols or the initials H A L over crossed pistols. Marks were separately struck into the underside of each barrel ahead of the barrel flats. The reason for these marks is a puzzle. Early firearms with the crown/pistol mark do not show German proofs. With few exceptions, doubles with the H A L stamp do. Crown marks as well as later H A L ones were never an indication as to who made a gun or its components. The assumption that Lindner himself only crafted shotguns with the H A L stamp cannot be substantiated. As a matter of fact, early hammer and hammerless Daly doubles without any maker marks or ones stamped only with crown marks were more likely to have originated and been finished in the workshop of Georg Lindner and the early establishment of Heinrich A. Lindner at Rüssenstrasse. All crown or H A L marked doubles, whether created in their shops, supplied in part by outworkers or other makers, are Lindner guns by virtue of their maker's marks.

The implementation and regulation of German proof marks caused confusion for a while. Lindner crown logos could easily be mistaken for the new German imperial

This 20-gauge double was manufactured about 1910.

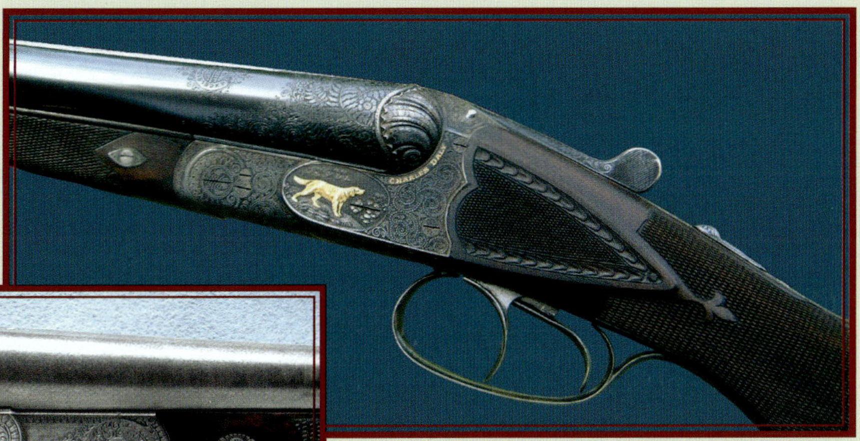

Scalloped action, 1890s.

Later hammerless double with straight-action contours, 1880 vintage.

crown insignia stamped above letters S, W, V. These emblems identified shotgun barrel proofs as part of the newly established proof law. They were stamped at the barrel location where, until then, makers had placed their marks. H. A. Lindner was compelled to remove the crown, so he replaced it with his initials H A L. Gold inlaid or engraved crown symbols on the outside of Daly firearms were obviously a part of embellishments and not affected by the law, which was passed by the Reichstag in May 1891 but not made public until June 1892. It became law in April 1893. For this reason a number of "cross-over" shotguns (for the lack of a better term) with crowns and proof marks may have reached the United States.

While Daly tried to keep most Lindner models in stock, he also accepted custom orders. Special-order shotguns were crafted according to the (sometimes eccentric) wishes of each customer and required time-consuming hand fitting and finish. It was apparent from the beginning that the Lindner shop was not able to furnish enough firearms to satisfy Daly's needs and that of the German domestic market at the same time.

Conversations today with Suhl gunsmiths familiar with Lindner's name confirm that he built few guns entirely by himself. Instead, he relied on skilled artisans from a vast talent pool available in Suhl and surrounding towns to satisfy the ever-increasing requests for his doubles from abroad. Over a period of several decades, his shotguns evolved into a harmonious blend of perfectly finished components supplied by independent craftsmen. Much of the machining was done in shops of gunmakers Schilling and Triebel. They supplied partially completed guns to Lindner "in the white" to be hallmarked, engraved, finished, and then sent to New York. Lindner reportedly often worked alone fitting barrels, checking, perfecting, and completing firearms one at a time.

When he journeyed to the United States at the turn of the century, Heinrich A. Lindner took along a number of his shotguns destined for the Daly firm. As related by fellow gunmaker Richard Bornmüller to his son Hans, Lindner traveled as a first-class passenger to the New World. On board he organized shooting competitions, for which he also provided ammunition. On his arrival in New York, the firearms cleared customs as used goods at reduced duty under 1891 U.S. tariff laws. Arriving at the Schoverling, Daly & Gales location, the doubles were disassembled, checked, rechecked, and thoroughly cleaned. They were then sold as new with descriptions of extended trials during the Atlantic voyage, which further enhanced their appeal.

At the start of WW I in 1914, the aging gunsmith was getting ready to retire or had already retired. He was sixty-six years old. Former employees and tradesmen now produced guns for the military as part of a Suhl work force estimated at 12,000 at the time. Great Britain effectively blockaded all sea lanes to the Atlantic, and the export of any goods to the United States ended. At the conclusion of the war in 1918, the New York importer was eager to reestablish former ties with H. A. Lindner, J. P. Sauer & Sohn, and other suppliers. The special relationship that the Lindner family had previously enjoyed continued with Charles Daly (who had passed away in 1899), Schoverling, Daly & Gales, and their successors. Although H. A. Lindner remained Daly's contact in Suhl, forwarding and filling orders for Daly shotguns, he did not actively work on firearms after his retirement.

An article published in a 1935 German trade publication commemorating 100 years of gunmaking by Suhl manufacturer August Schüler has to be noted. It reported that the Schüler firm had taken over the production of Daly guns after the war (probably in the early 1920s but the date was not specified), replacing makers Schilling, Triebel, and a Mr. H. A. Lindner. (The property and machinery of Val. Chr. Schilling, maker of military and luxury firearms, at Rimbachstrasse 37 in Suhl was acquired by Heinrich Krieghoff for $23,810, or 100,000 reichsmarks in 1919.)

It is interesting to note the distinction made among these makers: Gun manufacturers Schilling and Triebel, while not dealing directly with Daly except through

Lindner, were named as substantial establishments. Lindner was referred to only as a Mr. Heinrich A. Lindner. This "honorable mention" not only signified his special association with the Daly firm but was also indicative of the retired status of the premier gunmaker and his relatively small operation as compared to other firms at that time. Gun manufacturer August Schüler, who maintained sales rooms in Berlin and a factory in Suhl, subsequently took over production and continued to supply Daly after the death of Heinrich August Lindner in 1933. Lindner's wife Hedwig was still alive and, although only a supposition, possibly permitted the continued use of the Lindner logo for a time.

Dates in H. A. Lindne's Life

1848 H. A. Lindner was born.

1850s to 1870s Georg Lindner built unmarked hammer shotguns.

1865 The firm of Schoverling & Daly was established.

1874 The H. A. Lindner firm was founded; doubles are marked with crown/pistol logo and serial number.

1875 Schoverling & Daly start selling firearms.

1877 H. A. Lindner marries.

1891 The United States requires country of origin logos (Prussia) on imported firearms.

1891 Germany passes proof mark laws for firearms.

1893 Proof marks become law.

1891–1893 doubles are marked with HAL/pistols and proof marks.

1914–1918 H. A. Lindner retires at some point during World War I.

1914 Schilling and Triebel discontinue work for Lindner.

1920s Schüler supplies doubles to Lindner for export to Daly.

1921 The United States requires the logo "made in" added to country of origin.

1924 German-made guns have to show a proof date in addition to proof marks.

1926 Akah offers Diamant (Diamond) brand doubles.

1933 H. A. Lindner dies.

Imperial crown.

Shot-barrel proof mark.

Choke-bored rifle barrel mark.

Choked barrel mark.

Lindner made many side-by-side shotguns, and this example is typical of Lindner's work.

Early hammer gun by Georg Lindner.

Early hammer gun by Georg Lindner.

Gun aficionados classify Lindner-made doubles that were retailed by the New York importer "Lindner Dalys." Shooters and collectors have treasured Lindner shotguns for years, long before this author heard of Lindner-Daly doubles and appreciated their beauty and function. To this day, gun enthusiasts discuss their performance and appealing lines, marvel at new acquisitions, and agonize over serial numbers and initials.

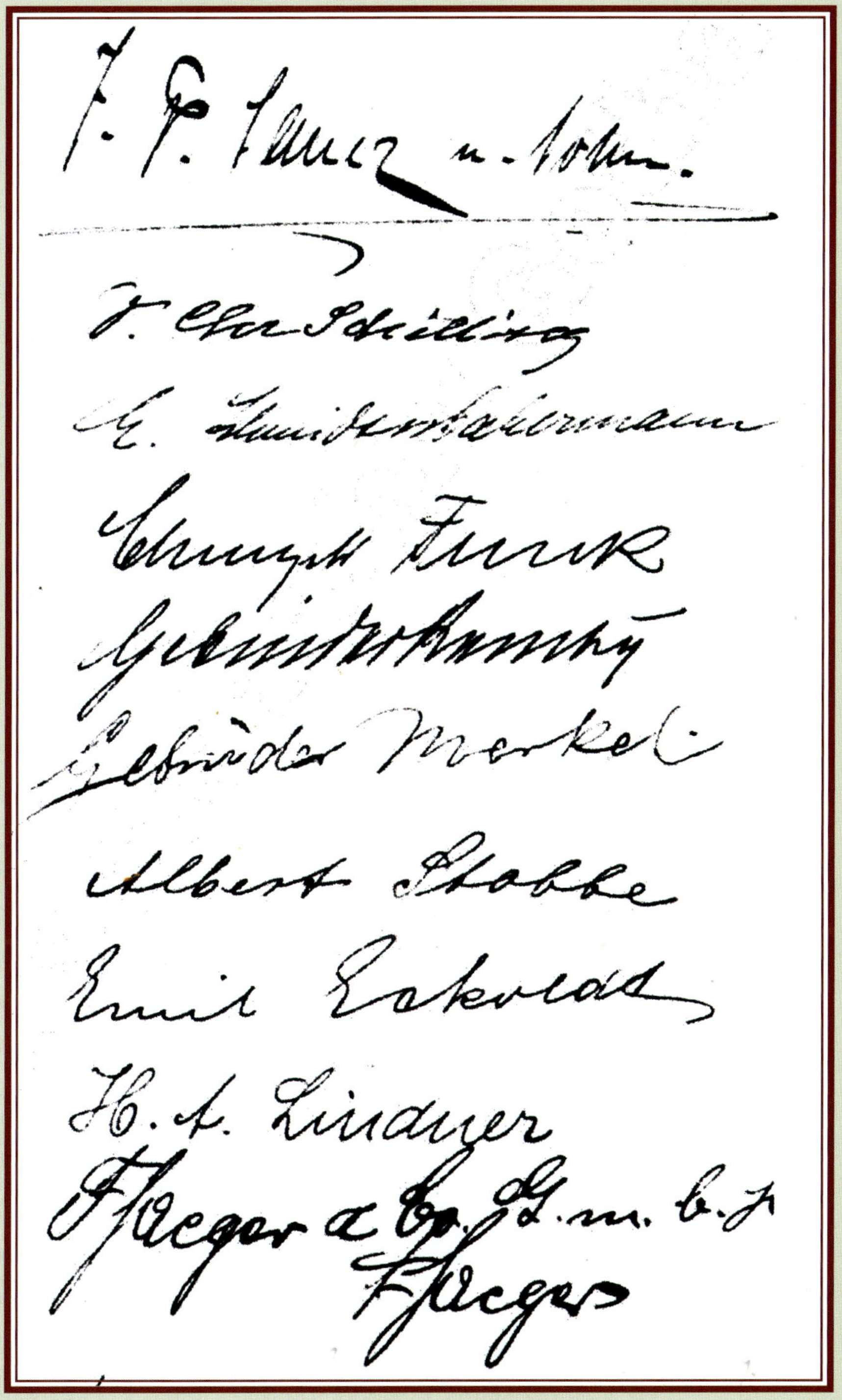

H. A. Lindner was in famous company when he affixed his signature to the founding charter of the Suhl Gun Manufacturers Association on 10 November 1911. These firms were also represented: J. P. Sauer & Sohn, V. Chr. Schilling, E. Schmidt & Habermann, Christoph Funk, Gebrüder Rempt, Gebrüder Merkel, Albert Stobbe, Emil Eckoldt, H. A. Lindner, Franz Jäger for the F. Jäger Co., G.m.b.H

Author's notes:

This chapter is a minor contribution when measured against the labor of other researchers intrigued by magnificent Lindner shotguns. Its pros and cons will doubtlessly spark further debate, as it should. The author is indebted to friends and collectors who allowed him to use their photographs. He gratefully acknowledges information given so freely by versed collectors and scholars here in the United States as well as by master engravers and gunmakers in Germany.

The 1907 Schoverling, Daly & Gales and J. P. Sauer & Sohn catalog reprints are available from the German Gun Collectors Association at www.germanguns.com.

KAISERLICHES PATENTAMT.

AUSGEGEBEN DEN 5. AUGUST 1914.

PATENTSCHRIFT

— № 277253 —

KLASSE **72a.** GRUPPE 18.

H. A. LINDNER GEWEHRFABRIK IN SUHL I. THÜR.

Umstellvorrichtung für Mehrläufer, bei der das vorzeitige Abfeuern des zweiten Schusses durch ein beim Rückstoß vorbewegtes, federbelastetes Trägheitsgewicht verhindert wird.

Patentiert im Deutschen Reiche vom 20. Dezember 1912 ab.

Die Erfindung betrifft eine automatisch arbeitende Umstellvorrichtung eines an mehrläufigen Gewehren anzubringenden Einabzugs, bei welchem die Umschaltung nach erfolgtem Schuß und durch denselben, und zwar in dem Augenblick bewirkt wird, in welchem der zum Abfeuern des Schusses an den Abzug gelegte Finger den Abzug nach stattgehabtem Rück- und Wiedervorstoß des Gewehres wieder freiläßt.

Umstellvorrichtungen für Einabzüge an mehrläufigen Gewehren sind bekannt.

Durch den Umstand, daß bei der Erfindung die Umschaltung erst vor sich geht, nachdem die durch den Schuß verursachte Bewegung des Gewehres, sowohl Rückstoß als Vorstoß, vorüber ist, ist ein gleichzeitiges ungewolltes Abfeuern beider Läufe unmöglich, im anderen Falle wird aber auch eine zu spät eintretende Schußbereitschaft für den anderen Lauf vermieden.

Die Erfindung ist in der Zeichnung dargestellt.

Fig. 1 zeigt die Seitenansicht des Systems, rechts gestellt, abgeschossen und in der Lage zwischen Rückstoß und Wiedervorstoß mit in die Umschaltung eingetretener Sperre.

Fig. 2 gleiche Ansicht nach erfolgtem Vorstoß, durch welchen die Sperre aufgehoben und die Umschaltung auf links erfolgt ist.

Fig. 3 Rechts- und Linksstellung auf dem Abzugsblech, von oben gesehen.

In der Basküle ist in einem Block a ein Trägheitsgewicht b der Länge nach verschiebbar gelagert. Dieses Trägheitsgewicht trägt an seinem vorderen Ende in der Querrichtung verschiebbar einen Schieber c, der einen mit der Spitze nach vorn gerichteten Dreikant c^1 und zwei Ansätze c^2 trägt.

In dem Block a ist ferner der Umstellschieber e querverschiebbar gelagert, der einen Dreikant e^1 trägt. An dem Umstellschieber ist, unter Federdruck stehend, der Umsteller f angelenkt, der sich mit seinem Hinterende unter die rechte oder die linke Abzugstange legen kann.

Durch den Rückstoß des Gewehres während des Schusses wird zunächst das Trägheitsgewicht b vorwärts bewegt, bis es die in Fig. 1 dargestellte Lage einnimmt. Der in diesem Trägheitsgewicht querverschiebbar gelagerte Schieber c trifft während der Vorwärtsbewegung mit dem an ihm befindlichen Dreikant c^1 gegen den ihm entgegenstehenden Dreikant e^1 des Umstellschiebers e und wird an demselben rechts- oder linksseitig so verschoben, daß einer der an ihm befindlichen Ansätze c^2 dem Ansatz d^1 oder d^2 eines hinter dem Umstellschieber e gelagerten Drehhebels d gegenübergestellt wird. In diesem Augenblick und kurz vor dem Ende der Vorwärtsbewegung des Trägheitsgewichtes b ist die in einem besonderen Stollen g angebrachte Sperre i durch Federdruck hinter das

Throughout his life, Heinrich A. Lindner kept a low profile, moving unassumingly among his fellow gunmakers without making any significant contribution to the development of firearms. He patented a single-trigger design for double-barrel shotguns in 1912, but apparently his invention did not see widespread use.

Zu der Patentschrift 277253

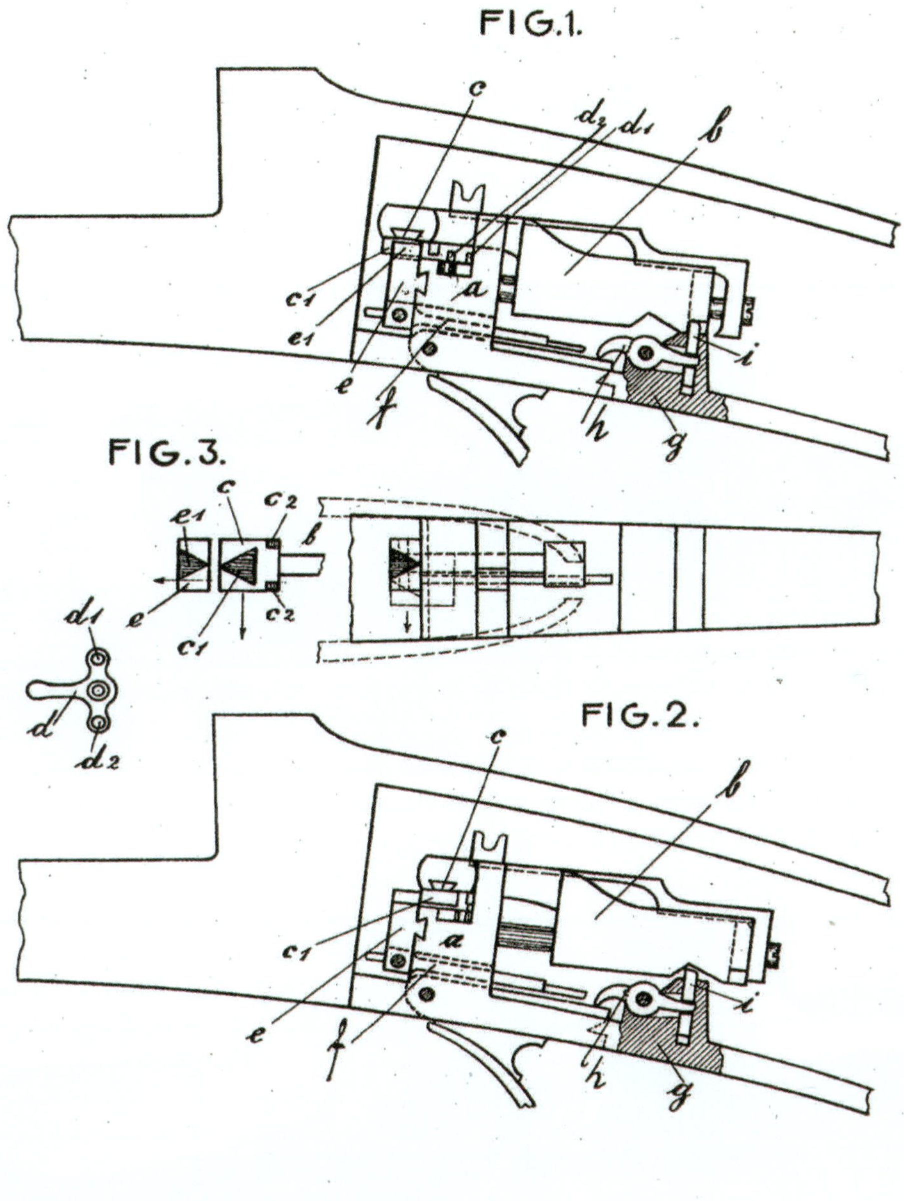

PHOTOGR. DRUCK DER REICHSDRUCKEREI.

IMMANUEL MEFFERT

Not much is known about the origins of gunmaker Immanuel Meffert. The history of the family can be traced back to Hans Meffert who seemed to have been a gunsmith in Suhl in the mid-1600s. There is a record of a Georg Meffert circa 1834 and a P. Meffert in 1846, also in Suhl. Immanuel Meffert founded his gunmaking enterprise under the name of "Imman. Meffert, Suhl."

From its beginning in 1839, Meffert's firm produced a number of popular target rifles and pistols. Immanuel Meffert experimented with several actions and systems as is evident from patents issued in 1882, 1909, 1910, and 1912. The company crafted combination guns—drilling and vierling—and small-bore rifles under the trade name Hubertus. It was also

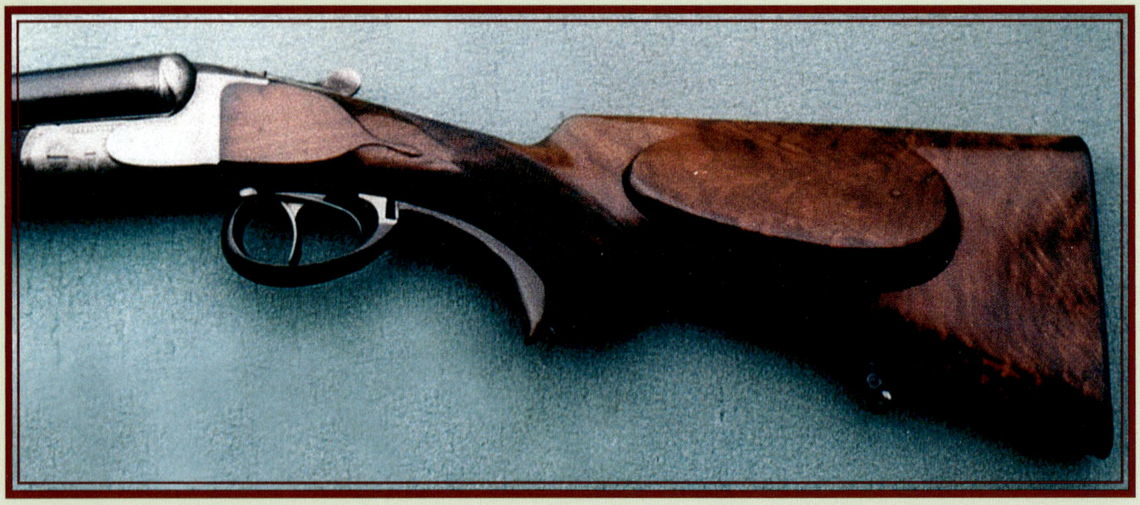

The Hubertus Gewehr model is shown in the firing position with the action cocked and the safety lever activated and pulled against the pistol grip.

Here the hammer spring is in the "safe" position.

"Light and strong" was a slogan for Meffert guns with aluminum receivers.

the company's name for the safety device used in its Hubertus-Gewehr double-barrel shotgun.

In 1914 the drilling Treff model was initially introduced with a Roux underlever lockup, the standard and widely used bolting mechanism for break-open guns at that time. A later version featured an unusual battery lock that was placed below the upper tang with a Greener crossbolt and side clips. The company's Treff battery lock design was discontinued in 1929, probably due to high production costs; it was replaced with a Blitz system action.

Immanuel Meffert was the first gunmaker to pioneer and sell drilling and vierling models with aluminum alloy frames to reduce weight without compromising the strength of the receivers. Advertised as light metal guns *(Leichtmetallgewehre),* they were in demand despite their higher price. As a rule, vierling models were available only with duralumin (*dural*) receivers. The gun was about one-half pound lighter than a vierling with a steel action. *Dural* was developed by the Dürener Metallwaren AG. It was a forged and heat-treated alloy of aluminum, copper, magnesium, and manganese of extreme toughness. All guns with *dural* receivers featured bushed firing pins and were available etched gray, anodized black, white, or gold.

At the start of World War II, the entire production of the company was shifted to support the war effort. In the postwar years, the firm struggled like so many other gunmakers to survive in the face of materiel shortages and destroyed production facilities. In 1962, the firm was liquidated and eventually absorbed by the Gunmakers Trade Association (*Bühag*).

This Meffert drilling is in caliber 8x57JRS with 16/16 barrels. It is equipped with an independent extractor for the rifle barrel, which could be cocked by the top tang slide. The dural receiver is etched gray with full hunting scenes, oak leaves, or English scrolls and a horn trigger guard. This model was also available with ejectors for shotgun barrels.

This Meffert drilling in caliber 7x57R with 16/16 barrels has a dural receiver and Blitz system, top-lever, cocking indicators. The top tang slide activates the rear sight and acts as a safety for the rifle barrel. The Greener safety on the left side is for the shotgun barrels.

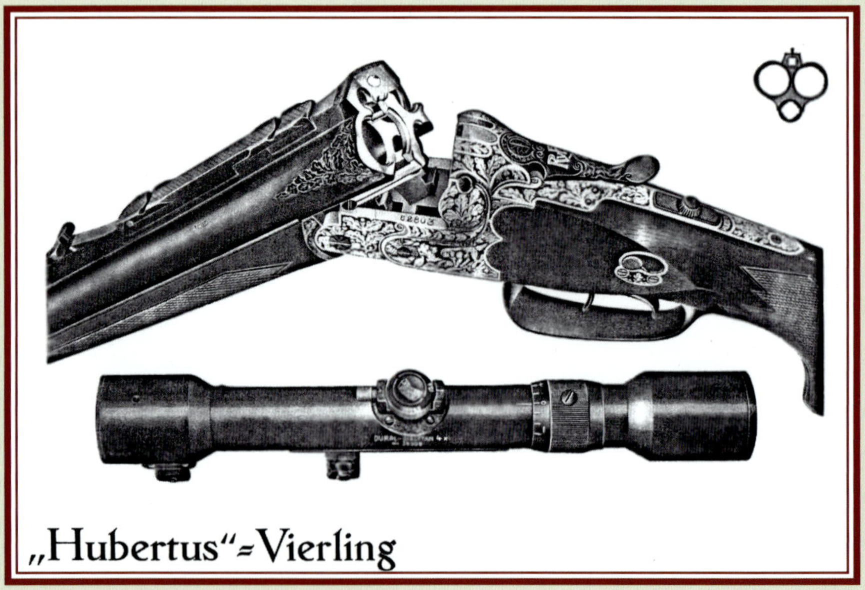

This Meffert vierling has an aluminum (dural) receiver, side clips, and Greener crossbolt. Note the rib extension to the right of the .22-caliber rifle barrel. The weight of the gun without the QD rail-mounted scope is only six pounds.

This Meffert drilling has a "Dural" action.

Gebrüder Merkel

The name Merkel is forever linked with Suhl, the central German provincial town in Thüringen, where steel was forged for centuries into weapons for nobles and citizens alike. Friedrich Ernst Merkel (1828–1901) was an independent engraver in Suhl. Working not only on guns, he also embellished precious metals, trophies, and medals. He met and married Auguste Louise, the daughter of respected gunmaker Heinrich Gottfried Funk. Of the thirteen children born to the Merkels, seven were sons. All learned the gunmaking trade and became master gunsmiths or master stockmakers. All formed companies of their own or went into business with their brothers, partners, or associates.

The factory owned by Ernst August Merkel (1853–1912), the oldest of the brothers, produced many kinds of hunting and sporting arms and sold these under the name E. A. Merkel. At times, he also employed his brothers Otto Gottlieb and Louis Franz Ferdinand Merkel. Bernhard Emil Merkel (1874–1954) was the

The Merkel brothers with their partners and customers.

The patriarch of the Merkel family was Friedrich Ernst Merkel, who was also an engraver. Here he is pictured with his wife, Auguste Louise, and one of their thirteen children.

Owners and employees posing with an eight-foot steel-and-wood model of a side-by-side shotgun during a celebration at the Merkel plant on 1 May 1933.

owner of the gun factory B. Merkel, Suhl, between 1908 and 1937. His company built a whole array of sporting firearms and also furnished them to several gun traders, including such notable firms as Barella in Berlin and Eduard Kettner in Cologne. At one time Franz Merkel was affiliated with the Udo Anschütz Gewehrfabrik located in Zella-Mehlis near Suhl. Besides manufacturing hunting and target rifles, the company specialized in the development of target pistols for Olympic competition.

Gebhard (1867–1933), his brother Albert Oscar (1864–1931), and master stockmaker brother Karl Paul (1870–1942) founded the firm Gebrüder Merkel, Suhl, in 1898, thus laying the foundation for a prestigious enterprise with a worldwide reputation. In the year 1916, the company changed its name to Suhler Waffenwerk Gebrüder Merkel. The firm produced conventional single-shot and bolt-action rifles, side-by-side shotguns, drillings, and double rifles. It pioneered the concept of firearms with superposed barrels designed for interchangeable barrel sets *(Einlegeläufe)*. Barrels individually hand fitted to the same receiver were available in a number of different gauges and/or calibers.

Because the Merkel brothers were mindful of the importance of a well-dimensioned stock, fitting guns *(Gelenkgewehre)* were sent to Merkel dealers throughout the world to take exact measurements of their customers. Attention to detail is evident on a Merkel sporting firearm in the cast of the buttstock. The cast did not start behind the receiver but was incorporated into the action. For a right-handed shooter, the angle measured 1 to 2 mm at the tang, resulting in a 5 to 10mm cast-off at the butt plate. On O/U guns *(Bockgewehre)*, the straight stock absorbed recoil better and reduced side swing.

In cooperation with successful big-game hunter Alexander Florstedt, the company also produced the Carpathian rifle *(Karpathenbüchse)* as one of their many specialties. The name was derived from the game-rich Carpathian Mountains in Eastern Europe. This light, break-open, ¾-stock, single-shot rifle was easy to handle. It had a two-part forearm and a double set of triggers,

Finishing touches on an O/U shotgun.

Waffen tips

On the Continent, any change made in the length of a shotgun chamber required a re-proofing of the barrels.

and it was ideal for stalking in trackless, mountainous terrain. It was designated as Model 180, which was available with various barrel lengths in caliber .22 HP (4½ pounds) up to 9.3x74R (6½ pounds).

Albert Oskar Merkel left the Merkel Company in 1907 and a year later founded his own firm, Oskar Merkel & Company (MERCO). A partner in this venture was Karl Merkel, the son of his brother Otto Gottlieb Merkel. The company produced side-by-side shotguns and double rifles, cape guns, hammerless and hammer guns of every description, and stalking and bolt-action rifles; in addition, the company developed trigger systems for Mauser and Mannlicher rifles.

In 1925, the firm of Abesser & Merkel was registered as a sporting firearms manufacturer in Suhl by Paul Abesser and Ernst Merkel. Ernst Merkel appears to have belonged to another branch of the Merkel family, possibly a descendant of a sibling of Friedrich Ernst Ferdinand, father of the Merkel brothers. Abesser & Merkel Co. was in competition with other Merkel companies and at times took unfair advantage of the Merkel name and reputation.

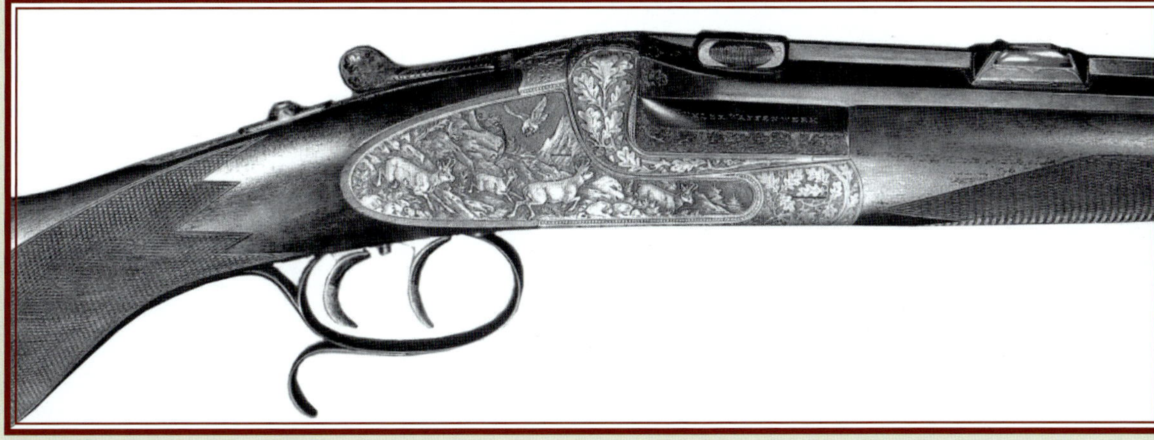

This 7x57R Carpathian rifle is engraved with an oak leaf and game scene, and it has a double set of triggers and a trigger guard finger hook.

His Highness, the Maharajah of Java, posing with his trophy tiger and his Merkel side-by-side double rifle.

Karl Paul Merkel (left), Gebhard Merkel (seated on right), and Oscar Merkel (below) founded the firm Gebrüder Merkel, Suhl, in 1898.

Gebhard Merkel was a partner for a time in the Gewehrfabrik Gottfried Funk und Söhne.

Karl Paul Merkel.

Oscar Merkel.

Ernst Merkel.

In 1925, Paul Abesser and Ernst Merkel established the firm of Abesser & Merkel, which was registered as a sporting firearms manufacturer in Suhl. Ernst Merkel was from another branch of the Merkel family and not directly related to the siblings in Gebrüder Merkel, Suhl.

The single-shot Carpathian rifle on top uses the Anson system and has Kersten fasteners.

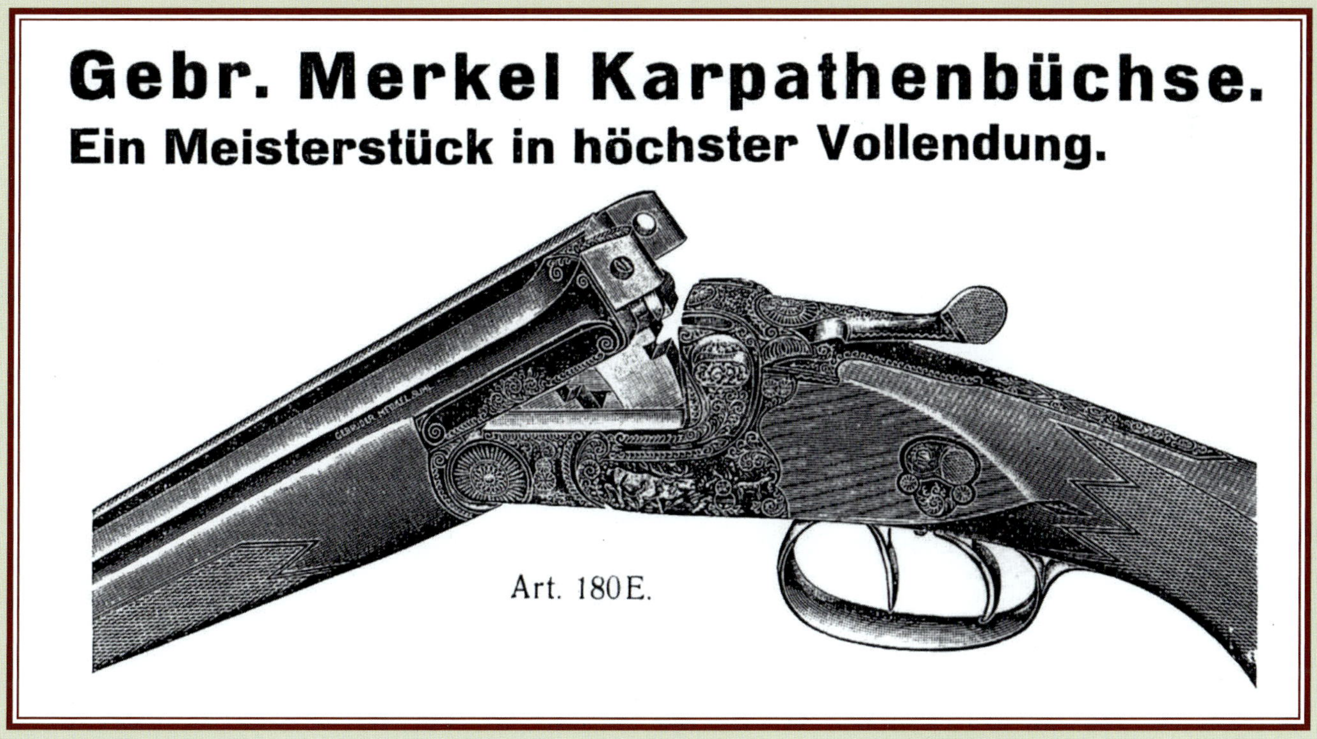

This advertisement for Merkel Carpathian rifles states, "A masterpiece in the highest perfection."

Note the beautiful engraving on this Merkel sidelock, over-and-under shotgun.

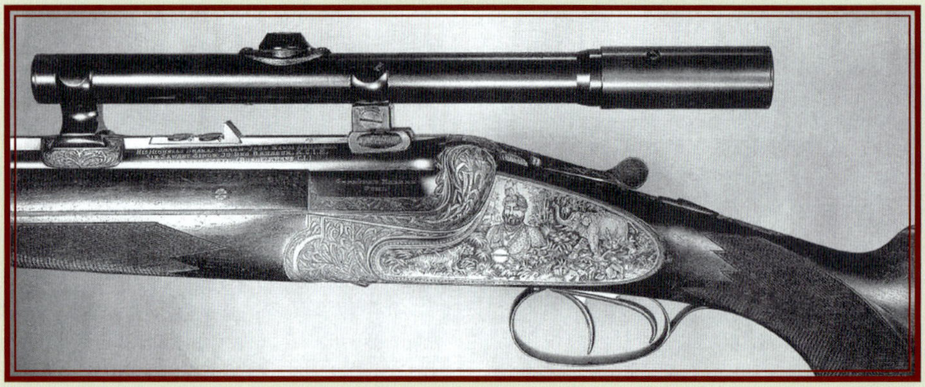

This O/U double rifle has custom sights, a Q.D. scope, custom wood, and was engraved for the Maharajah of Java.

J. PETERLONGO & R. MAHRHOLDT,

AUSTRIAN GUNMAKERS

Innsbruck, a town in the southern Tirolean region of Austria, was the home of gunmaker Johann Peterlongo, who started trading in sporting arms in 1854. At the end of the century, he had added a gun shop to his business. It became so successful that even before World War I, the company employed a large work force. The firm was known as the Tirolean Weapons Factory (*Tiroler Waffenfabrik*). Peterlongo developed and produced several new cartridges in calibers 8mm and 9mm and custom guns for these loads.

Faced with stiff competition, gunmakers often referred to their gun shops as factories to enhance their image when, in reality, the business might consist only of the proprietor and a helper. Because of this ever-increasing advertising practice, regulations were eventually passed to curb it. In these regulations, it was stipulated that a

Catalog No. 9, printed in 1931.

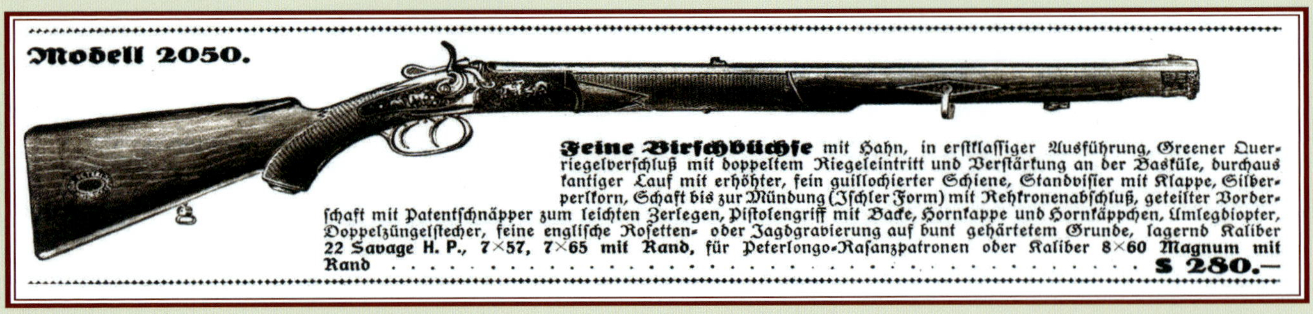

Advertising text for Model M2050: "Elegant hammer rifle for stalking in first-rate finish with Greener crossbolt, hexagonal barrel with integral raised rib, two-part stock (Ischler shape) with staghorn tip at the muzzle, horn butt-cap, pistol grip-cap, and folding peep sight. Tasteful English scroll or hunting scene engraving on case-colored background. In stock in caliber .22 Savage H. P., 7x65R, or 8x60R magnum." S280. (Austrian shillings)

J. Peterlongo

R. Mahrholdt

company had to have a minimum number of employees before the owner was allowed to use the term "factory" *(Fabrik)* in its advertising literature.

Between the years 1898 and 1918, the gunmaker Richard Mahrholdt took over the helm of Peterlongo's company. Mahrholdt is also known as the author of a dictionary entitled *Waffen Lexikon* (*Weapons Dictionary*), published in 1931. It is presently in its tenth printing.

In 1919, Mahrholdt founded his own company under the name of R. M. & S. After his death in 1947, Mahrholdt's son, Herbert, and eventually Mahrholdt's grandson, Erwin, a master gunmaker of the Ferlach school, took over. The company is famous for its target rifles and high-performance hunting arms. It built special sporting firearms for the tropics and drillings with a patented Peterlongo safety, as well as custom and luxury guns.

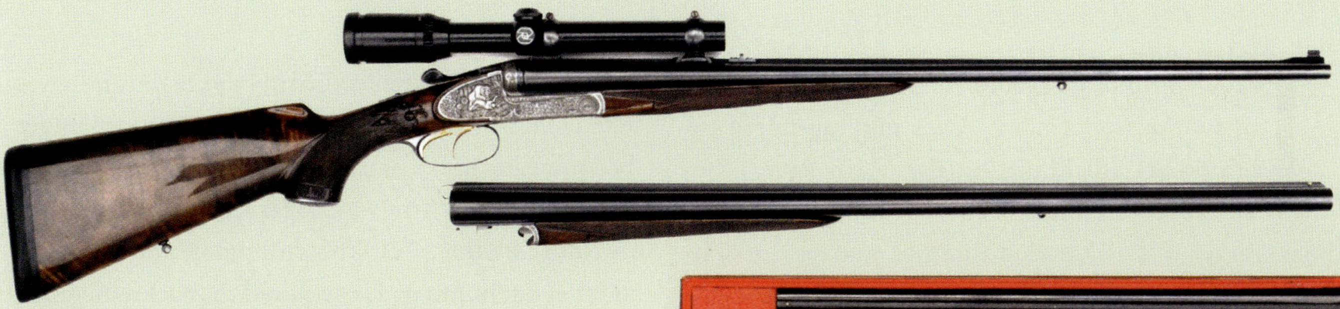

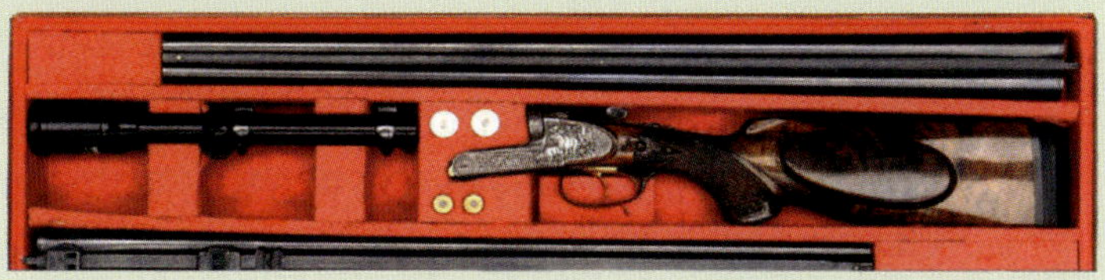

3403. ***MAHRHOLDT SIDE-PLATED EJECTOR DOUBLE RIFLE WITH EXTRA SHOTGUN BARRELS, SCOPE, AND CASE.** SN 41/ 170. Cal.

Note the exquisite engraving on this Mahrholdt double rifle.

Jacob Sackreuter

Jacob Philipp Sackreuter (1799–1850) grew up in southern Germany. After moving north to Frankfurt am Main (on the Main River), he worked as a gun trader in 1827. From his gun shop, Sackreuter initially traded flintlock and percussion guns of several designs. Later the firm also sold Suhl-made sporting arms and acted as distributor for several English, Belgian, and French gunmakers. Regionally he gained a reputation for crafting excellent short-barrel, large-caliber boar guns. These were double rifles *(Saubüchsen)* for stalking wild pigs.

An interesting accessory for his cape guns and double rifles was a unique one-piece muzzle protector. It prevented snow and dirt from entering the barrels, since these guns were often used for hunting wild boars on moonlit, snowy nights or during inclement weather in the winter months. Plugs were individually carved from a solid piece of walnut for each barrel combination.

After Jacob Sackreuter died in 1850, his business was sold to Phillip Friedrich Behrends but continued under the Sackreuter name, as was the custom. The next owner of the Sackreuter firm was Edgar Conrad A. Andreae, a wealthy banker, well-known hunter, and writer of books about hunting. He acquired the Sackreuter firm in 1872. Under his leadership, the firm expanded and prospered until about 1913.

Andreae promoted the sale of an "automatic" hunting firearm, System Roth, Vienna, an autoloader in caliber 8mm. This gun was apparently manufactured by Suhl gun manufacturer C. G. Haenel in 1902–1903. An example of this five-shot autoloading rifle was displayed at the German Colonial Hunting Exhibition in the city of Karlsruhe in the summer of 1903. At the time, an autoloader as a hunting firearm was not accepted by the conservative hunting fraternity. Sackreuter might have sought approval for its use in the

These photos show a hammer cape gun in caliber 11.15x60R and a 16-gauge barrel of 65mm length. It is fitted with a matching set of Damascus exchange barrels in caliber 16/16 and a straight English stock with rounded cheekpiece. It was made in 1890.

German colonies in Africa (and, therefore, the display at the Colonial Hunting Exhibition). The gun was not a commercial success.

In addition, the firm offered various sporting arms, hunting outfits and equipment, dog-care supplies, game calls, hunting horns, targets and target guns, fishing outfits, nets, ammunition, loading supplies, and miscellaneous staghorn furnishings for the hunting lodge.

These three owners of Sackreuters apparently were not gunmakers themselves, but traded in guns and accessories and employed a staff of highly qualified gunsmiths who made and repaired guns on the premises in Frankfurt.

A Sackreuter ad from the 1890s for the Andreae double-rifle drilling states, "Excellent shooting performance and handling weight only 3.2 kg (7 pounds, 1 ounce). Rifle barrel in caliber 12.5x60R (a large-caliber, black-powder, Mauser-based cartridge), large entrance hole, shot barrel 20/76. Easy selector, practical, clear sights. Price: 350 German marks; hammerless version, 500 Marks."

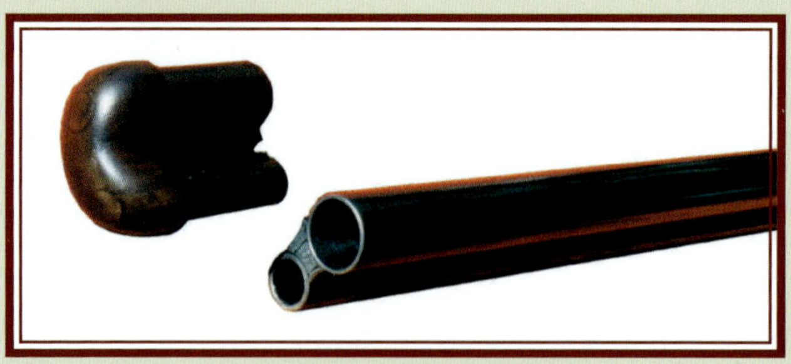

These walnut muzzle protectors were slipped over the front sight, barrels, and into the bores. The same protectors were also available for drillings.

A Sackreuter hammer shotgun.

J. P. SAUER & SOHN

The renowned firm of J. P. Sauer & Sohn was founded by Johann Paul Sauer in 1751; it is the oldest and one of the largest gun factories in Suhl, Germany. This family-owned business flourished under the leadership of many generations: Johann Peter Sauer, 1720; Johann Sauer Jr., 1755; Franz Sauer, 1790; Rudolph Sauer, 1830; Franz Sauer Jr., 1840; Hans Sauer, 1875; Rolf Sauer, 1882; and Franz Joachim Sauer, 1914.

The company crafted sporting arms of high quality and precision for the commercial market. It also sought commissions from the military, and in 1811, it was awarded the first contract for muskets by several of the German states. This was due in part to the great demand for military armament during the Napoleonic Wars.

Production facilities had to be expanded when, in 1837, two other firms joined Sauer to build firearms for the military. The company at that time was named Spangenberg, Sauer and Sturm, and by 1858 it employed 260 people. To meet the increasing demand for the new needle-fire rifle used in the Franco-Prussian War of 1870–71, the Sauer factory and work force expanded once again. When the Mauser factory was unable to handle the production for its new Mauser Model 71, Sauer was called upon in 1872 to build these new Mauser rifles.

With the war over, Franz and Rudolf Sauer decided in 1882 to stop producing military arms and to concentrate on its sporting firearms line, which would be sold under the old logo "J. P. Sauer and Sohn." Although still working together with other gunmakers on different projects, the sporting-arms sector of the Sauer factory constantly sought technological improvements. In cooperation with the firm of Friedrich Krupp A.G. in Essen and beginning in 1899, new barrel steels were developed and used exclusively on Sauer guns.

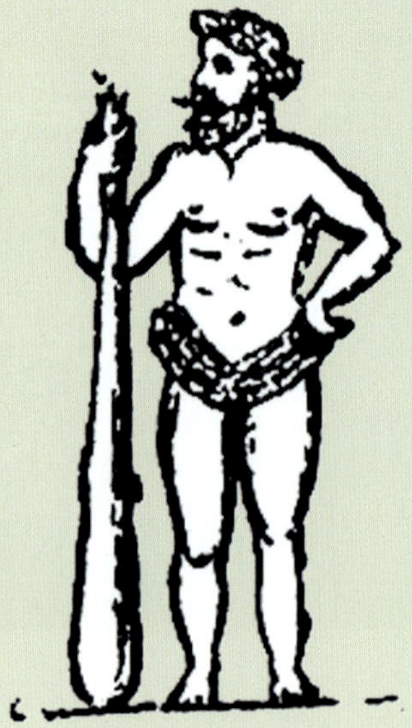

Sauer trademarks.

Shot with a Sauer & Son hammerless three barrelled gun in Mexico

This 16-gauge double shotgun with Damascus barrels is complemented by fine scroll engraving on the action and sidelocks.

Klasse 32

32 434586 S 31515

FORTUNA

3/9 1930. J. P. Sauer & Sohn, Suhl i. Thür. 18/6 1931.

Geschäftsbetrieb: Maschinenfabrik. Waren: Schreibmaschinen, Schreibmaschinenteile. (GK. 32)

[31. 1354]

Sauer advertisement for typewriters, September 1930.

The outbreak of World War I in 1914 brought a change to small-arms production worldwide. Not only the German army but the armies of the Allies as well—French, American, British, and British Empire—demanded "a machine gun that could walk." Like so many other businesses, however, by the end of the war Sauer had to find its way back to the commercial market. While continuing to craft firearms for the hunter and sportsman, in 1919, the firm diversified with the production of typewriters under the trade name "Fortuna."

In 1939, the Sauer program included shotguns, cape guns, drillings, double rifles, bolt-action rifles, and break-open stalking rifles such as the light and accurate Tell rifle. A few of the numerous improvements on Sauer guns included single selective triggers, separate hand-cocking features on combination guns, safeties to prevent doubling, interchangeable barrels, and reinforced breeches on drillings and double rifles.

With the outbreak of World War II, Sauer had to switch to military production once again and, consequently, produced few sporting firearms during the war years. After the war, the company relocated to the West German town of Eckernförde in northern Germany and started to rebuild.

The Sauer factory at the height of its success.

ENTRANCE TO WORKS
AND ADMINISTRATIVE OFFICES

Forging works.

Machine tool room.

Steam turbines delivered power to the various gunmaking facilities.

Waffen tips

Oskar Will, owner of Venuswaffenwerk in Zella-Mehlis, offered a Tell air gun in its catalog.

Late model "Tell" with a lever pivot bolt. Gunmaker Sauer & Sohn's popular single-shot rifle, the Tell, was named after the legendary Swiss freedom hero, William Tell, who was forced by a tyrant to shoot an apple off the head of his young son.

In the 1890s, the company introduced a single-shot rifle, called the Tell. It was initially offered in caliber 5.6x35R. The rifle became popular and was later also offered in calibers 6.5x52R (25-35 W), 6.5x58R, 8.15x46R, 8x48R, and 9.3x57. On early model Tell rifles, the pivoting bolt had to be removed with a screwdriver to disassemble the rifle. Later models featured a lever bolt for a quick take-down.

This Sauer shotgun with a single trigger was made for Charles Daly.

Another view of the same J. P. Sauer shotgun shown on facing page.

GUNMAKER STIEGELE

Founded in Munich in 1837 by Carl Anton Stiegele, the firm Carl Stiegele initially produced popular parlor rifles (*Zimmerstutzen*), air guns, and target rifles. Stiegele target rifles and hunting firearms became famous and were exhibited at the World's Fair in Paris in 1867 and in Vienna in 1873, where they took gold medals for their excellent shooting performance, meticulous workmanship, and tasteful execution. In 1867, Stiegele patented a new locking system for his guns which resulted in increased business and made possible the opening of his rifle factory in 1868. Made Purveyor to the Court of the King of Bavaria—*Kgl. Bayr. Hof-Gewehrfabrik*—and to several princes and other royalty in Europe, Stiegele also furnished sporting arms to the emperor of Germany, Kaiser Wilhelm II.

Between 1929 and 1934, the company delivered several sporting firearms to the emperor of Japan. One of these guns, a gold and silver inlaid drilling, can be seen today in a museum in Tokyo. During World War II, most of the business records were destroyed in bombing raids on Munich, and in May 1945, all remaining guns and tools were confiscated by order of the Allied command.

In the 1950s, the Brandl family acquired the Stiegele business. Under gunmaker Victor Brandl Jr., the company was renamed Stiegele Jagd, and it branched out to South Africa and the United States. Today it also maintains a shooting range outside Munich and conducts well-attended auctions of new and used sporting arms. It is interesting to note that the sales facilities are still at the same location on Maximilianstrasse in Munich as they have been since the inception of the firm in 1837.

Top: A Stiegele percussion drilling.
Bottom: The storefront of the Stiegele firm in Munich displayed merchandise and awards.

CHARLES DALY

Charles Daly guns are listed in this volume because many of this company's firearms originated in Germany. Daly was not a gunmaker but a gun importer in New York. From the late 1800s until the present day, the Daly Company imported guns into the United States. Sales catalogs entitled Charles Daly are rare, but they do exist. Other catalogs circulated under the name Shoverling, Daly & Gales. They offered hunting and fishing equipment, shotguns, rifles, pistols, and drillings to the sporting public in the United States around the turn of the twentieth century. Both catalogs—Charles Daly and the Shoverling, Daly & Gales—also invited orders for one-of-a-kind, custom-made firearms.

Some of the earliest guns imported by Daly in the 1800s were made in Belgium by a variety of companies. They were well made Scott-action hammer guns and hammerless guns of Anson & Deeley design with quality Damascus steel barrels. These came in a variety of patterns, including Bernard and Cluny. Charles Daly also contracted with the German firms of August Schüler, Abesser Merkel, J. P. Sauer, and H. A. Lindner. Schüler and Merkel sporting firearms accounted for few of the Daly imports, the majority coming from J. P. Sauer & Sohn. These Sauer/Dalys are high-grade examples of the gunmakers' artistry.

Perhaps the most appealing arms to appear under the Charles Daly name were the Lindner/Daly guns. They first showed up as double-barrel hammer shotguns. Grades ranged from a plain hunting gun to ones that were highly ornate. The workmanship, finish, and quality of Lindner guns excelled in every aspect, including their outstanding Damascus barrels. Later, Lindner guns were found in a variety of grades but in a modified Anson & Deeley hammerless design. Damascus barrels were used with the Anson & Deeley action, but fluid steel soon became standard.

These guns featured a longer special action for greater leverage when working the bolt and overhanging safety sears to prevent an accidental discharge. A

Charles Daly (1839–1899).

A Lindner-made 12-gauge Charles Daly diamond-grade rifle.

Greener crossbolt was standard, its cross-section square instead of the usual round shape. The barrels were either made of Witten Excelsior or Krupp Special steels. The hammerless actions were beautifully sculpted with side clips and scalloped frames. Regular-grade and single-barrel trap guns made by Lindner showed the same attention to detail.

In the United States, guns have surfaced with the "Lindner" signature on the barrels but without the Daly name. On the majority of the guns, there is no name other than "Charles Daly," but identifying marks are found in the shape of a crossed dueling pistol stamp on the underside of the barrels along with the initials "H. A. L." These guns are also found with the words "Prussia," "Saxony," or "Thuringia" stamped on the action.

The reason for this disparity is a mystery. Possibly Lindner exported a few guns under his own name. It is more likely that a few Lindner guns that had been sold under the maker's name in Europe were brought to the United States from Germany after World War II. This information confirms what Swedish firearms authority Frederick Franzen recently observed: "Lindner-made guns are not seen in Europe."

H.A. LINDER - SUHL

Founded 1874

Berlin Salesrooms
P. HELBIG WILHELMSTRASSE 53

SPECIALTY
CHARLES DALY GUNS
FOR
EXPORT TO NORTH AMERICA

This is an advertisement found in the old German shooting magazine Schuss and Waffe, *(Vol. 6, Nos. 8, 9, and 13). A. Englehardt of Buenos Aires, Argentina, discovered it. The translation is: "The Lindner specialty was the export of guns to North America."*

The top is enlarged on this stamp while the lower is full size.

On opposite page: A Robert Schüler shotgun made for Charles Daly in New York.

Opposite page: Wild boar, a game animal highly favored in Europe for centuries.

PART 3
THE GUN ITSELF

HISTORY

The natural development of weaponry by the Germanic tribes was on par with the rest of Western civilization, if not more advanced in certain technological developments. Steel making has long been recognized as a Teutonic area of expertise. The blades of Solingen are legendary and the foundries of the Ruhr world famous. Along with the ability to master working materials and technology, the Germanic people have always had a love of craftsmanship and an aptitude for innovative engineering.

The years between 1880 and 1939 are thought by students and collectors of Germanic sporting arms to be the "Golden Age." This period saw an extraordinary number of innovations and changes in sporting-arms technology. Into this time period fell the monumental change from muzzleloader to breechloader, the shift from hammer to hammerless design, and a move from black to nitro or smokeless powder. Along with these improvements came numerous advancements in materials and methods that led to the development of the modern sporting arm.

Within the Golden Age itself, generally speaking, the finest work in terms of craftsmanship was produced between 1880 and World War I. Before the First World War, there was a substantial amount of handwork and fitting done on each gun. Many examples of exceptional quality sporting arms *(Feine Gewehre)* were still produced after 1918, but the trend was toward less handwork and more machine finish in gunmaking, mainly because of labor costs that spiraled exponentially after the war. By utilizing more machinery, gunmakers were able to increase output and reduce firearm prices, yet at the same time still retain a high level of quality.

It is interesting to note that handwork and craftsmanship at the time, as much as we admire and seek it out today, were not very profitable because of labor costs and, as a result, gunmakers did not value them as we do today. When the quality was maintained and labor wages reduced, gunmakers embraced modern production methods, as is evident in their catalogs with pictures of large, modern (for that time) production facilities that featured rows upon rows of lathes and metal shaping machinery of the latest design.

The large firearms firm of J. P. Sauer & Sohn is said in a 1907 Schoverling, Daly & Gales catalog to have begun mechanizing twenty-five years earlier, in 1882. By 1907, the company reportedly was fully mechanized with at least one thousand electric power tools. Simson & Co. of Suhl proudly announced that they had reached that stage by the early 1920s.

As costs for hand finishing became more prohibitive, machine-made parts produced a perfectly functional and reliable gun. Therefore, the unadorned product became more plentiful. The outbreak of World War II put an end to fine "prewar" craftsmanship, although examples of exceptionally high-quality sporting arms were produced right up until 1945 in Suhl. There were also a few excellent sporting guns assembled in the early 1950s from components made before the war.

Today in Germany and Austria, there are several firms that can produce a gun of any barrel configuration, any caliber, and whatever feature and level of quality a customer might desire. The quality of a modern German fine gun compares favorably to that of any reputable firm in any other country, but, as is the case with any gunmaker today, prices for their handmade firearms have risen to heights not thought possible.

The Frank Drilling

The Frank drilling, with its detachable rifle barrel, was an attempt to lighten the weight of the gun during hunts for upland game. Advances in technology, resulting in lighter steel alloys and the use of aluminum, rendered the design obsolete.

The 1910 ALFA Catalog describes the Frank Drilling as follows:

"By detaching the rifle barrel, the Frank three-barrel can quickly be converted into a light gun and vice-versa into a three barrel. Only universal firearm of the twentieth century, in use for twenty years. More than 2,000 specimens. Full five years' guarantee. Splendid shooting owing to free position of barrels.

"The advantage of the Frank three barrel: Because of the free position of the rifle barrel and the vibration connected therewith, this firearm is never in danger of bursting as is the case of a three barrel with soldered rifle-barrel—consequently it's the safest rifle of modern times.

"Proof: The 8mm rifle barrel of a Frank three-barrel was fired in the Royal Testing Establishment at Suhl with 3 grams of nitro-powder and stamped. The rifle barrel was then soldered on, and the Royal Testing Establishment then again fired it in this condition with the same quantity of nitro-powder, and on this occasion it burst. Certificate of the Royal Testing Establishment is at hand.

"A proof that the rifle-barrel does not alter its position, although put to the most severe test, is given by the following original report by the Royal Testing Establishment at Suhl: Royal Testing Establishment Day book No. 646 95.

"After the legally prescribed trial with black and nitro-powder, the detachable rifle barrel of the three-barrel gun No. 9356 submitted by you, has also, in accordance with your wishes, been tested with 1,000 rounds, using nitro powder. The locking mechanism acted perfectly. The barrel and bolt remained intact.

Signed: Fritsche, Director."

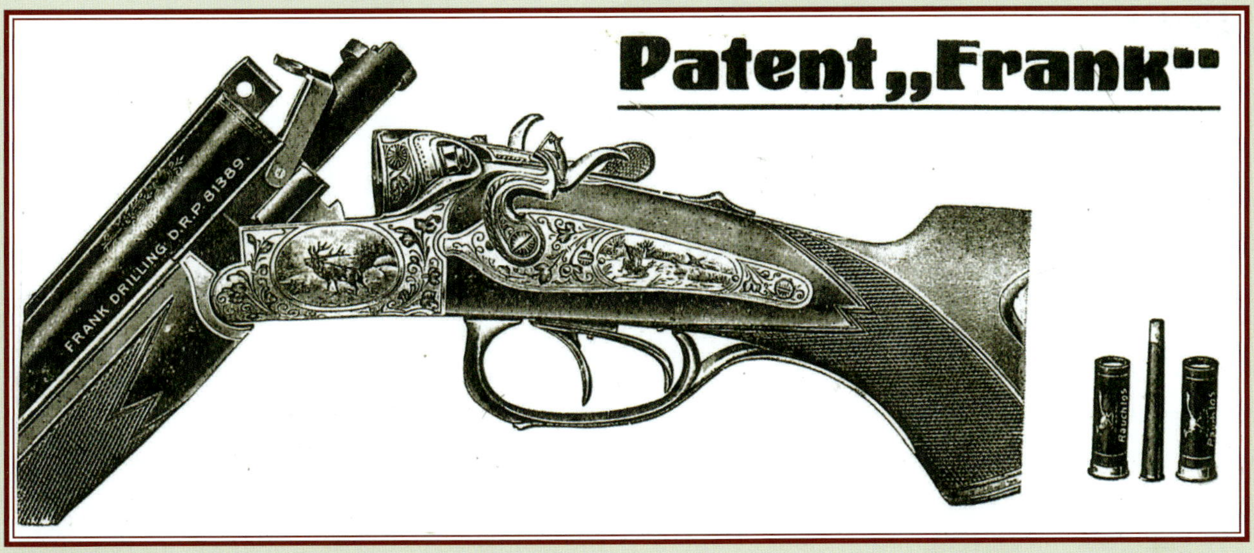

Hammer top-lever drilling with detachable rifle barrel.

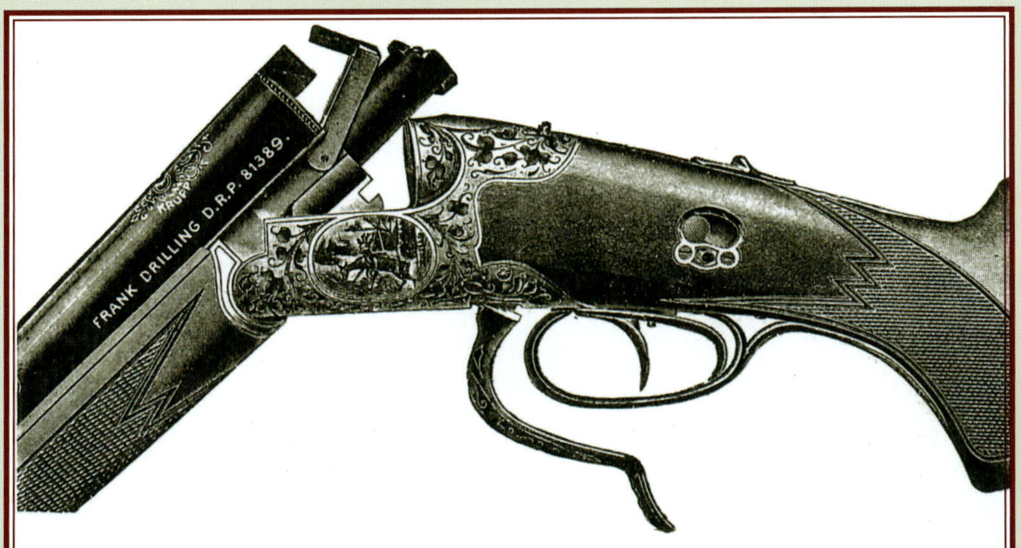

Hammerless Frank drilling with Roux locking lever.

The Barrel

The Making of the Barrel

The barrel was the main part of an early firearm. It contained the powder charge and projectile, to which it also gave direction. Initially barrels were forged entirely by hand from a billet of iron. The thickness and length of the barrel to be forged determined the size of the iron bar that would be obtained from the smelter.

Working the metal required great skill and a knowledge of the material and the tools. The barrelsmith had to work fast, heating and reheating the iron and stretching it into the desired shape by precise hammer blows. Heating the metal too many times weakened the structure of the material. Forging it when it had already cooled too much made it brittle.

Barrelsmiths often worked together with a skilled helper or journeyman, and under ideal circumstances this team would be able to forge up to twelve barrels a day. They settled in locations that had waterpower, suitable iron ore for mining, and timber for making charcoal. Water-powered hammer mills eventually took over much of the barrel forging and shaping work. After the desired shape had been attained, the resulting thin metal strip was pounded into a half-round depression on the anvil and hammer-formed around a hardened mandrel.

The centuries-old method of forging steel for Damascus swords, known first in the Orient, was later applied to crafting superior gun barrels. Small iron rods

Anvil for forging barrels.

Working the water-powered hammer.

Twisting the barrel.

or wires of different carbon content were twisted and hammered into flat iron bars. When wound around a steel pin and welded, they imparted hardness and elasticity to the resulting barrel blank.

The arrangement of these rods and the way they were hammered determined the various patterns visible on gun barrels. The surface of the barrel was etched with acid, then polished to a beautiful, nonreflective finish. The process of making Damascus steel and the subsequent acid treatment, handed down from father to son, remained the secret of the Damascus-smith for generations.

With demand increasing, makers on the Continent first started to import Damascus barrels from Spain. A gold-inlaid master mark stamped on a barrel crafted by a famous Spanish gunsmith was a sign of quality and made a gun highly desirable. Incorporating these barrels in their firearms was an accepted and fashionable practice, even for famous European gunmakers.

With many customers insisting on Damascus barrels in their firearms and requests for them ever-increasing, it comes as no surprise that the makers' marks were sometimes faked. Barrels stamped with imaginary or forged hallmarks by fellow Spanish or Continental gunsmiths were difficult to detect.

Gunmakers in and around the Belgian town of Liege became masters in forging excellent quality barrels with beautiful patterns. A number of relatively small

Sanding and polishing the barrel.

Honing the bore.

companies employed hundreds of barrel makers in that region. Shotgun tubes and rifle barrels were exported to other countries, either finished or unfinished, to be used by German, Austrian, and English makers. Although firms in the gun centers of Suhl, Ferlach, St. Etienne, or Birmingham made barrels of their own design, they increasingly imported Damascus barrels from Belgium because they were not able to compete with Belgian prices.

In 1811, well-known gunsmith and trader Heinrich Anschütz observed gun-barrel making in his hometown. In his book *The Gun Factory in Suhl (Die Gewehrfabrik in Suhl)*, he wrote: "Regular, twisted, turned, or Damascus barrels are delivered by the factory here in excellent quality. Barrel making for hunting firearms does not differ from that of military guns, but the finish on hunting arms is superior, requiring more care and attention to detail."

It was in Liege that the art of manufacturing fake Damascus *(faux damas)* steel barrels was perfected. Inexpensive cast steel barrels were etched with beautiful designs and patterns imitating real Damascus steel. They were then labeled with fanciful authentic-sounding French names or descriptions. The most brazen makers even advertised them as genuine Crollè, genuine Rubans, or genuine Chainette. Because of their appeal, Damascus designs were also applied at a later time to fluid steel barrels when these became available.

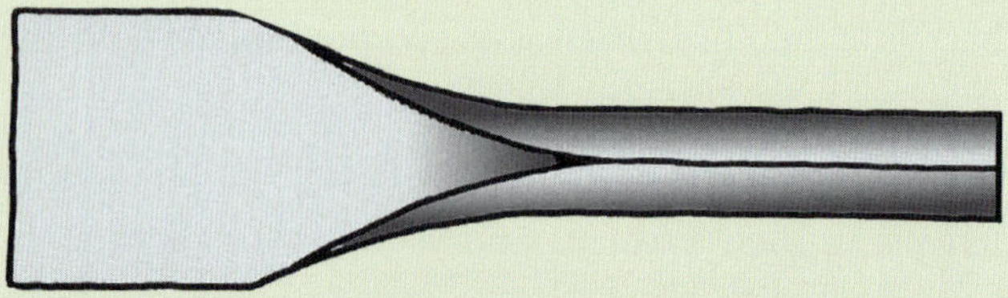

Overlapping ends were forge-welded to form the barrel tube, the weld running parallel to the axis of the bore.

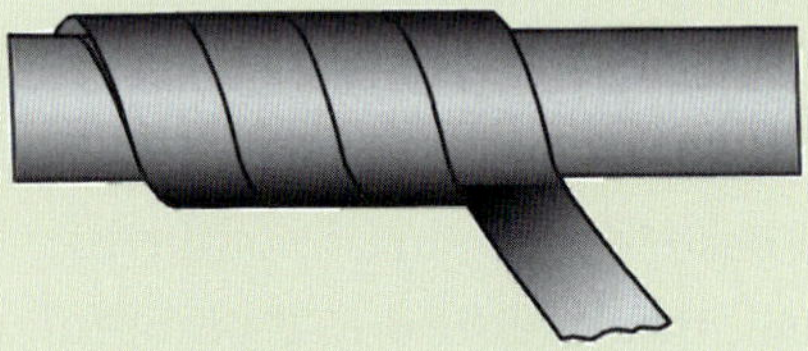

An alternate method required the material to be wound diagonally around the mandrel. This also resulted in a stronger barrel.

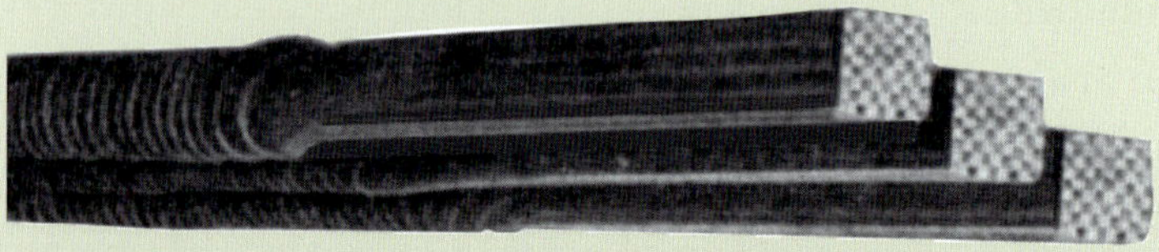

Initially barrels were formed from a billet of steel.

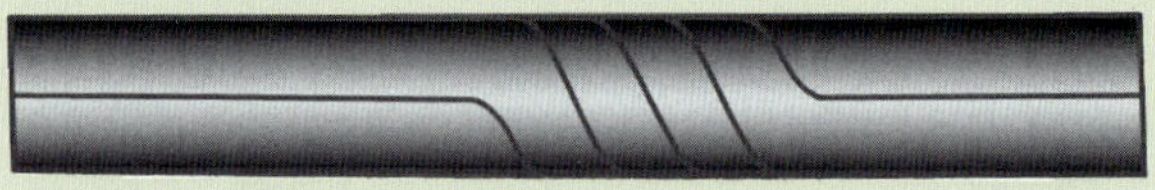

In another procedure, the barrel was reheated and turned, twisting the weld for increased durability.

Damascus barrel wound diagonally around a mandrel.

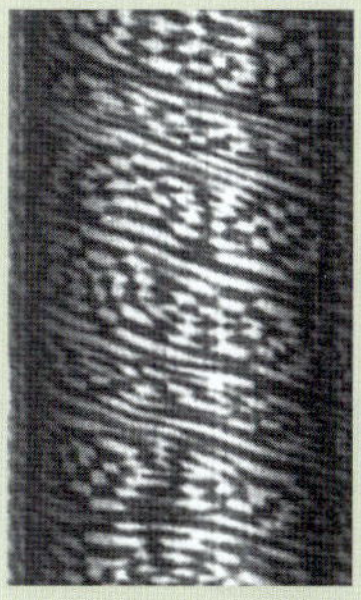
Bernard II

Bernard I

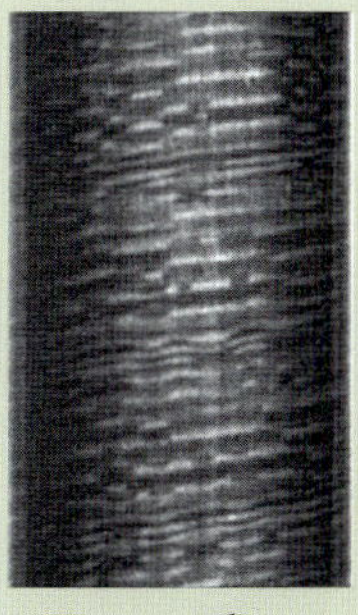
Birmingham

Boston Extra

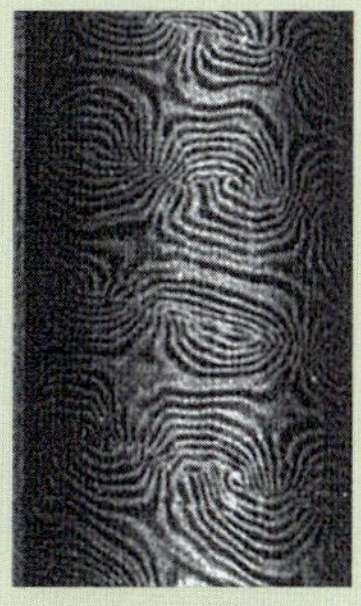
Boston II

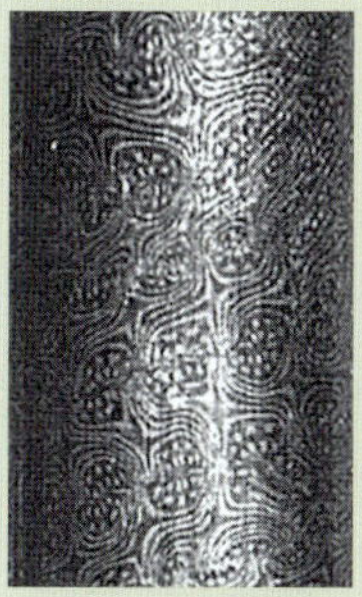
Turk Extra

Wellington

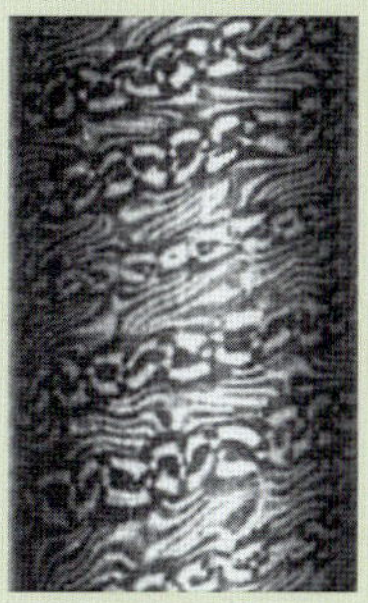
Chainette

Wellington Fin

Crollè Extra

Crollè I

Crollè II

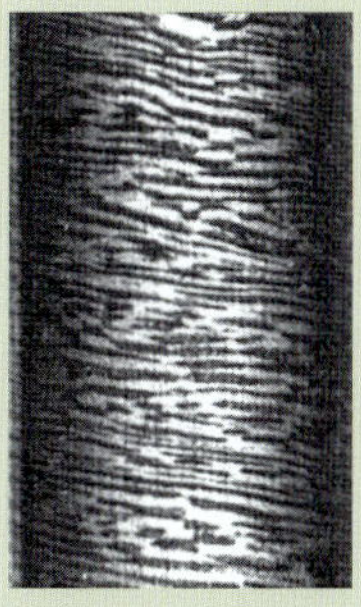
Leopold Bernard

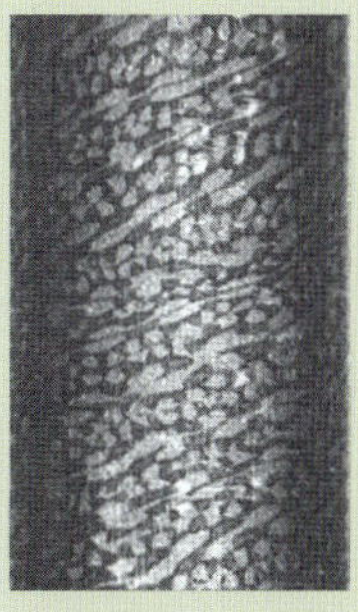
Manufacturer Extra

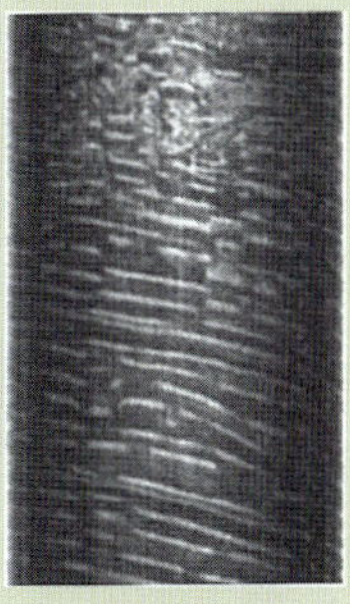
Rubans Fins
Fine Twist

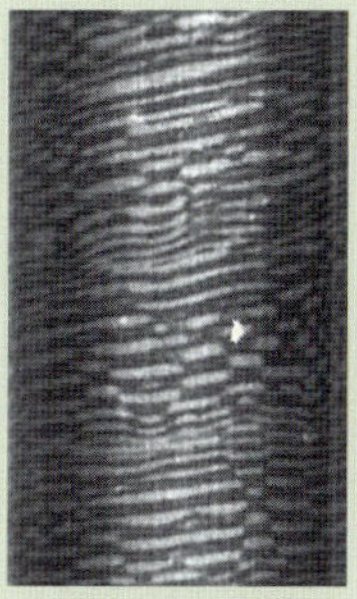
Rubans III
Twist III

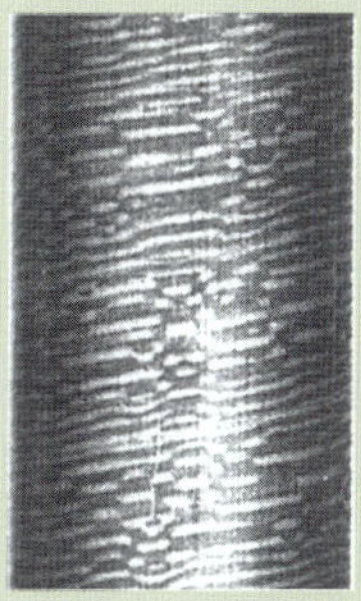
Rubans Royal Extra
Royal Twist

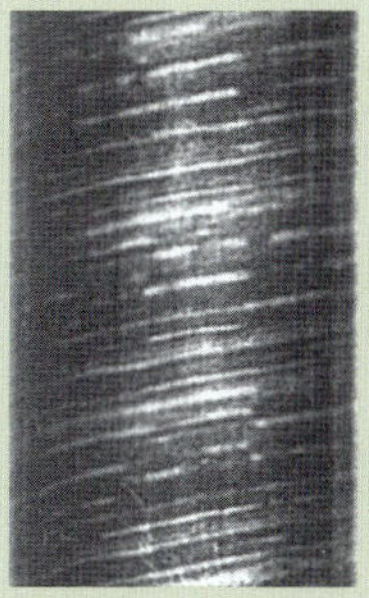
Rubans Royal
Twist

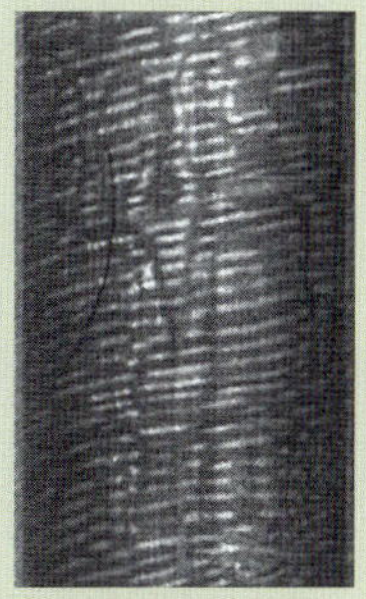
Rubans II
Twist

Clou Fin

These Damascus barrel patterns are from the Belgium barrel steel maker Manufacture Liegeoise d'Armes a'Feu. These barrels were offered finished or unfinished. Many other Liege manufacturers offered similar patterns in their catalogs.

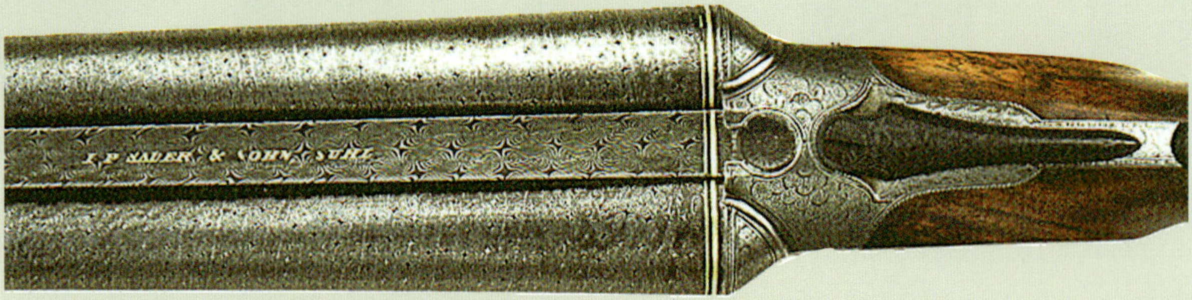

This is a 16-gauge Sauer shotgun with Damascus barrels.

Other firms in Europe also produced fake Damascus. These barrels entered the world markets by the tens of thousands under various names and in several languages. Birmingham, Ruban, Plaintwist, Ribbon, Royal Twist, Fine Twist, Stub Twist, or Skelp barrels were a few of hundreds of available labels. Intricate Crollè Damascus designs were more costly. They had names like Chainette, Bernard, London, Rosè, Wellington, or Turk. German makers marked their barrels as Streifendamast, Türkischer, or Rosendamast and Hufnageldamast.

Forging barrels by hand demanded long experience, skill, and manual labor, even with the use of new machinery. With the introduction of cast and fluid steel *(Fluss Stahl)*, steelmakers saw an opportunity to mechanize the production of steel barrels, which could be manufactured in large numbers at a cheaper price. When alloyed with chromium, vanadium, nickel, or manganese, their hardness, durability, elasticity, and/or resistance to corrosion made them superior to the Damascus barrels of the time. On the Continent and in England, fluid steel barrels were produced in different grades. Regular steel barrel blanks were supplied for inexpensive arms. For luxury guns, heat-treated and alloyed ones were available on special order.

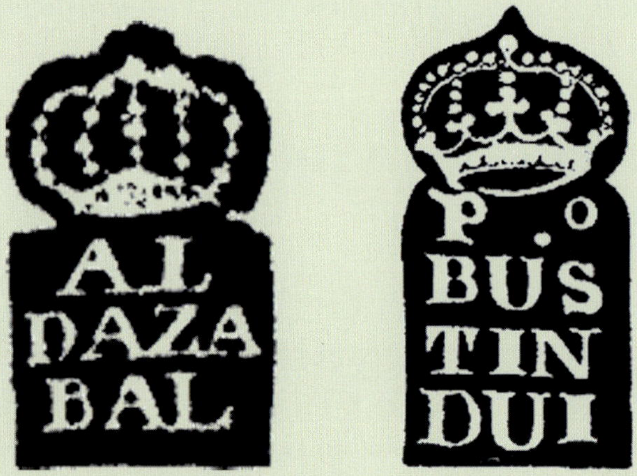

Hallmarks of Spanish barrel makers.

The largest steel manufacturer in Germany at the turn of the twentieth century was Friedrich Krupp A.G., a company with headquarters in Essen in the Ruhr Valley. The firm produced steels in many shapes and forms for the metal industry and was a leader in the field of metallurgy. The variety of Krupp steel blanks for barrels achieved world-famous reputations for their quality and were ordered by gunmakers from many countries.

Higher-priced barrels were produced from refined and alloyed metals, so-called precious steels *(Edelmetalle)*. They were annealed by a controlled-temperature process. When tested, Krupp barrel steels were superior in hardness, flexibility, toughness, and resistance to expansion. In 1918, the Poldi Steelworks *(Poldi Hütte)* in Austria became part of Czechoslovakia (present-day Czech Republic and Slovakia). The steelmaker developed the first rust-resistant barrel steel in 1910.

GUSS STAHL	CAST STEEL
Fluss Stahl, Krupp, Essen	Fluid steel, Krupp, Essen, was an early name for Krupp steel barrels.
Krupp Stahl	Krupp steel—heat-treated steels for medium-quality guns.
Krupp Laufstahl	Krupp barrel steel—improved and heat-treated alloy steel. Around 1900, this logo replaced Fluss Stahl.
Spezial Gewehrlaufstahl Friedr, Krupp, Essen	Special rifle-barrel steel—Friedrich Krupp, Essen.
Dreiläufer System	Three-barrel system.
Prima Krupp Stahl	Krupp steel (prime, super), excellent, refined, and alloyed steels for heavy loads.
Krupp-Inerso-Laufstahl Dreiring System	Krupp stain-resistant barrel steel for heaviest loads.
Nirosta, Friedr. Krupp, Essen	Krupp stainless steel for heaviest loads.

Advertisement for Witten barrel steel.

In 1853, Alfred Krupp invented a centrifugal process to cast steel wheels for railroad cars. They were manufactured by the thousands and laid the foundation for the tremendous wealth and growth of the Krupp empire. The Krupp logo, three interlocking wheels or rings (Dreiring), was designed in recognition of this important innovation.

Krupp Dreiring logo.

GUSS STAHL	CAST STEEL
Poldi Fluss Stahl	Fluid steel
Poldi Extra	Alloyed electro steel
Poldi Electro	Improved electro steel
Poldi Wolfram Spezial	Special tungsten steel
Poldi Anticorro	Stain resistant
Poldi Anticorro Spezial	Stainless special

German *Stahlwerke Röchling Bruderus A.G. produced:*

Röchling Electro Gewehrlauf Stahl	Steel for shotgun barrels
Röchling Ferro-Platin	Stainless steel for strongest loads
Röchling Elektro-Spezial	Improved steels for shotgun and rifle barrels
Röchling Electro	Improved steels of medium quality

Gebr. Böhler & Co, A.G. of Austria produced:

Böhler Blitz	Excellent, high-alloy barrel steel
Böhler Tanne ML	Excellent, high-alloy barrel steel
Böhler Antinit NG	Stain resistant, light-weight barrel steel
Böhler Spezial W 43	Stain resistant, light-weight barrel steel

BARREL CONNECTIONS

In gunmakers' catalogs of the time, we frequently find references to soldered barrel joints and how they differed from and were superior to those of the competition. On multibarreled sporting arms, special attention was given to the method of fastening barrels together. In the past, the soldering of steel and Damascus barrels, extensions, and related parts was done extensively with hard solder using brass. When refined steel barrels became available, hard solder, with its high melting temperature, could change the metal structure of heat-treated alloy steel. Reheating or overheating barrel steel damaged the very properties the barrel manufacturer sought to incorporate into the material.

Prior to soldering, the garnishing smith *(Garnierer)* aligned the shot tubes and rifle barrels. Components were then fastened together with wire and special wedges that pressed the barrels and ribs together. If barrels on double rifles did not shoot well together and the gun could not be regulated with different loads, the gunsmith had to de-solder, clean, regulate, and blue the barrels again.

Heat distortions of double-rifle and drilling barrels changed the point of impact after firing several shots. On a drilling with the rifle barrel above the shot tubes, successive shots fell short of the target. On traditional double rifles, the point of impact could change to either side contingent upon which barrel was discharged and was subject to pauses or intervals between shots.

Depending on steel category, strength required, and location, gunmakers changed to tin or copper/silver solder with a lower melting point. Generally, two, three, or four barrels were fastened together only at the breech and sometimes at the muzzle with hard solder. Likewise, wedge-shaped underlugs *(Laufhaken)* were hard soldered for strength at the chambers. The center part of barrels, top, and side ribs *(Reifen)* were connected with soft solder. Hard-solder seams with higher temperatures were completed first; soft solder with lower temperatures finished the process. Ribs often consisted of two parts: solid rear sections including rib extensions and hollow, soft-soldered center ribs.

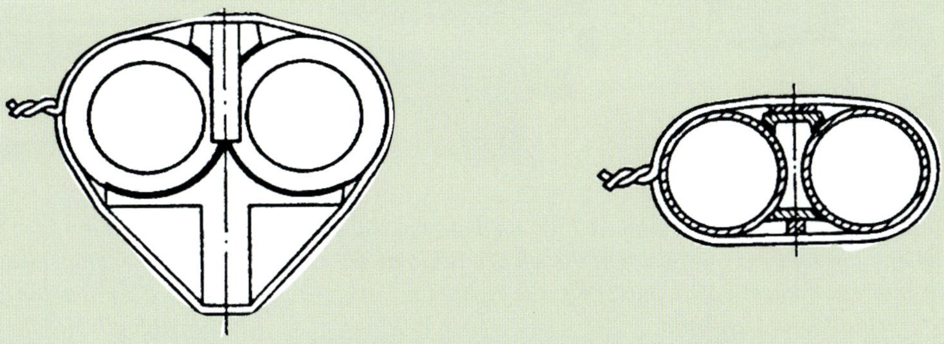

Barrels fastened together before soldering.

Soldered barrel connection on a :

Shotgun Drilling O/U double rifle

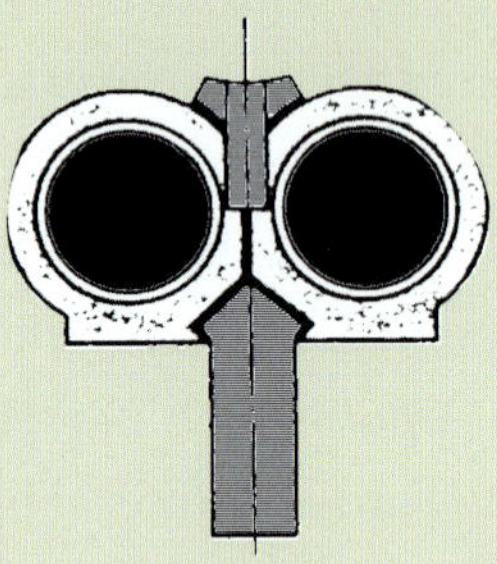

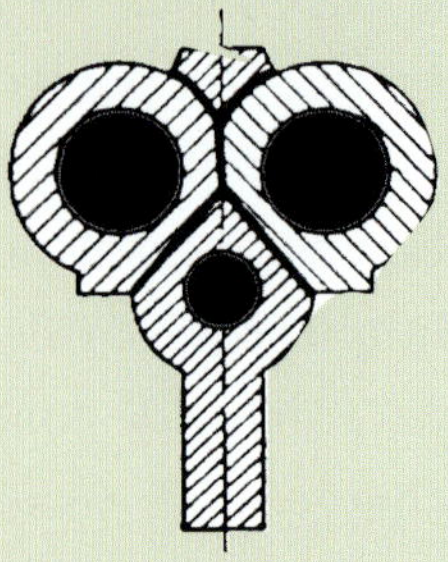

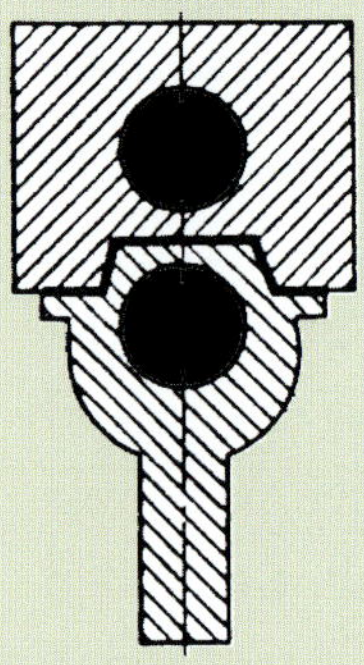

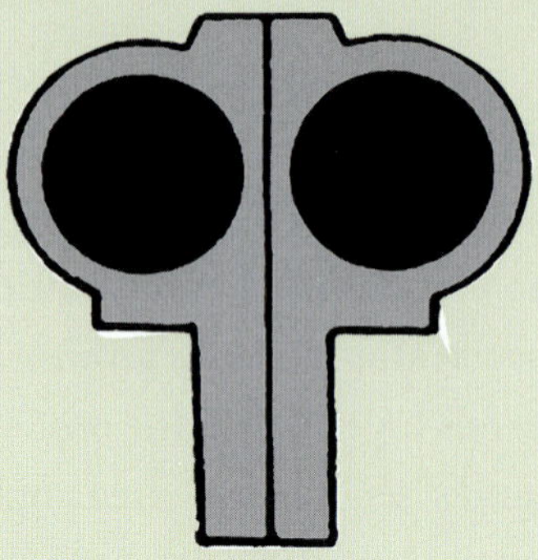

Demibloc

The demibloc technique employed underlugs and ribs that were each half forged to the barrels to avoid a high-soldering temperature; it also retained strength. Although it provided a strong barrel connection, it was expensive to manufacture and, consequently, was used mostly on high-priced sporting arms. Side-by-side shotguns were produced in this manner by several gunmakers, including Carl Walther in Suhl and Belgian gunmaker Bayard.

The disadvantage of using soft solders lay in the fact that barrels had to be cold-blued in a time-consuming, brush-on operation. Hot dipped bluing solution attacked and corroded soft-soldered seams, turning the solder into a white powder.

Steelmaker Gebrüder Böhler furnished electo-welded demibloc barrels to the trade. Heat, generated during the welding process, was ventilated away from the chambers.

Electro-weld

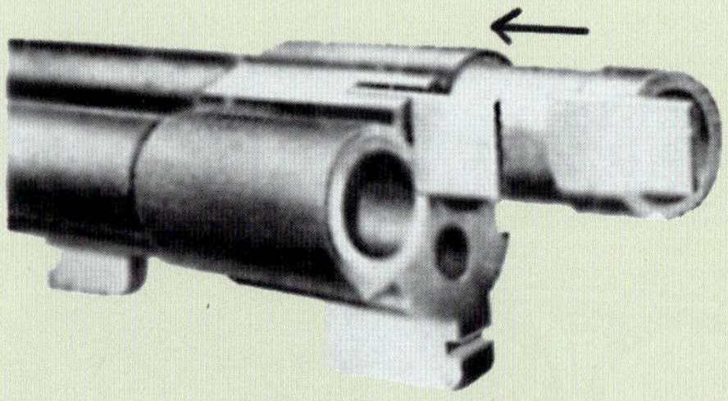

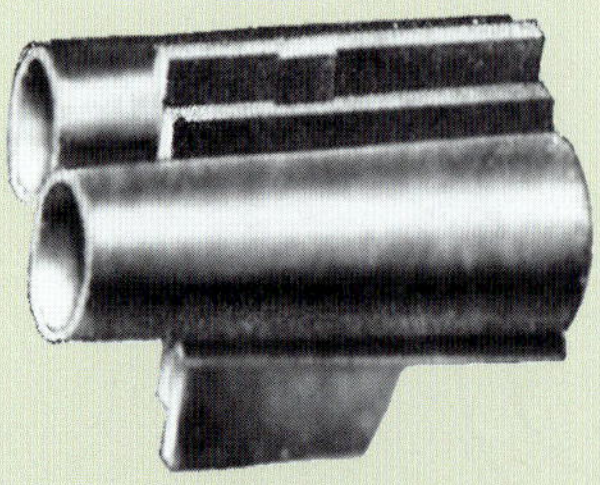

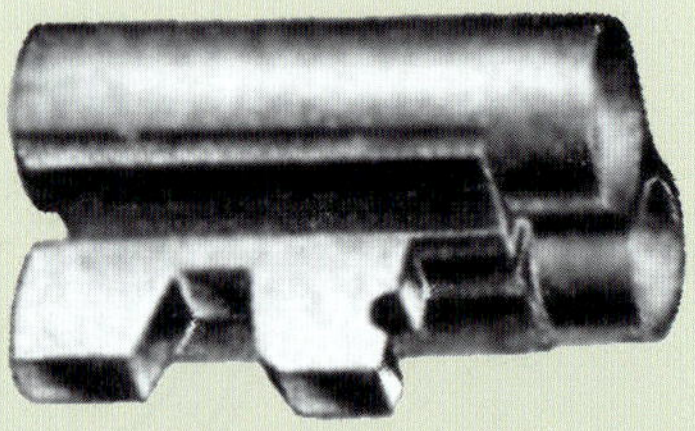

Several gunsmiths and steel manufacturers developed dovetailed mechanical joints that were fitted and soft soldered together. On the left is a Schmidt & Habermann drilling with mechanical barrel joints. On the right is a Carl Walther shotgun with vertical dovetailed joint.

Above is a monobloc barrel section of a shotgun. The monobloc system as developed by Belgian gunmaker Henry Pieper strengthened the critical part of the barrels by inserting and soft soldering the tubes into a forged chamber block. Similar techniques were used in the firm of Schmidt & Habermann, Suhl, and W. Collath of Frankfurt a.d. Oder.

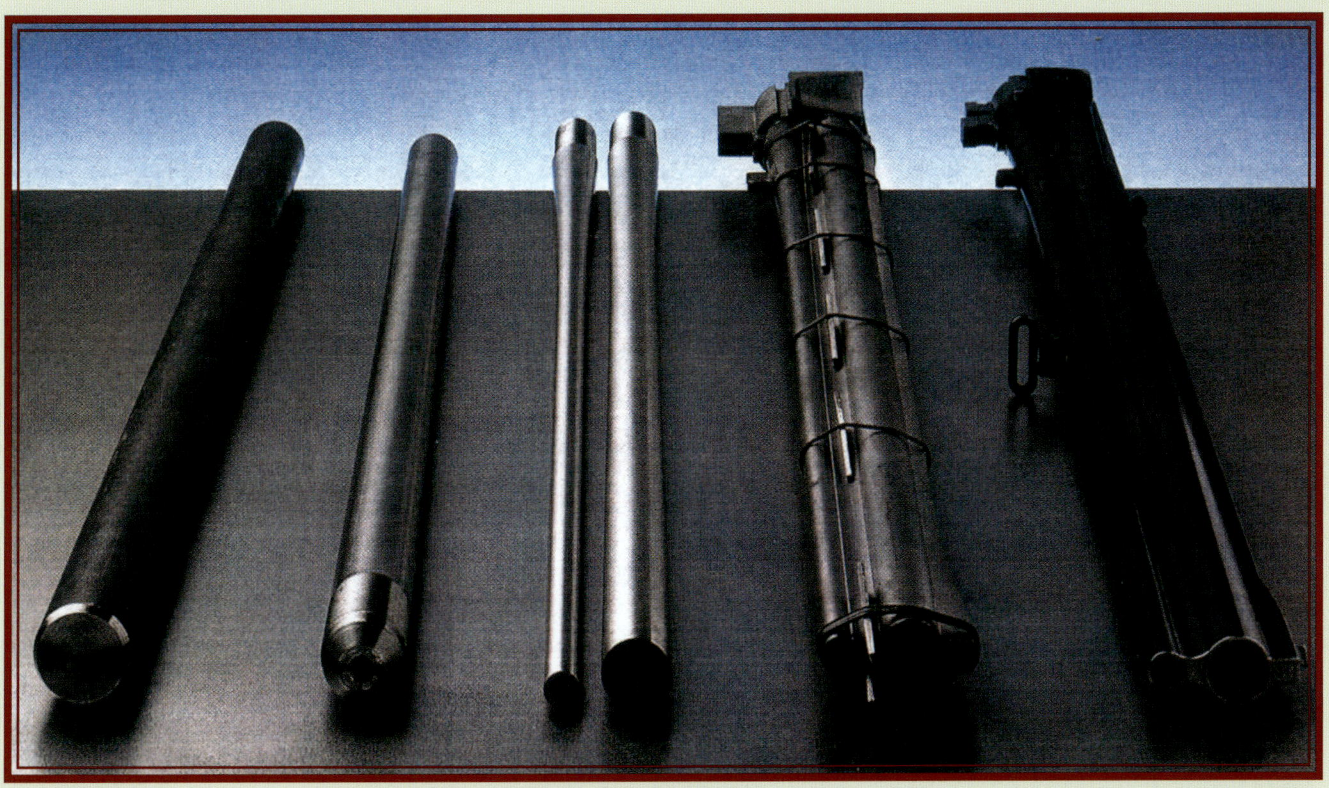

Stages in the manufacture of a Heym shotgun/rifle (Bockbüchsflinte).

This shows the barrel connection of a Collath drilling. Collath gun barrels were screwed into a threaded monobloc housing before being soldered together.

DEUTSCHES REICH

AUSGEGEBEN AM
11. OKTOBER 1930

REICHSPATENTAMT

PATENTSCHRIFT

№ 509 779

KLASSE 72a GRUPPE 27

72a S 9. 30

Tag der Bekanntmachung über die Erteilung des Patents: 2. Oktober 1930

Zu der Patentschrift 509 779
Kl. 72a Gr. 27

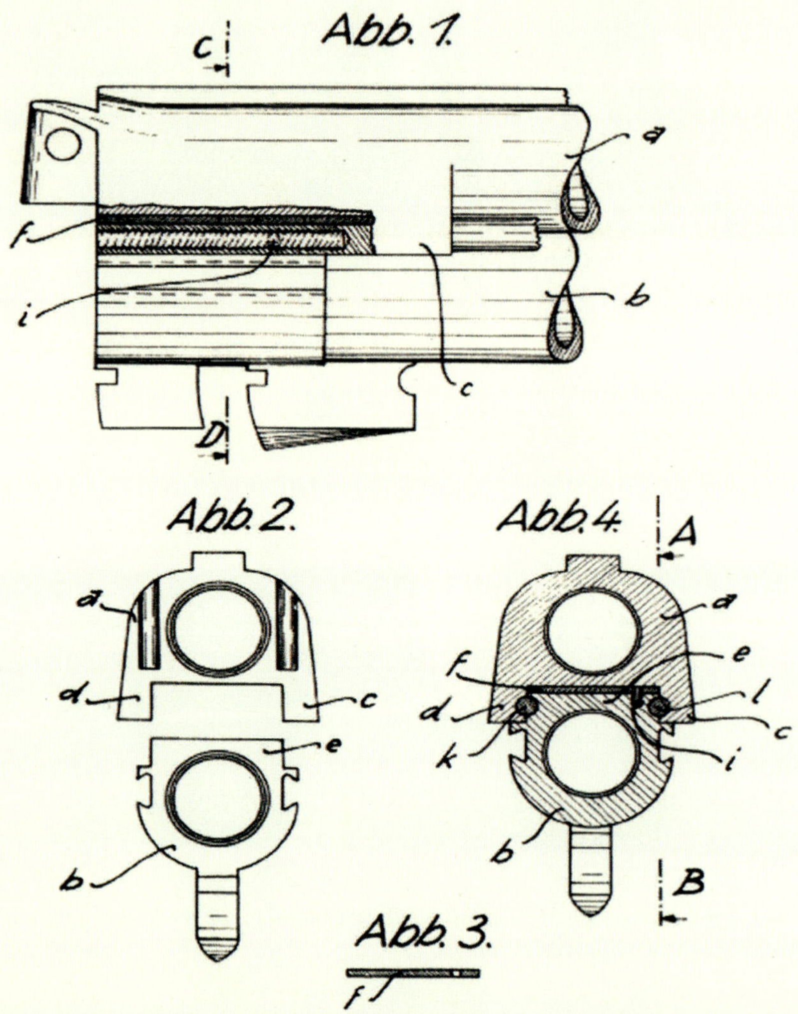

Gebrüder Merkel, Suhl, used a patented design on its O/U sporting arms. The lower barrel was dovetailed into the upper barrel and fixed into position by two threaded studs running parallel to the axis of the bores.

BARREL CONFIGURATIONS

Already by the middle of the nineteenth century, several German gunmakers had crafted three-barrel percussion drillings that functioned with two hammers. One hammer was hinged to fire the third barrel. Another form of a percussion drilling had a third hammer centered on top of the action.

After the development of the metal cartridge, the Munich gunmaker Peter Oberhammer patented the first breechloading drilling in 1878. This gun was fitted with two locks, hammers, and triggers. By means of a small knurled lever, the front trigger could fire either the right shot tube or the rifle barrel. Different gun manufacturers over the following decades produced a variety of this first breechloading, three-barrel hammer gun. Gunmakers sometimes improved on existing drilling designs or incorporated their own ideas.

Hammer guns were popular and continued to be featured in gun catalogs of most makers for a long time, even after the Suhl gunmaker Friedrich Wilhelm Heym invented the first hammerless drilling in 1891.

The name "drilling" derives from the German word *drei* meaning three or triple. Initially, these popular combination guns were called *Dreiläufer* (three barrels). The word *Büchse* means "rifle." A *Flinte* is a shotgun, but in the past it also designated any gun with a smooth barrel. The name of an O/U gun is preceded by the German word *Bock*. (The first O/U guns in the seventeenth century were so heavy that they could only be handled using a support, a *Bock*.) The position of gun barrels in relation to each other determines the designation of a gun.

The typical and most often used drilling has two 16-gauge shotgun barrels and a rifle barrel underneath. The 16-gauge tubes give the gun pleasing lines and reduced weight. It's important to know that the drilling was customized in many gauges and calibers. It always was and still is important for the sportsman to know his specific needs before ordering a drilling.

Oberhammer drilling with opening lever in front of trigger guard.

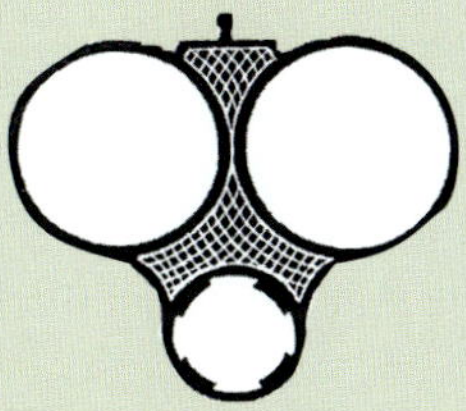

The most popular of the combination guns is the drilling with its side-by-side shot barrels and a rifle barrel mounted centrally below them.

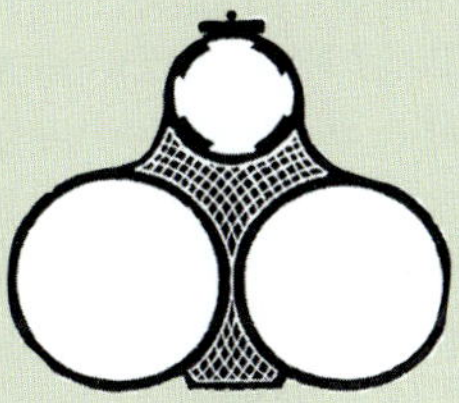

Several gunmakers, including W. Collath of Frankfurt/Oder developed early drillings with the rifle barrel above the two shotgun tubes. This design brought the line of sight closer to the top barrel but also put more stress on the action when the rifle barrel was fired.

Double-rifle drilling

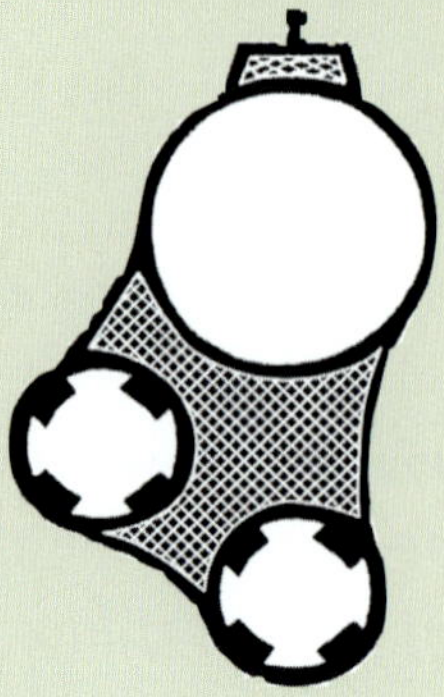

Bock double-rifle drilling

For the hunter stalking wild boar, red deer, or elk-size game, a double rifle drilling (Doppelbüchsdrilling) *was available with both rifle barrels side-by-side above the shot barrel, which was used for the occasional hare or pheasant. Many hunters preferred the Bock double-rifle drilling with its slimmer shape. Double-rifle drillings were heavier than regular ones. Built to the specification of the customer, they also carried a higher price tag.*

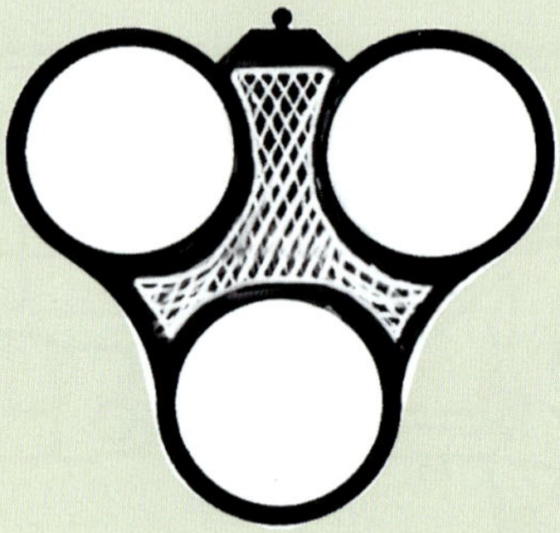

Shotgun drilling

The shotgun drilling (Flintendrilling) *was custom built for hunters of mostly small animals* (Niederwild) *who wanted to be able to fire three shots in rapid succession. To eliminate time-consuming switch-overs, these shot drillings were equipped with a single selective trigger or with two triggers. The front trigger fired the top barrels, the rear trigger fired the lower barrel. This lower tube often was loaded with a shell containing different shot. Gunmaker Greifelt in Suhl also supplied shot drillings with three triggers acting on three locks. With the introduction of semiautomatic and pump-action shotguns, these drillings were discontinued.*

The rifle drilling (Büchsdrilling), *used by the big-game hunter, is today made only by special order.*

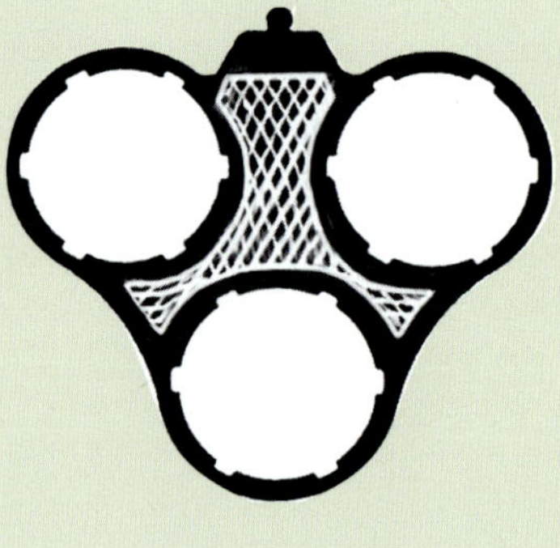

Rifle drilling

The shotgun/rifle combination in the O/U configuration with an added .22-caliber rifle barrel on the side was first built in Ferlach, Austria, in 1934. Called the Bock drilling or Triumpf Bockbüchsflinte, it was available in these calibers: .22 LR, .22 WM, .22 Hornet, and later in .222 Remington as the small caliber.

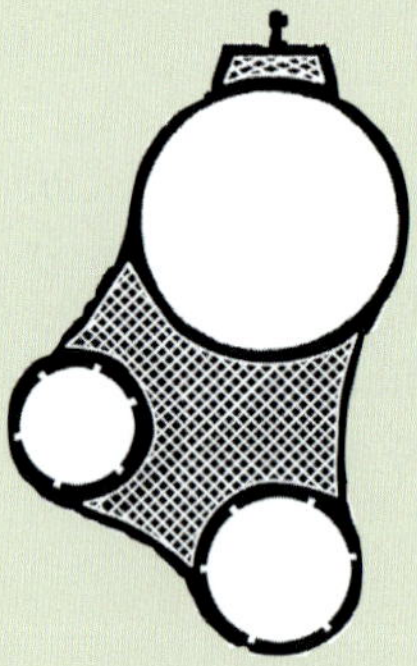

Bock drilling

The gunmakers Benedict and Josef Winkler, together with Hans Michelitsch, developed this version specifically for hunting in the Austrian Alps where a second shot barrel was seldom needed. The larger rifle caliber was used for deer-size animals while the .22-caliber barrel was used for small game in the off-season and to shoot woodchuck-size game.

Bock drillings became popular in Austria and Germany and are built by most sporting-arms manufacturers. Handcrafted on special order, they combine function with slim, elegant lines.

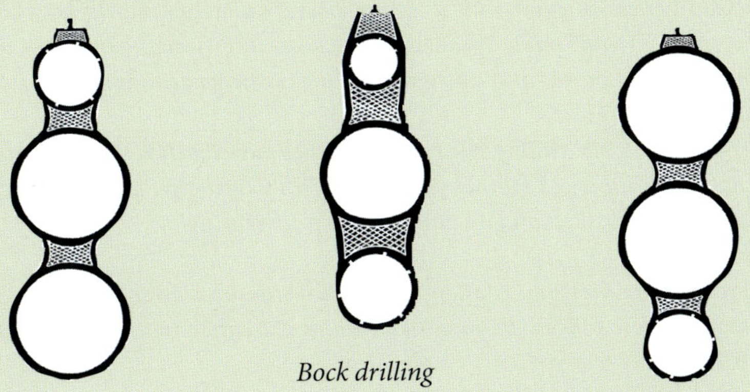

Bock drilling

Gunmaker Siegfried Günther in Suhl designed a Bock drilling in several caliber variations with all three barrels placed in line vertically. One trigger functioned for both shot barrels. The rifle barrel was cocked separately and fired with the second trigger. These guns are rarely seen today.

The Bergstutzen, a break-open rifle often used in the mountainous Alps, evolved in Austria from a light single-shot rifle in a caliber suitable for deer and chamois. A high rib contains a second barrel normally in caliber .22 Long Rifle, 5.6x35R (22WCF), or .22 Hornet for hunting woodchucks. Today these guns are built using the Blitz or Anson & Deeley system with one trigger and a sliding selector on the upper tang or with two triggers and two locks. They are available in several modern calibers.

Austrian drilling with rifle barrels arranged horizontally.

Bergstutzen

The cape gun (Büchsflinte) *was common in the late nineteenth and the early twentieth centuries and is still custom-made today. Hunting arms in this configuration date back to the flintlock and percussion era when double guns were in use with a rifled and a smoothbore barrel or two rifled barrels, one of which was equipped with straight grooves for use with shot or ball.*

Cape gun

Bockbüchsflinte

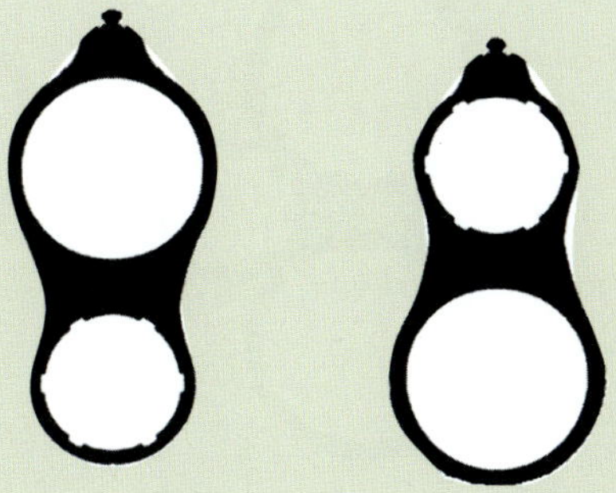

The O/U combination gun (Bockbüchsflinte) *can have the rifle barrel either below the shotgun tube or above it. The version on the left is the most common one today.*

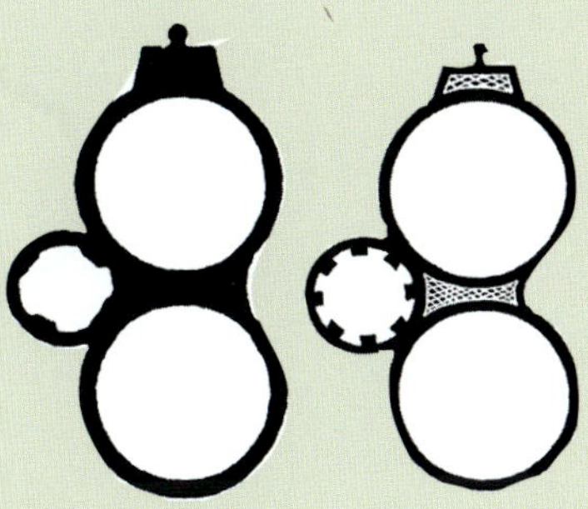

This is an example of an O/U shotgun with a .22 Long Rifle barrel on the side.

The gun factory Schmidt & Habermann in Suhl developed and marketed a light (six pounds) hammerless shotgun with a .22 LR barrel built into the rib between the barrels. The company's trade name Waldläufer *translates into "woods runner" or better, "backwoodsman." The gun was also called rib drilling* (Schienendrilling).

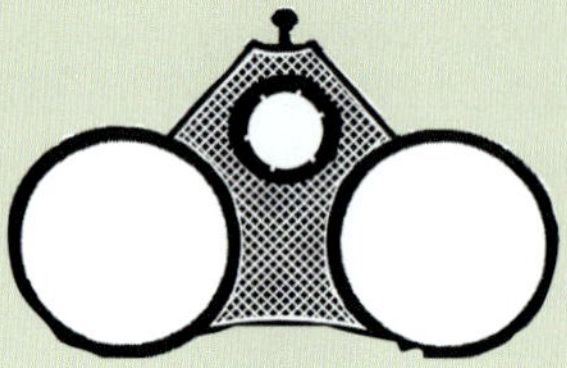

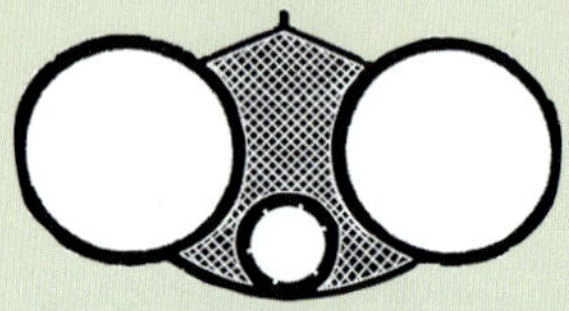

Rib drilling (Waldläufer)

On a later version of this rib drilling, the rifle barrel was moved below the shotgun tubes and was available in caliber .22 Hornet (5.6x35R). This new design made it possible to incorporate a Greener crossbolt and an automatic flip-up rear sight.

The four-barrel gun, or vierling, is often found with side-by-side shot tubes, a large game rifle barrel centered below them, and a second .22-caliber rifle barrel mounted in the top rib.

Earlier guns were chambered for the .22 Long Rifle or the 5.6x35R vierling cartridge, which was the .22 WCF loaded to higher velocity in Europe. The vierling was also available in .22 Hornet.

Gunmakers H. Burgsmüller & Söhne and E. Kerner & Co. positioned the small-caliber rifle barrel on their models into the center between the shot and rifle barrels. Combined with the Greener lockup and the automatic rear sight, they featured either three or four locks with two triggers and a selector on the tang.

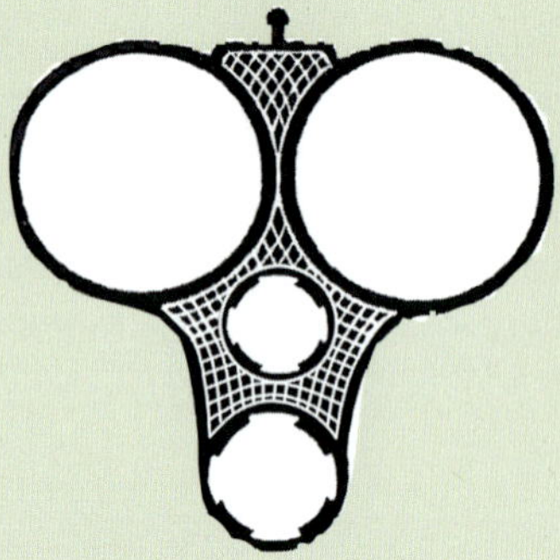

Burgsmüller vierling

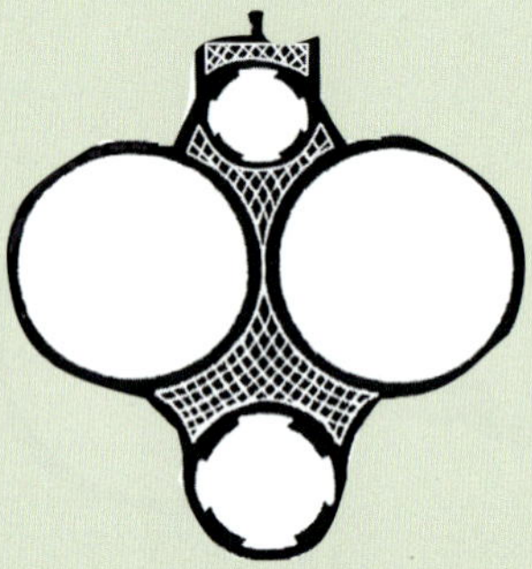

Vierling

The use of heat-treated, aluminum alloy actions and improved barrel steels reduced the weight of the initially heavy vierling to 6½ pounds. The gunmaker Immanuel Meffert in Suhl specialized in these aluminum alloy receivers. Several other barrel arrangements are known, like the examples below.

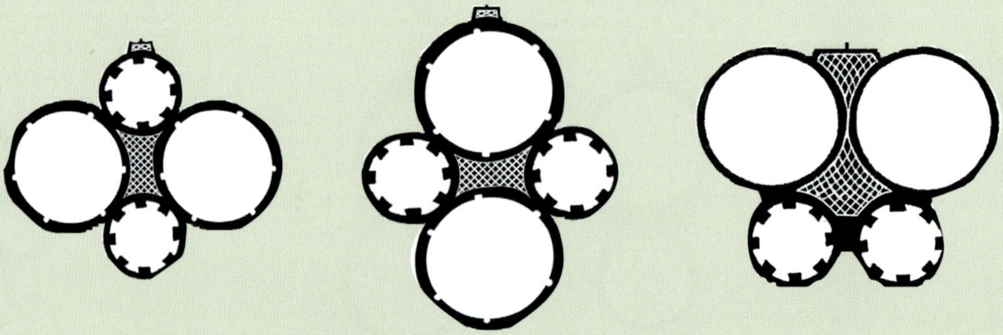

Different vierling barrel arrangements

BARREL ARRANGEMENTS

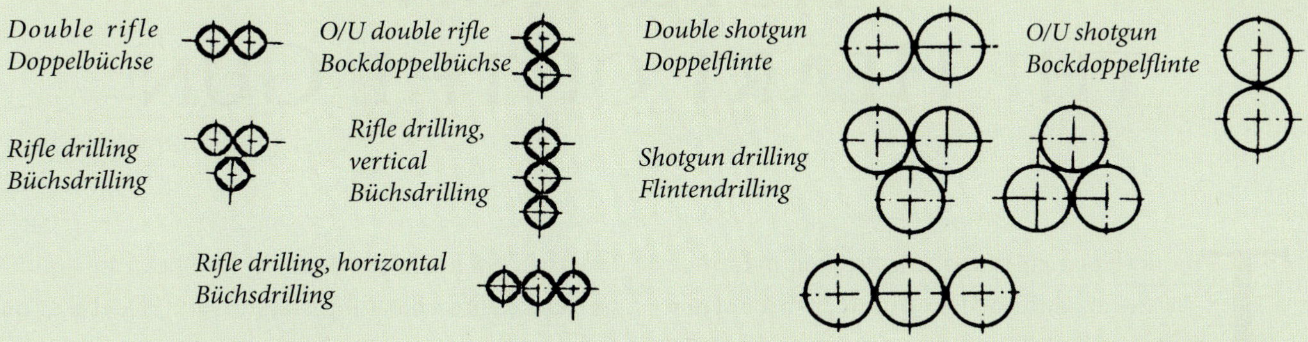

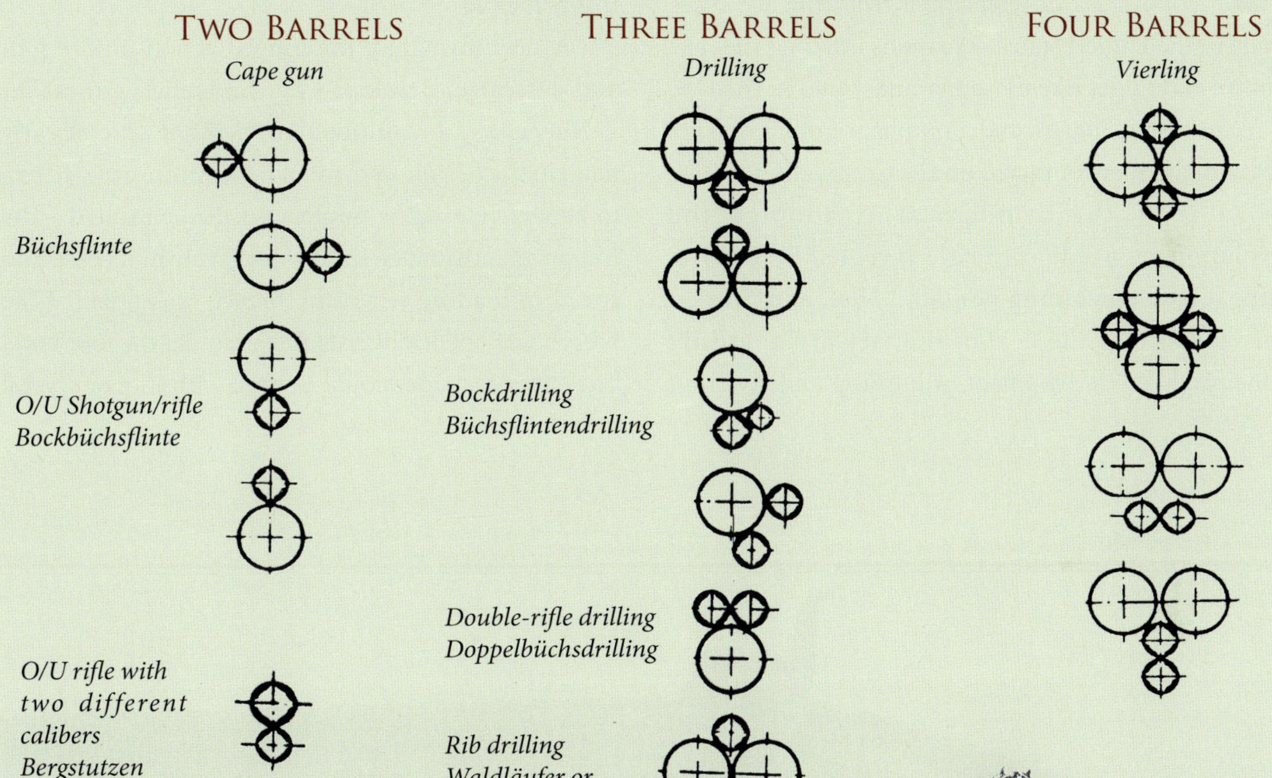

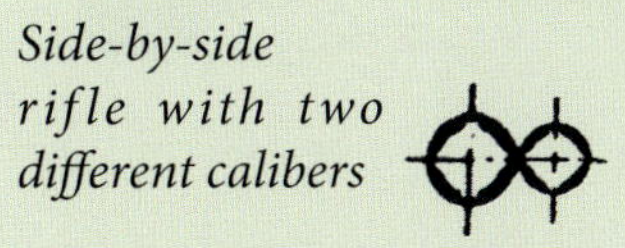

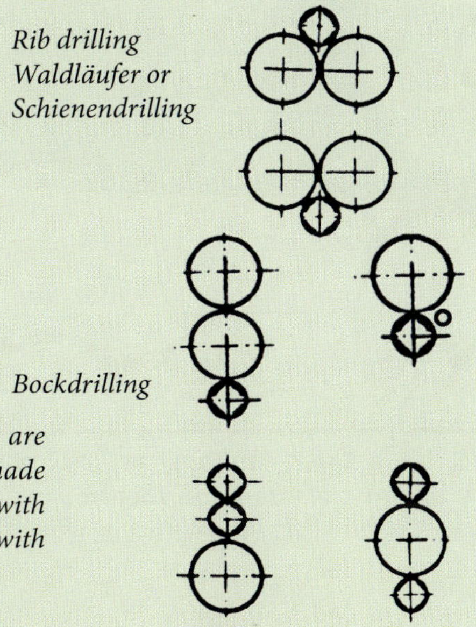

In addition, other barrel arrangements are known, mostly one-of-a-kind, custom-made curios. An example is a drilling or vierling with each barrel of a different caliber or a gun with five barrels (Fünfling).

Waffen tips

The term combination gun dates back several centuries to when firearms were first attached to edged weapons.

THE ACTION: THE HEART OF THE GUN

The development of sporting firearms in Europe in the middle of the nineteenth century followed a different path from the advances made in the United States. Weapons utilizing the new rimfire cartridges like those manufactured in the U.S. by Winchester, Sharps, and a number of other makers were not often encountered on the Continent.

In 1840, the Prussian army adopted the revolutionary needle-fire rifle invented by Dreyse, using a case containing powder, bullet, and primer. This advance in the field of military arms greatly influenced the development of hunting and sporting firearms. For a brief period many European gunsmiths introduced breechloading shotguns and rifles based on this principle.

A new invention, the hinged-action pinfire gun and cartridge, developed by the French gunmaker Lefaucheux, grew in popularity. After several early flaws in the design were remedied, pinfire arms began to be widely used by hunters on the Continent. The important advantage in this design lay in its ease and speed of loading when the breech was open. (The breech was opened by a steel lever under the fore-end.) The paper cartridge could be used with shot or several

A 16-gauge pinfire shotgun signed J. Giglot Aror à Anvers (Antwerp) on the rib of the 30-inch barrels. It features rear-action sidelocks, an English straight stock, and a metal fore-end with a Godin double lever. (On the Godin system, the lower lever opens the breech; the small one above it at the tip of the fore-end facilitates removing the barrels.) Proof marks on the gun indicate it was manufactured before 1893.

This double-barrel, pinfire 16-gauge shotgun is signed "L. Bruns, Braunschweig." It has 29-inch Damascus barrels; rear action sidelocks; half-horn pistol grip; cheekpiece; and a metal fore-end and action. It also has leaf and vine engraving.

It is proof-marked "V." In 1891, a new German proof law required arms in inventory to be marked "V." This is taken from Vorrat, *the German word for "inventory under the crown."*

sizes of balls. Projectiles and empty primed paper cases were available at any gun shop or village trader.

In Britain the first appearance of the new break-open guns caused barely a stir. English gunmakers were secure in the knowledge that they crafted the best and most accurate percussion muzzleloaders in the world; consequently, they were slow to recognize the advancement that the pinfire system represented. As W. W. Greener put it: "A breechloader will never attain the accuracy and performance of a muzzleloader." Eventually they realized the potential of the hinged breech, and their many outstanding improvements and safety features are still in widespread use today.

It was a time of experimenting for numerous gunmakers on the Continent and in England. Notable firms like Barella, Greener, Heym, Krieghoff, Purdey, Sauer, and Westley Richards, to name a few, all developed and improved actions and various methods of locking barrels to the breech by means of a hinge and additional fasteners. Many of the new breechlock innovations were short-lived because they were too difficult or awkward to handle. Some guns were technically too advanced and ahead of their time, or their manufacture was too expensive. Other designs used by regional gunsmiths did not get recognition because they reached only a limited clientele.

THE DEVELOPMENT OF THE BREAK-OPEN ACTION

LEFAUCHEUX'S NEW BREECHLOCK

The Paris gunmaker Casimir Lefaucheux (1802–1852) patented a new breech-locking device between 1825 and 1836. Shotguns using this locking mechanism utilized a lever under the fore-end that engaged a lug underneath the barrels in a T-shaped slot. By rotating this lever, the barrels tipped downward on a hinge, opening the breech. For this system, Lefaucheux developed special black-powder, pinfire cartridges with paper cases and cup-shaped brass bases. Metal pins protruding out of the sides of the bases fired caps when struck by the hammers. When the gun was loaded, the pins fitted into recesses on top of the barrel chambers.

In 1845, Casimir's son, Eugene G. Lefaucheux, developed a revolver with an improved brass cartridge that was based on his father's patent. Eugene later moved his factory to Liege, the gunmaking center in Belgium.

Lefaucheux guns became popular throughout Europe where numerous manufacturers and gunsmiths made and sold shotguns and handguns based on this system. These arms ranged from the utilitarian to very expensive versions with Damascus barrels and elaborate engraving and carving.

On early models, extractors were not fitted to the barrel chambers, and cartridges had to be pulled out by the pin. This proved difficult or impossible when wet paper hulls became swollen. Often a torn paper cartridge could only be removed by a ramrod.

Despite these initial shortcomings, hunters liked pinfire guns because they represented the first functional breechloader. It combined ease of handling with an affordable price.

Although long obsolete by then, Belgian-made Lefaucheux guns were still produced at the turn of the twentieth century. Ammunition was still available until the 1950s.

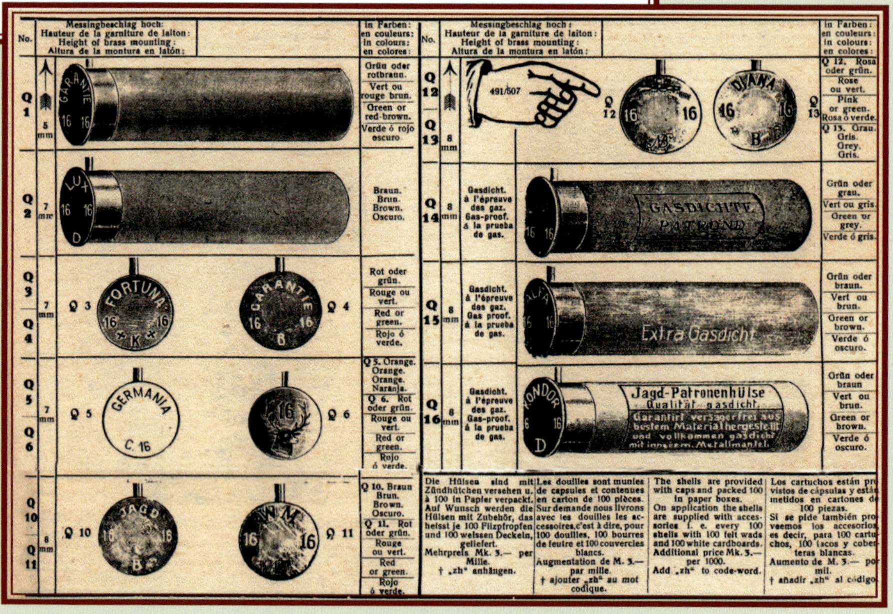

Pinfire cartridges advertised in the 1911 ALFA Export Catalog.

OTHER DEVELOPMENTS IN ACTIONS

This 16-gauge, double pinfire shotgun is signed "Christoph Funk, Suhl" on the rib of its 30-inch Damascus barrels. It also features a half-horn pistol grip, cheekpiece, and oak-leaf engraving. The gun has no proof marks, indicating it was produced and sold before 1891. In catering to the tastes of the German hunter, the gunmaker fitted this shotgun with a short underlever covered with buffalo horn and a half-horn pistol grip with one scroll. In addition, the trigger guard was modernized and simplified with only an ornamental protrusion or nose.

In 1851, the English gunsmith Charles Lancaster was the first to sell a workable centerfire, breechloading shotgun. It rapidly gained in popularity to such an extent that the term "Lancaster," denoting a centerfire shotgun, is found in old gun catalogs of that period. With the increased demand for and the improvement of centerfire arms, the sale of pinfire guns slowed over the years and eventually production ceased. Initially steel was used for the opening levers, but it was soon replaced by buffalo horn or wood clad ones in order to lighten guns and to make them more comfortable to the touch on cold days.

A long horn lever under the fore-end locks the action by means of a friction nut. Barrels are fastened to the frame by a wedge, as on this cape gun.

A short horn lever locks the barrels to the fore-end. The small second metal handle at the fore-end tip on this double rifle fastens the barrels to the forearm.

With the development of the centerfire cartridge, improvements of break-open actions continued. They were variously called break-down, drop-barrel, hinge-frame, tip-up, hinged-breech, break-open, or tip-barrel *(Kipplauf)*. Whatever they were called, they connected the barrel to the stock. They also contained fasteners, locks, and lock parts, and were designed to provide a gas-tight seal between barrels, chambers, and the breech. Ideally, they required as few motions as possible to load and to unload the gun.

Actions often took the name of the inventing gunsmith; others were named after the technical features of their locking system. In many countries, different designations were in use for the same or nearly identical version of a certain breechlock. Minor modifications on an existing system often justified a new name. This could include the name of the original inventor (for example, the improved Purdey lock; the Kersten lock, also sometimes referred to as Double Greener; and so on). Out of literally dozens of designs, three principal action types emerged that are still being produced today: the Anson & Deeley, the Blitz, and the sidelock.

THE THREE ACTION TYPES

1.

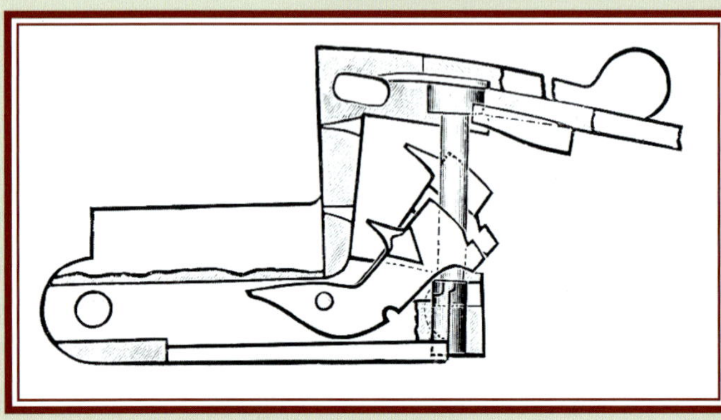

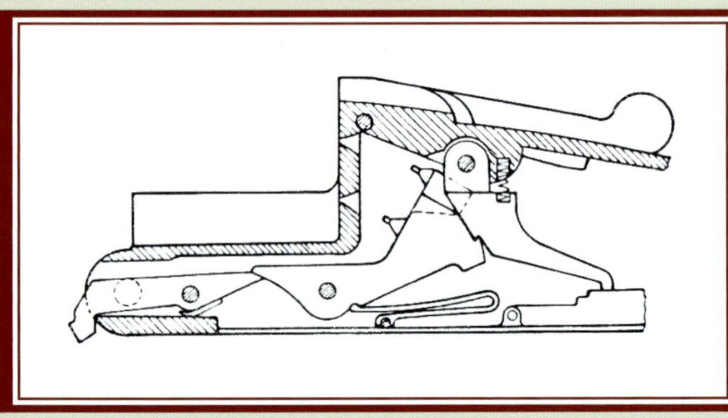

The Anson & Deeley system had hammers (strikers), mainsprings, cocking levers, and sears mounted forward in the bar of the action, allowing the gun to be made shorter. The hammers served as firing pins, striking the primers through the firing pin orifices in the face of the standing breech. On the left is the Anson & Deeley lock for O/U guns by Ernst Kerner, Suhl, and on the right is the Anson & Deeley lock by Simson & Co.

After removing the blind lockplate, lock parts were easily accessible on the Anson & Deeley design by Berlin gunsmith E. Steigleder.

2.

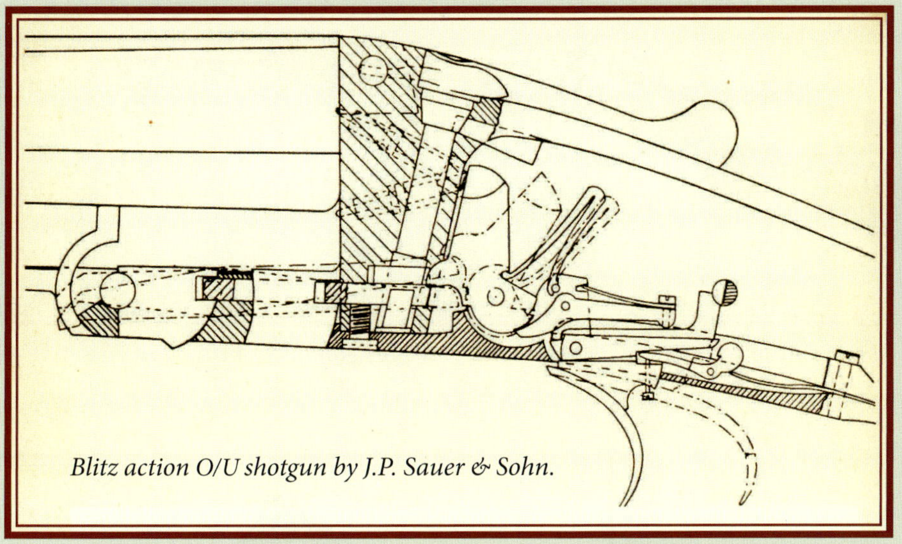

Blitz action O/U shotgun by J.P. Sauer & Sohn.

The second action type is the Blitz or lightning system, also called a trigger-plate action, with hammers mounted on the trigger plate, striking separate firing pins.

3.

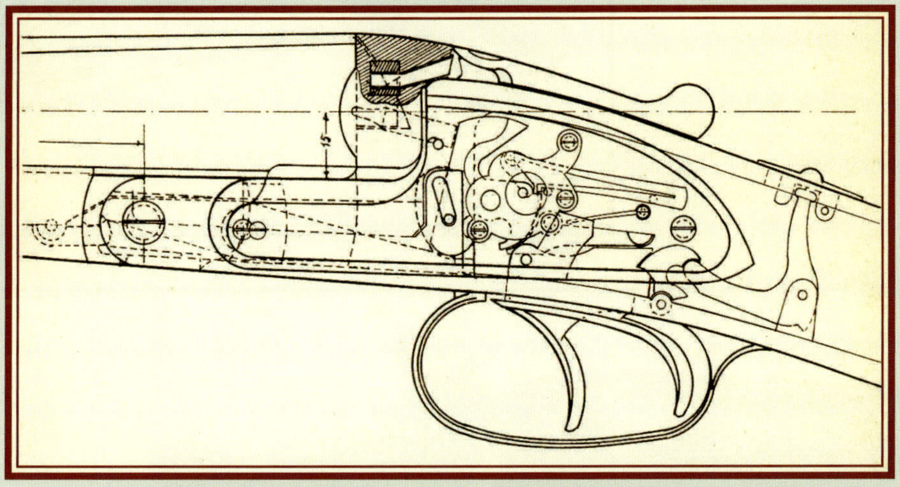

The third action type is the sidelock (Seitenschloss) *gun, furnished with mainsprings forward (bar action) or with mainsprings mounted toward the rear of the lockplate (back action).*

Most three- and four-barrel guns (drilling and vierling) were fitted with a combination of sidelock-mounted hammers (strikers) for the side-by-side barrels, with third and fourth strikers mounted on the trigger plate.

Blitz and Anson & Deeley actions were referred to as boxlocks (Kastenschloss) *and came in a multitude of configurations, designs, and shapes, depending on the maker. The rearward segments of boxlocks, where actions met the stocks, were often shaped into curving lines. This was done partially for appearance but also to strengthen the wrist area of the firearm by increasing the surface area between the wood and metal.*

On some models, boxlocks were fitted with sideplates (blind plates) to give the pleasing appearance of a true sidelock or to provide space for more engraving. To distinguish between sidelock and side-plated guns was often difficult when bolts and fasteners of the sidelock parts were not carried through the plate itself, but were instead concealed.

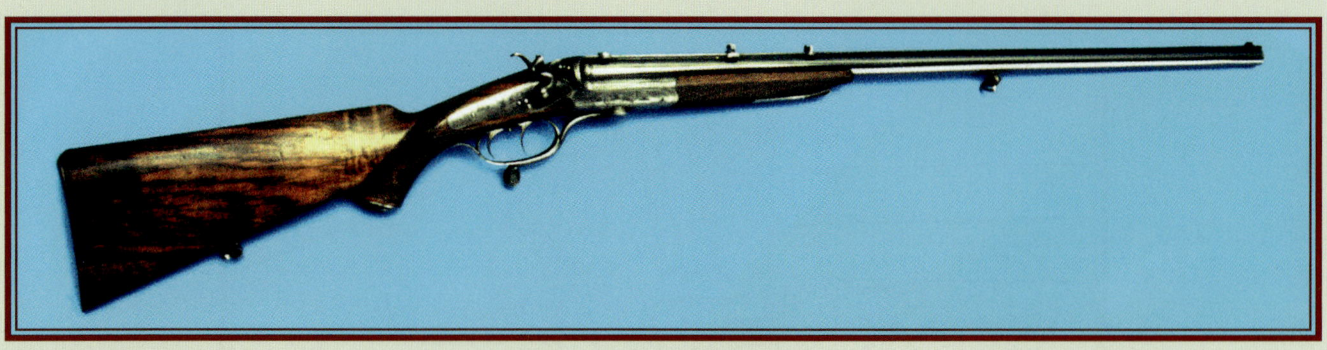

This light, elegant hammer rifle in caliber 9.3x72R with Jones lever is by gunmaker Ferdinand Fükert of Weipert.

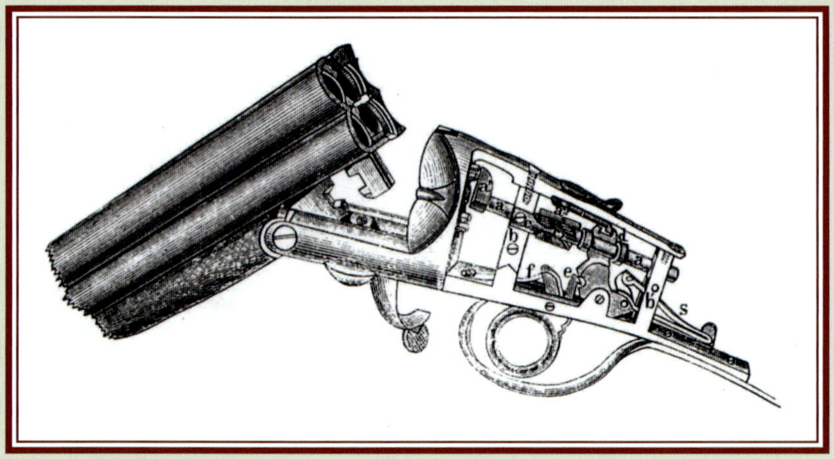

This early vierling shotgun has a Jones underlever and a doll's head third fastener. Note the old-style trigger on this four-barrel gun.

The Jones underlever, also called the T-lock or English lever, followed the contour of the trigger guard. Turning the lever to the right rotated a locking nut out of a T-shaped opening underneath the barrels. This drilling is in caliber 11x60R 16/16 and was made by Thieme & Schlegelmilch in Suhl.

This is a Collath drilling in caliber 9.3x65R 16/16. On some Dreyse and Collath actions, barrels backed up over bosses on the face of the standing breech when the action was closed. They were renowned for their strength and safety. This is important because the increased use of the new, smokeless powder called for reinforced frames, stronger breeches, and improved locking devices and fasteners.

The short horn underlever on a Collath drilling moves the barrels forward and away from the face of the standing breech by means of an eccentric disk. The barrels pivot around a pin in the forearm and tip down to expose the chambers. The recess for the disk and the rifle barrel extension that lock the action can clearly be seen below the extractor.

The Roux lock positioned the opening lever underneath the action over the trigger guard. The breech opened by moving the lever forward (Bügeldruckverschluss).

Waffen tips

Gunmaker Collath was the inventor of the automatic rear sight on drillings.

This Sauer drilling is in caliber 9.3x72R 16/16.

Examples of a sidelever (side opener) system include the right-handed example below and the left-handed one above. On each gun, the top lever activates the rifle barrels, simultaneously preventing the face of the hammer from contacting the firing pin of the right shotgun barrel when the gun is fired.

Waffen tips

Hammer guns remain popular and are still made to order by many gunsmiths.

A Kettner drilling in caliber 11x60R 16/16.

LOCKS & FASTENERS

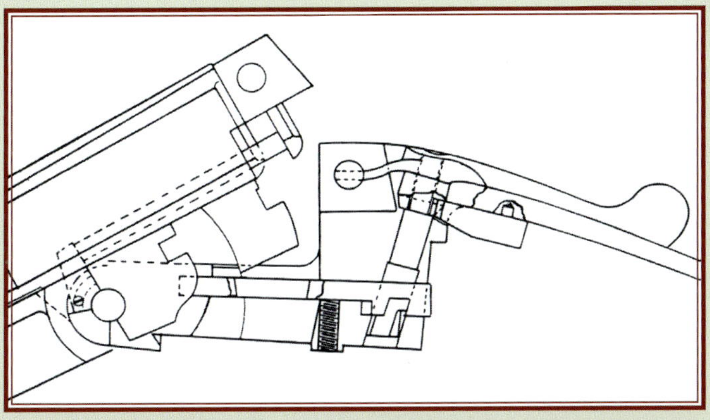

Gunmaker W. W. Greener of Birmingham, England, in 1874 developed the hammer and strong lock system. It featured a top lever–activated crossbolt through an extension of the barrel rib (Greener lock). This system was and still is widely used by gunmakers.

The crossbolt holds the barrels solidly against the standing breech at the moment of discharge, and the extension down in its mortise prevents any lateral movement of the barrels.

Round crossbolts are generally employed, but square or oval ones are also used. It was reasoned that these shapes increased the bearing area, and that they provide a stronger lock.

This Gustav Fükert double rifle with improved Greener fastener is in caliber 8x57R. Note that the crossbolt is concealed, not protruding out of the fences.

This H. Barella double rifle in caliber 10.75x70R has a Greener crossbolt, two massive underlugs, and a reinforced action, which can be seen protruding ahead of the hinge pin.

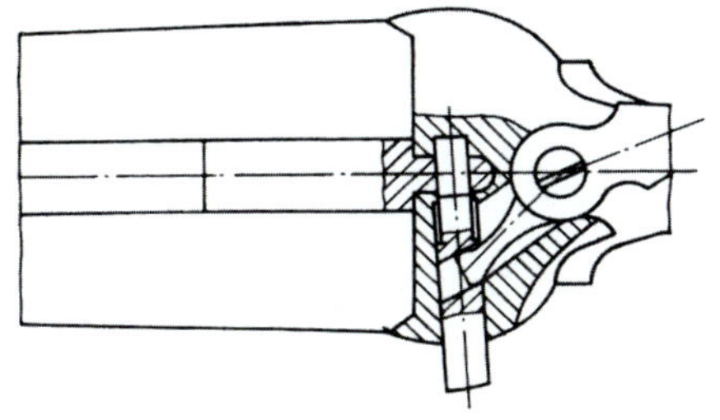

Greener lock open.

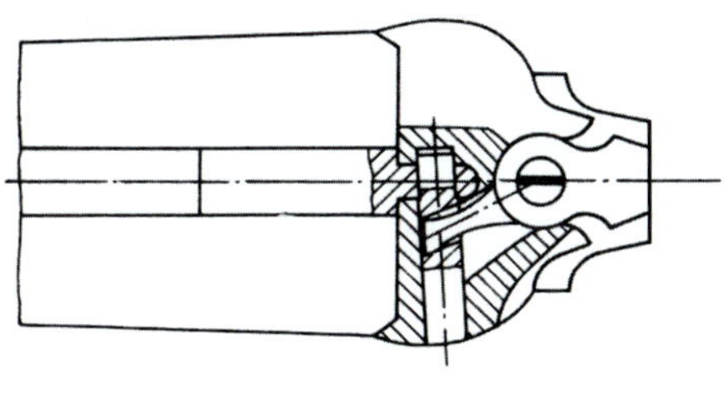

Greener lock closed.

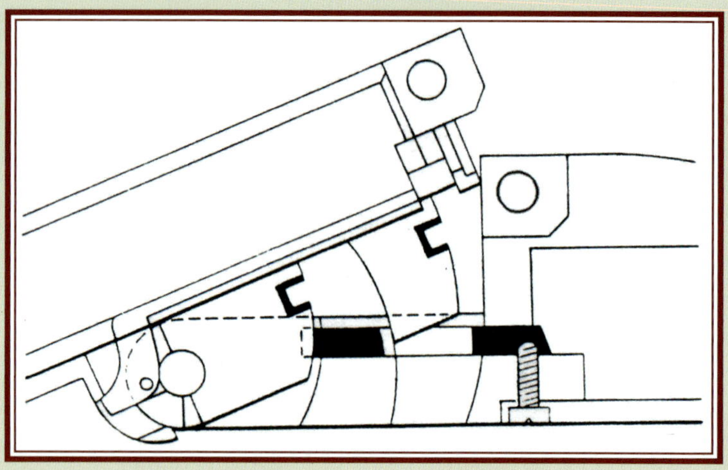

In 1862, the English gunmaking firm of Westley Richards first employed a lock that activated wedges by way of a lever that engaged matching openings in underlugs beneath the barrels. When fitted exactly, the front surface of the rear underbite supported the hinge by relieving pressure on the hinge pin. The activated wedges in the top lever prevented the pivoting of the barrels when the gun was fired.

On many break-open guns, the rear lug is designed to be shorter and does not extend through the frame. Only the forward lug is visible from the underside of the receiver. Other models are built without openings to strengthen the frame.

Black-powder arms, as a rule, featured smaller underbites. For more powerful smokeless loads, the underbites were larger. Note how the protruding lip was built into the frame to protect the underlug.

This shows the extension of a lug of a Sauer drilling. Guns made in Suhl or Ferlach were often equipped with small extensions or noses as part of the forward barrel lugs. While their specific triangular shape was ornamental, the design increased the surface of the curved rearward flat of the lugs. This prevented them from binding in the rectangular frame opening when closing the action.

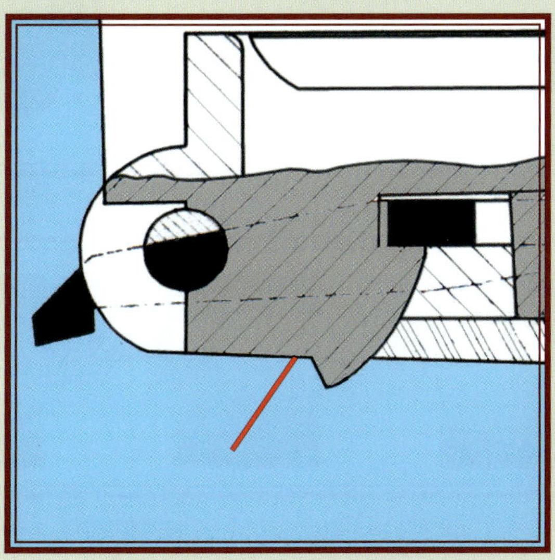

Nose protruding out of the action.

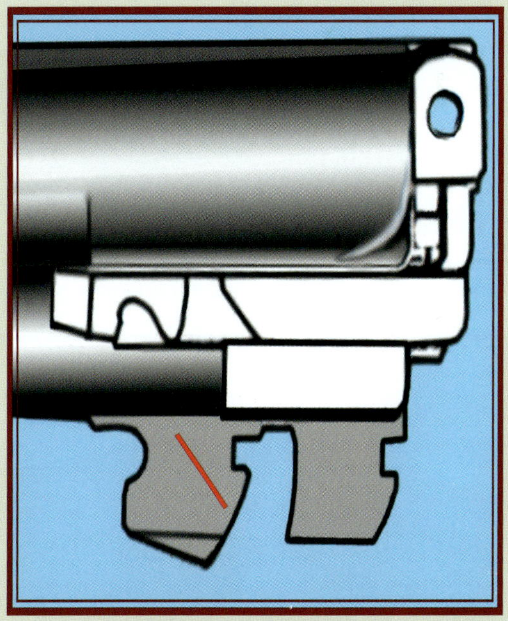

Nose on forward underlug.

Waffen tips

The letter "N" or the word "Nitro" stamped on a barrel designated that it was proofed with smokeless powder.

English gunmaker Purdey first invented the Purdey lockup that was later adapted by gunmaker Rempt of Suhl for his REMO O/U shotgun/rifle combinations. In the company's catalogs, the two fasteners, one on each side of the barrels, were advertised as an improved or double Purdey lock.

The doll's head extension was also called a third fastener. It worked in conjunction with underlugs on many shotguns and combination guns.

Many makers marketed similarly shaped fasteners to improve the bolting of their guns. Positioned on the top or on the sides of the frame, they functioned together with either one or two underlugs or underbites. Whether round, oval, triangular, square, lens, or T-shape, their effectiveness depended entirely on how well they were fitted.

Doll's head fastener.

Widely copied English fasteners: 1. Greener-Webley 2. Greener top-rib 3. Purdey 4. Westley Richards 5. Webley-Scott

Two underbites and an upright moving bolt (Vertikal Bolzen) *were the locking features on O/U shotguns and combinations crafted by E. Kerner of Suhl. An English invention called a rising bite action is still made by Max Ern.*

The Kersten lock, named after the Strassburg gunsmith, is found on many combination guns. Also called the Lux, Luchs, or Strassburg lock, it consists of two barrel extensions forged to either side of the upper barrel and a crossbolt that engages both barrel extensions. It is primarily used on O/U (Bock) guns.

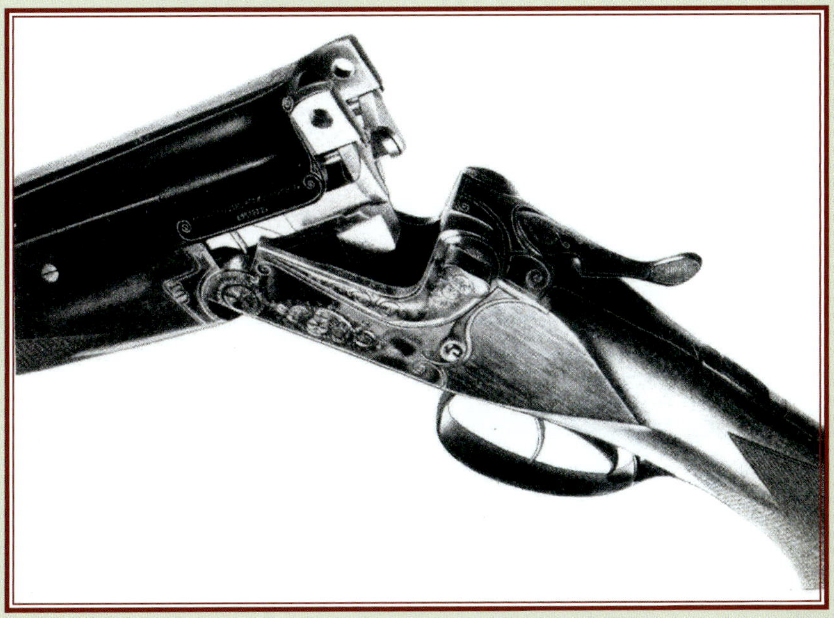

This Merkel shotgun has a Kersten lock; it is in gauge 16/16 and has separate extractors. The Merkel Company in Suhl uses it to this day.

A double rifle drilling (Doppelbüchsdrilling) *with Kersten lock in caliber 9.3x74R / 9.3x74R /16-gauge signed on the barrels: "Hofbüchsenmacher G. L. Rasch, Braunschweig (Brunswick)."*

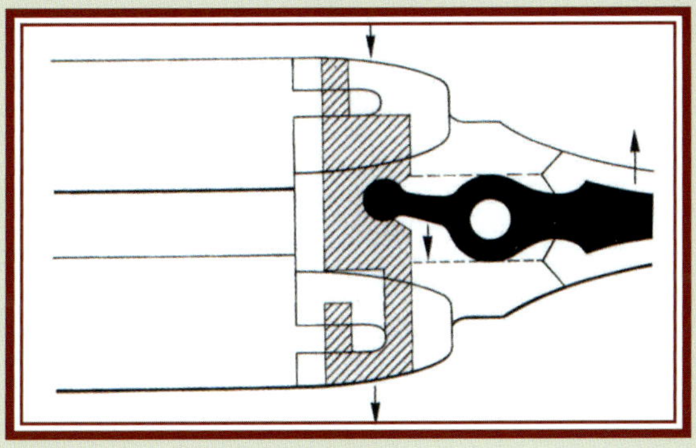

Crossbolt of a Kersten lock.

Waffen tips

The Kersten lock was also called double Greener.

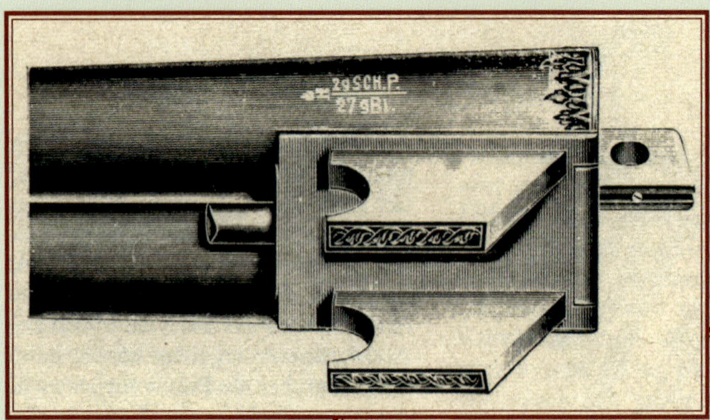

An important innovation by gunmaker Franz Jäger was his Simson-Jäger lock that had two underlugs positioned precisely under each barrel. This configuration in combination with a Greener crossbolt eliminated a side movement from either barrel. It was a feature on Jäger guns as well as on hunting arms made under license by the Simson company in Suhl.

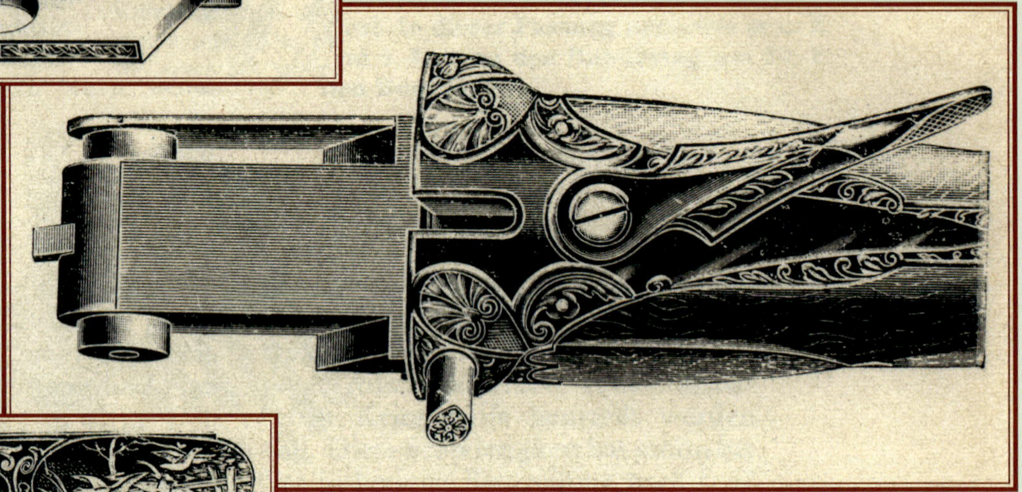

The Simson-Jäger lock with removable sideplate is also called a Record Verschluss.

Jäger advertisement states, "Safety above Everything."

According to the 1930s ad on the left, "The Simson-Jäger lock is the only one that provides a real strengthening of the action." The usual hinge pin of much smaller diameter is replaced by two much larger trunnions for extra strength.

This unusual lockup uses a T-shape bolt that slides out of the left side of the action of this hammer gun when the action is opened. This bolt matched openings in the locking bar on the underside of the barrels. The top lever simultaneously activates the Greener cross-bolt. The hinge opening is also clearly visible.

This sidelock double rifle drilling was made by Simson & Co., Suhl, in caliber 9.3x74R, 9.3x74R, 12-gauge with a pivot bolting design.

The Suhl gun factory of Schmidt & Habermann often used a locking system in its guns that was developed by gunmaker Fr. Karl in Lüneburg. Two underlugs were reinforced by a movable breech plate that engaged a wide rib extension. This lock was able to withstand high chamber pressure.

Vertikalblock-Kipplaufverschluss.

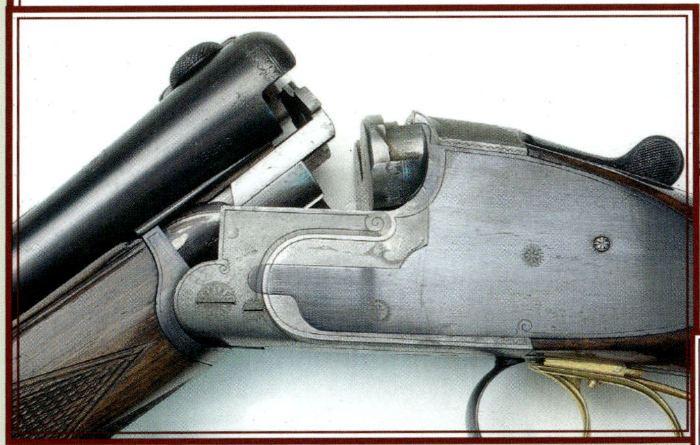

When opening the gun, the rear barrel underlug actuates the separate breechblock. It pivots away from the breech face and exposes the chambers.

When closing the action, the turning motion of the barrels seats the barrel extension over the breechblock and completely encloses the chambers.

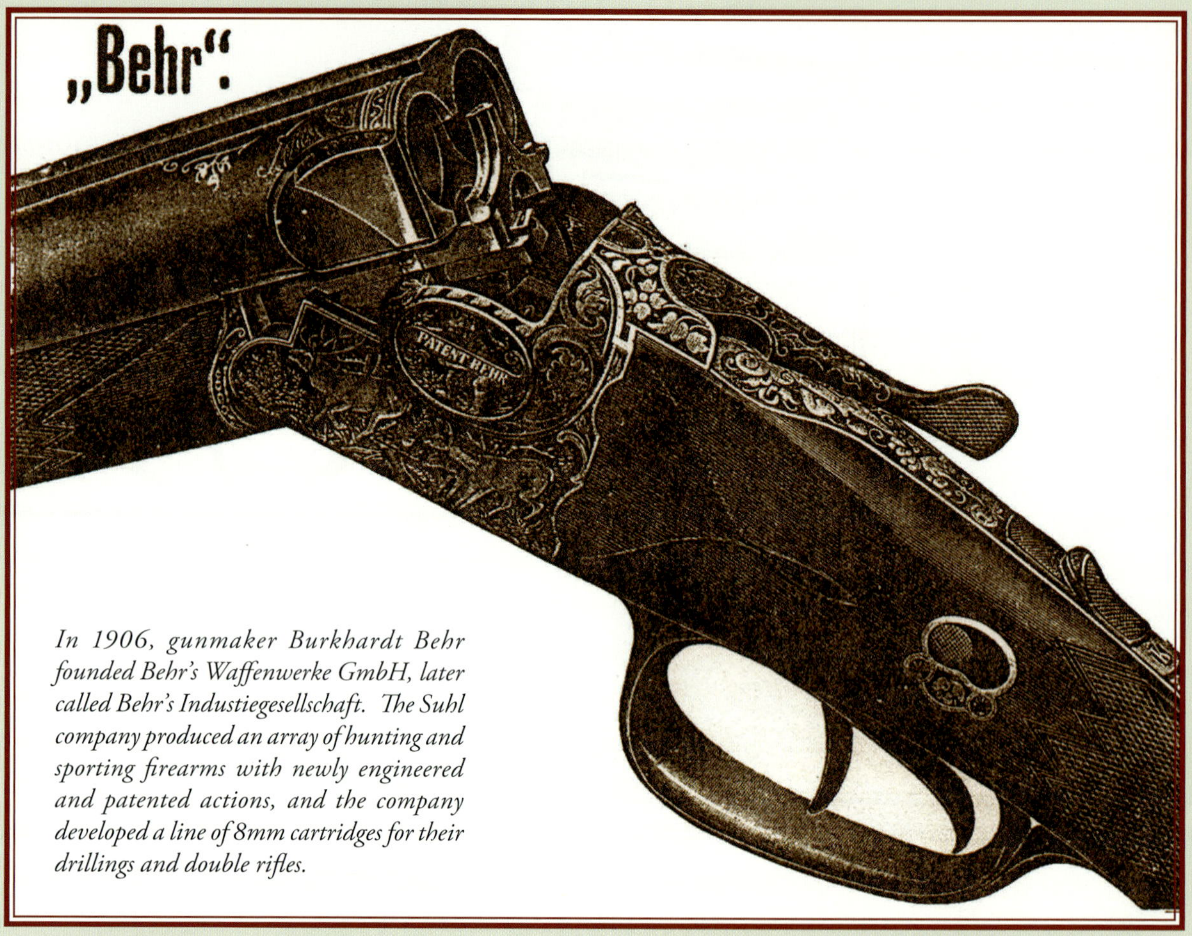

In 1906, gunmaker Burkhardt Behr founded Behr's Waffenwerke GmbH, later called Behr's Industiegesellschaft. The Suhl company produced an array of hunting and sporting firearms with newly engineered and patented actions, and the company developed a line of 8mm cartridges for their drillings and double rifles.

Behr's Waffenwerke promoted its version of a trunnion lock in conjunction with a Purdey-type fastener. The trunnion pins, in line with the barrel bores, prevented the barrels from swiveling when the gun was fired.

Waffen tips

At the turn of the twentieth century, many gun factories advertised multiple bolting features for their sporting arms.

Fükert's "Extra-Patent-Lock suitable for all guns" was especially recommended for use with smokeless powder. Patented in Austria, Hungary, Germany, Belgium, France, and England, it added rigidity to the lockup.

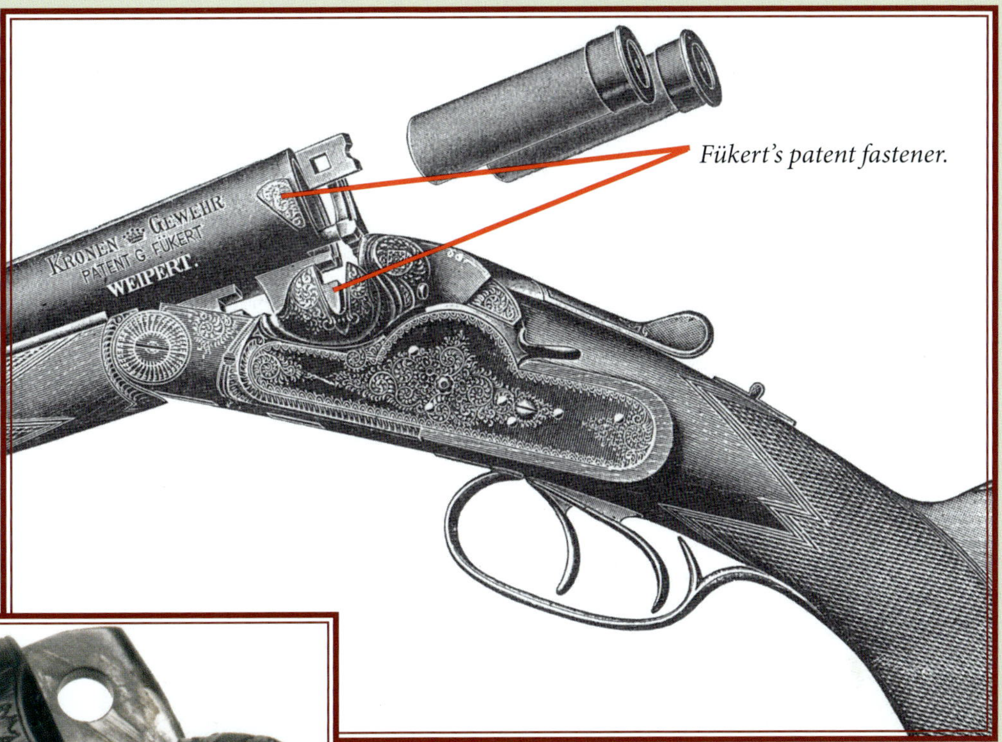

Gunmaker Thieme & Schlegelmilch in Suhl offered a patented lock on its doubles and drillings. Called the Nimrod (nose) lock, it worked in conjunction with two underlugs and a Greener crossbolt.

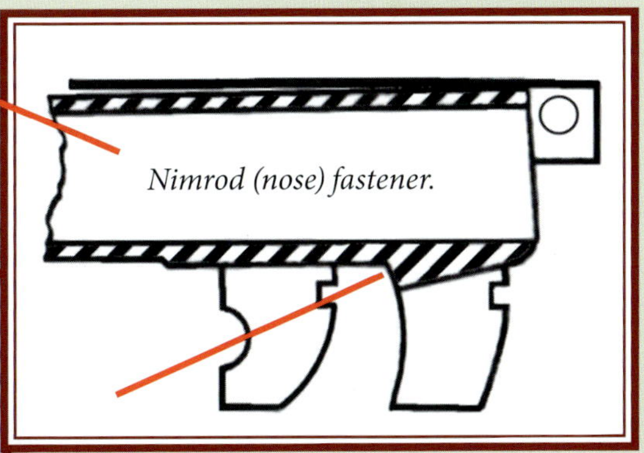

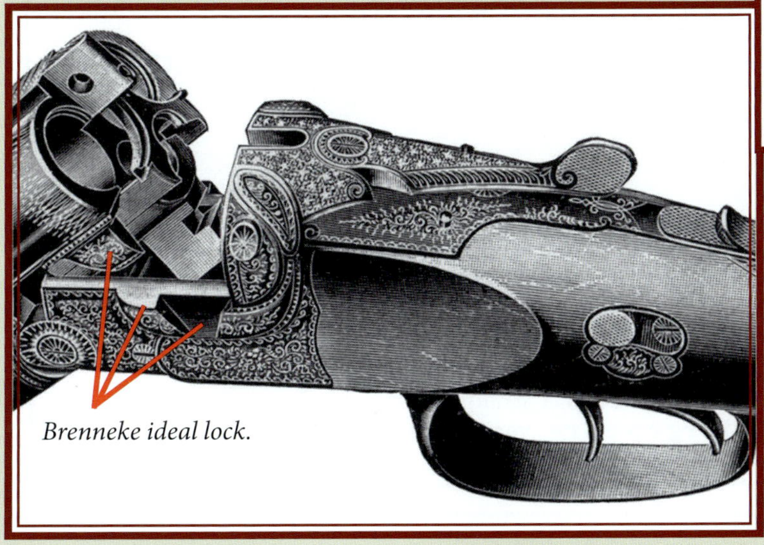

The Ideal Lock (Ideal Verschluss), *found on safety drillings promoted by Wilhelm Brenneke, reduced side movement and counteracted the tendency of the barrels to pull away from the breech. This added to the durability of the action.*

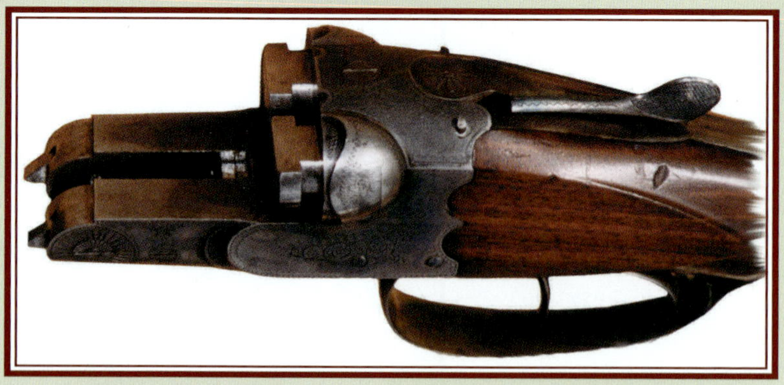

This double rifle in caliber 8x57IRS / 8x57IRS from the 1920s is signed "Bittman."

The top lever rotates the two rotary bolts. Also called a cannon breech (Zylinder Verschluss), *it consisted of a single, large underlug or locking block. Two top levers operated the rotary breechblocks or locking lugs that were fitted to recesses in each barrel when the action was closed.*

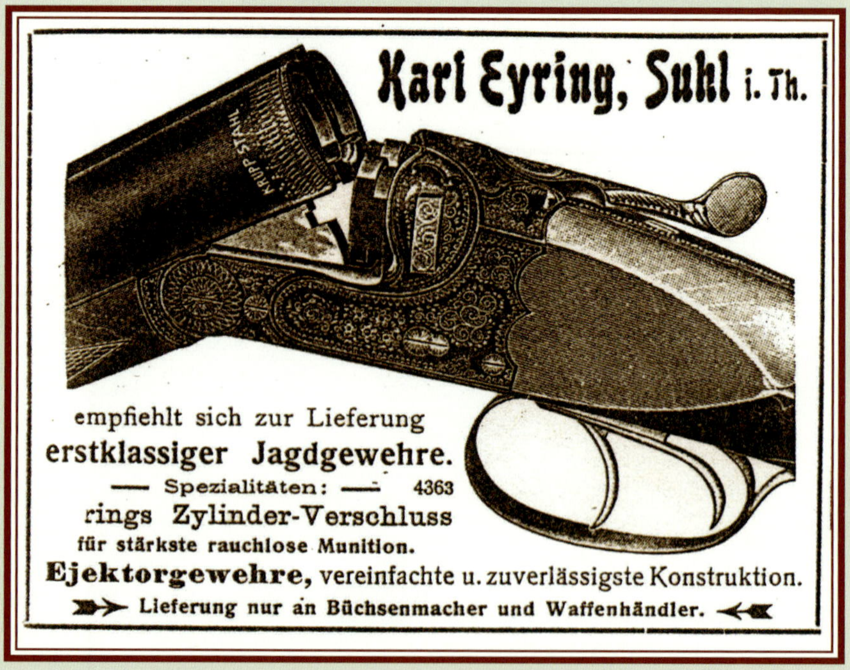

Karl Eyring marketed sporting arms with this strong cannon breech action.

Waffen tips

The additional cost for a reinforced aluminum receiver was between $25 and $50.

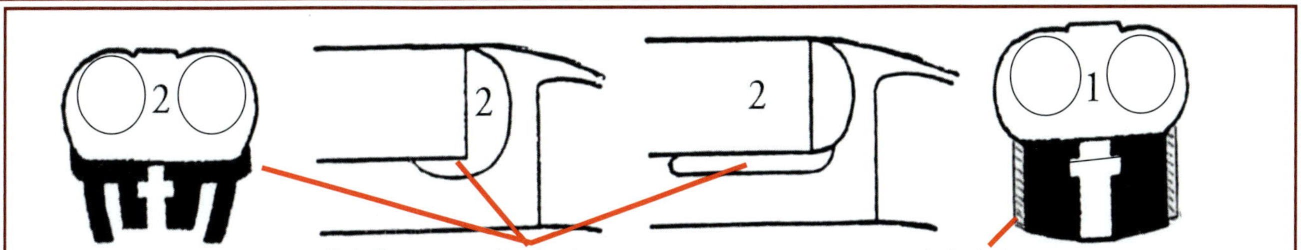

Shotgun drilling with reinforced frame.

The use of smokeless powder in heavy loads called for stronger frames. One method of reinforcement in critical areas was a solid action with the hammer locks fastened to the outside instead of inletting the lockplate into the frame.

The addition of small bolsters or cheeks (Backen) *to the sides of the action strengthened the standing breech at the critical right angle. These reinforcements came in several shapes, depending on the maker.*

Heavy, mussel-shell-shape reinforcements formed the sides of the clamshell action (Muschel-Stabil-Verschluss). *The barrels nestled down between them, reducing lateral movement when firing heavy loads.*

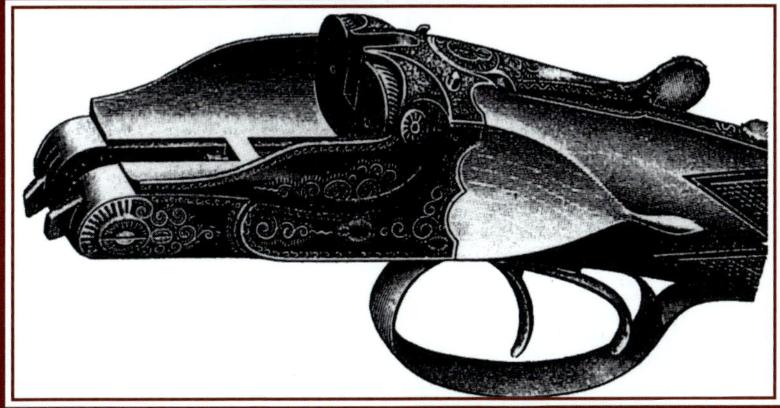

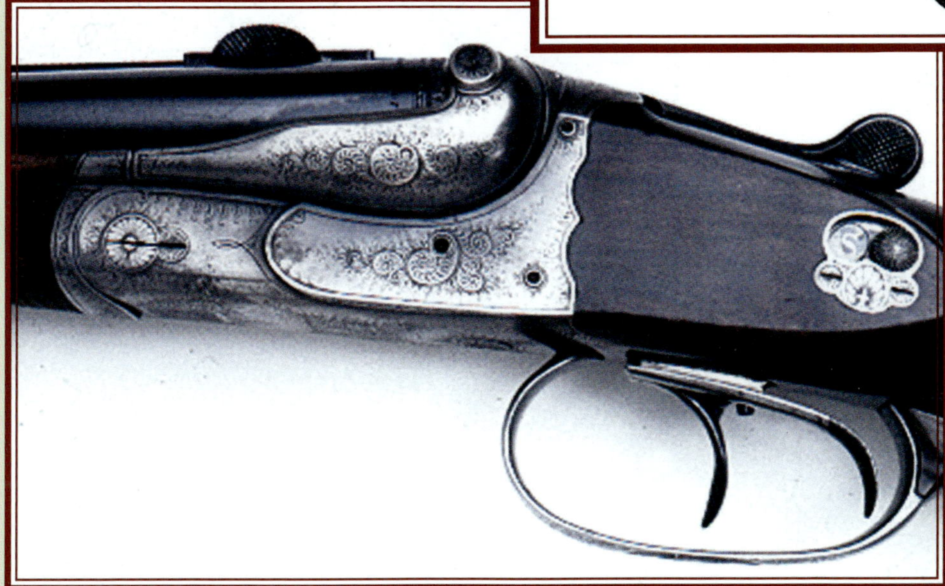

This is a double rifle with a clamshell action by gunmaker J. J. Reeb of Bonn in caliber 8x57IR / 8x57IR.

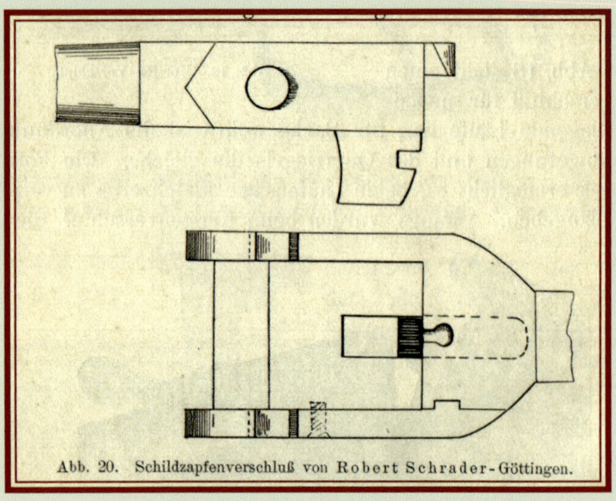

Gunmaker Robert Schrader of Göttingen, a city in central Germany, introduced the Schrader trunnion lock (Schrader Schildzapfen Verschluss). *With the action closed, the locking pins mated with corresponding openings in the receiver.*

Since the pins were aligned with the axis of the bore, the tendency of the barrels to pivot away from the breech was eliminated. The locking bolt under the barrels engaged a single underlug.

August Schüler, the well-known Berlin gunsmith, offered sporting arms with his patented Hercules action in the early 1930s. Similar French designs dated back to the late 1800s and English designs to the first decade of the twentieth century.

Made without underlugs (Hakenloser-Hercules-Verschluss), *the top lever activates two roughly oval-shape shields or wings, thus engaging round studs on each side of the frame and the outside of the barrels. This lockup was ideal for double rifles in heavy calibers.*

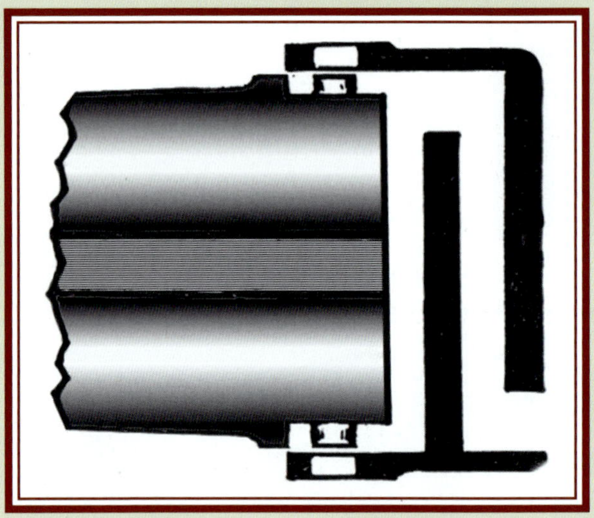

This Hercules action on a Kettner double rifle in caliber 9.3x74R / 9.3x74R has two underbites.

Hercules actions were also built using conventional underbites in addition to the sideplates.

The Ischler Stutzen, a Gunmaker's Gem

The Austrian town of Ischl lent its name to an interesting stalking rifle—a *Stutzen*—originally designed for use in the rugged Austrian Alps. Called a *Stutzer* in Austria, the Stutzen was a single-shot hammer gun favored by hunters stalking in the local mountains of Bavaria, Austria, and parts of Switzerland. Between 1850 and 1860, a gunmaker by the name of Wolfgang Leithner or Leitner of Ischl first crafted this short, big-bore percussion mountain rifle. In 1870, Leithner built a breechloading version with similar lines and features in caliber 12.5mm (.570).

The Ischler hammer guns featured a full stock and an octagonal barrel. In early models, the actions were opened by a lever under the trigger guard. The

A noon rest at one of many alpine huts was part of every royal hunt.

From the mid-1920s Schmidt & Habermann of Suhl made an Ischler Stutzen in caliber 6.5x70R. The long, sleek 6.5mm (.257) cartridge was introduced by S&H around 1912 in cooperation with a well-known German hunter. It permitted slender single shot and drilling actions, all the rage at the time.

staghorn-tipped stock was fitted with a cleaning rod, and its detachable handle was stored in a flat section on the underside of the butt. The right side of the stock contained a patchbox with a wooden cover. A harp trigger guard protected the double set triggers.

The gun attained fame as the favorite hunting firearm of Emperor Franz Joseph I of Austria. It was soon copied by several Continental gunmakers. Peterlongo of Innsbruck *(Tiroler Waffenfabrik)*, notable Ferlach gunmaker Franzoj, and famous German gunsmith Kuchenreuter produced their own versions of the desirable single-shot rifle.

The Stutzen underwent some modification when makers introduced modern calibers and replaced the early cast brass harp guard with a steel trigger guard. A two-part, detachable fore-end allowed a quick take-down and gave the gun its sleek lines. The cleaning rod was moved from its position under the barrel, and its sections were stored in a special recess in the butt cap. The gun connoisseur can still special order a modern version of the unusual and elegant Ischler Stutzen.

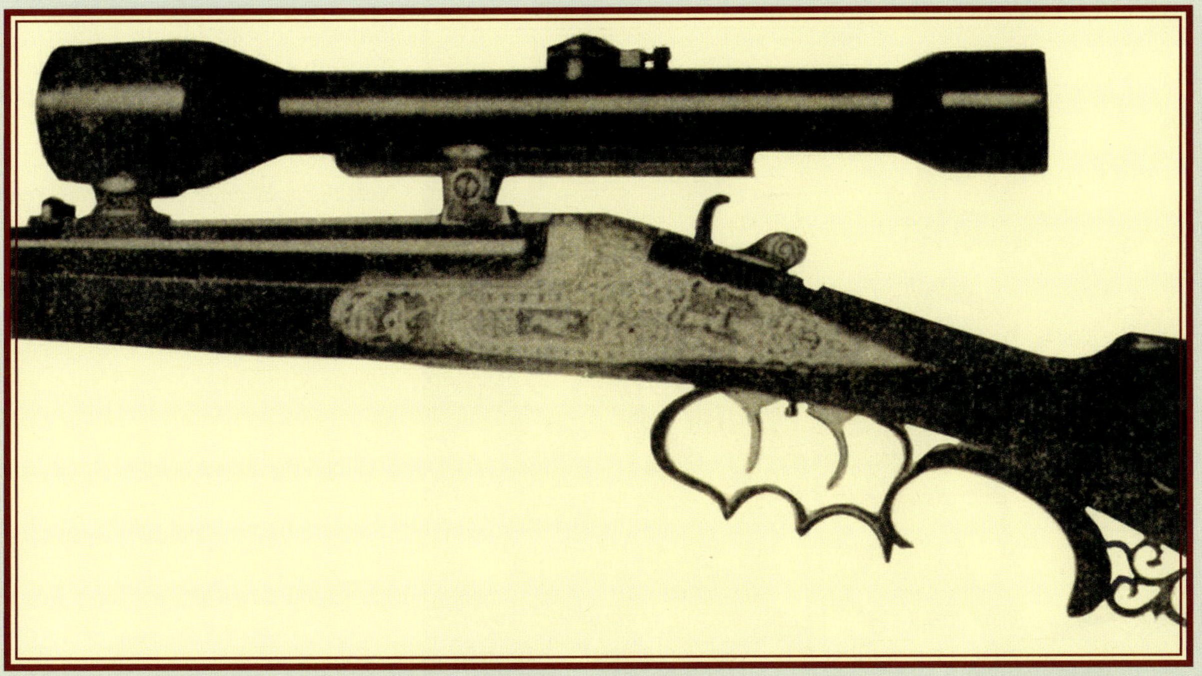

This handmade, elaborately stocked and embellished Ischler Stutzen was made for an Austrian customer by Peterlongo of Innsbruck in the 1930s.

In 1928 Heinrich Leue, a noted Berlin gunmaker, built this Ischler Stutzen. The gun measures 39 inches overall and weighs 7½ pounds. At the time it represented the elegant, slender style of a gentleman's stalking rifle much in vogue for the nobility and well-heeled patrons.

The gun is not signed on either the barrel or action. The maker would have remained anonymous had it not been for a tiny stamp in the shape of a lion on the water table. Magnification revealed the name Leue within the outline of the animal.

Emperor Franz Joseph I hunting in the Austrian Alps with his favorite Ischler Stutzen. He was a staunch advocate for the single shot—one barrel, one shot.

Note the position of the emperor's right hand: His fingers are curling around the harp trigger guard on the outside in the manner of target shooters.

Sportsmen named the 6.5x70R (rimmed) the Bleistift Patrone *(the pencil cartridge) as seen above. Compare it to an 8x57 in the .30-06 class*

THE BOXLOCK

BOXLOCK SHAPES

Actions on break-open sporting arms connect to stocks by bolts and/or wood screws through the wrist area of the firearm. The rear outline of boxlock frames *(Basküle)* where it meets the wood was often given a curved shape. In contrast to most English sporting arms with straight frame edges, Continental gunmakers contoured shapes by filing or milling, depending on the maker's preference and type of action used. When meticulously fitted, these profiles added pleasing lines to the gun and rigidity to the wood-to-metal connection.

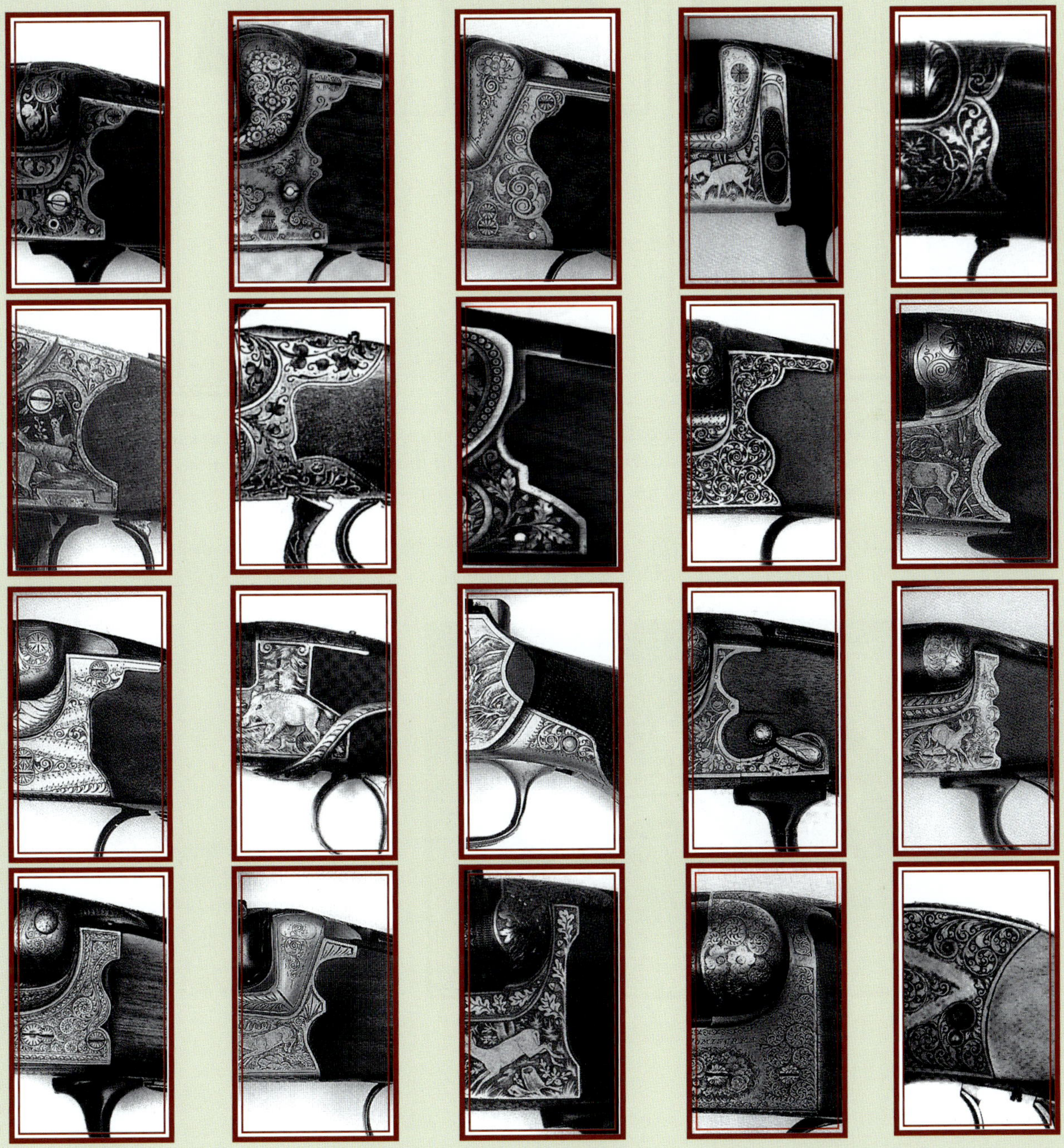

In the early twentieth century, gunmakers continuously designed lighter drillings with more slender lines to improve their handling characteristics. Smaller, more rounded actions were developed and used in conjunction with rimmed ammunition in caliber 6.5x58R, 7x72, or 8x72R, based on the English Nitro Express cartridges that were popular for deer hunting on the Continent.

This development was carried to the extreme in the ultra-thin pencil cartridge (Bleistiftpatrone), *a round with a 70mm (2¾) case length and a 6mm (.257) bullet, which made a slim action more graceful.*

This is a view of the production stages of a Heym O/U boxlock receiver machined from a solid block of high-tensile steel. The finished stage on the right shows the upper tang extension already forged to the frame.

Cocking Indicators

On hammer guns, the position of the hammers indicate at a glance whether they were cocked. For this reason, many hunters parted reluctantly with their beloved hammer guns when hammerless sporting arms became available. Once the hammers were enclosed, their position could no longer be seen. Because sportsmen wanted to see and preferably feel the state of the inside strikers, this presented a problem. Gunmakers resolved the issue in a number of different ways.

Cocking indicator pins projected approximately an eighth (⅛) of an inch through the top of the receiver when the locks were cocked. These pins were located either on the breech above the top lever, on both sides of the lever, or below the lever on the tang. Small spiral springs retracted the steel or brass pins when the hammers were not under tension. There was a weakness in this system, however, and that was the possibility that moisture could enter the receiver through pin openings.

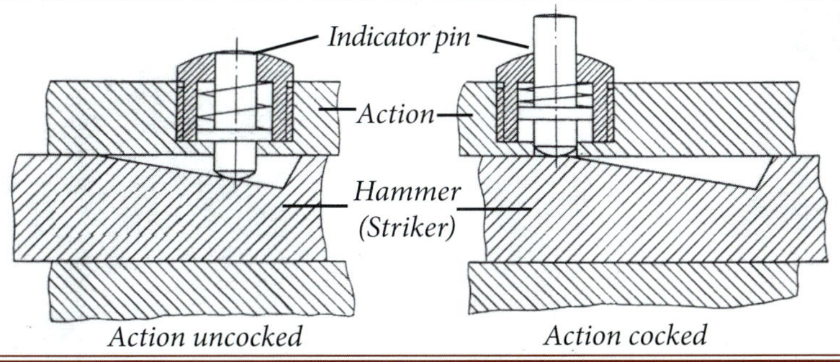

Pins were located either on the breech above the top lever, on both sides of the lever, or below the lever on the tang.

On this drilling by gunmaker Georg Link of Darmstadt, the indicators are located on the breech above the top lever. These pins are easily felt in the dark.

Here signal pins are situated on the top tang and below the top lever on a Meffert drilling.

Indicator pins on a Funk, Suhl, drilling are placed next to the top lever.

1 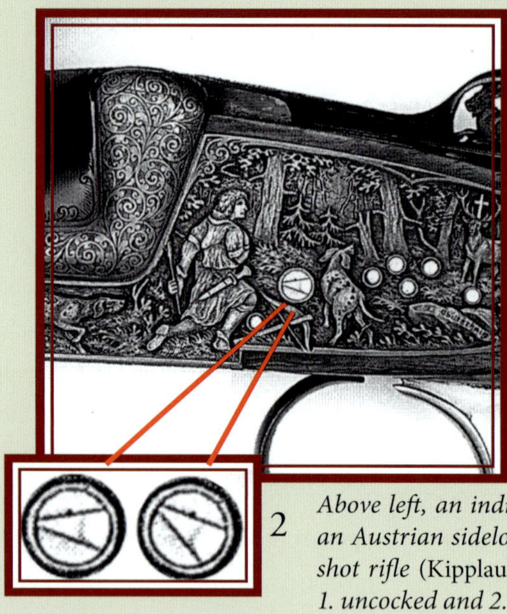 2

Above left, an indicator on an Austrian sidelock single shot rifle (Kipplaufbüchse)*: 1. uncocked and 2. cocked.*

1  2

Above right, indicator pins on a Merkel O/U boxlock: 1. cocked and 2. uncocked.

Sidelock indicators of different shapes.

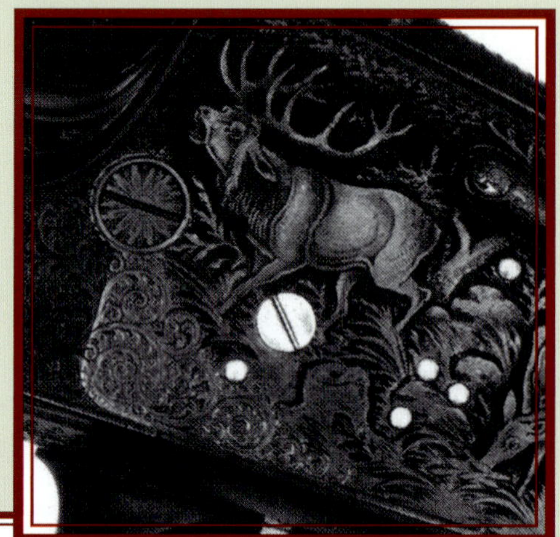

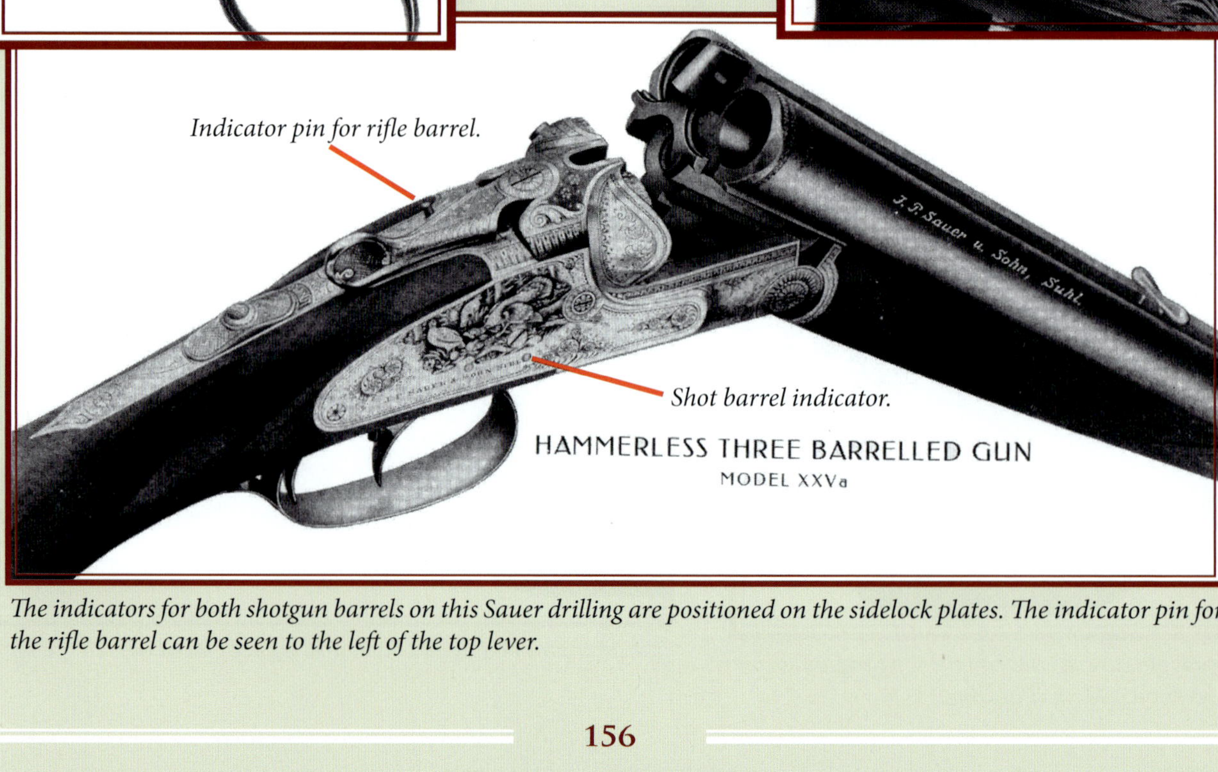

The indicators for both shotgun barrels on this Sauer drilling are positioned on the sidelock plates. The indicator pin for the rifle barrel can be seen to the left of the top lever.

On the left sideplate, a large, sculptured arrow indicates the condition of the barrel lock on this drilling made by J. J. Reeb, Bonn gunmaker. Note the Greener safety.

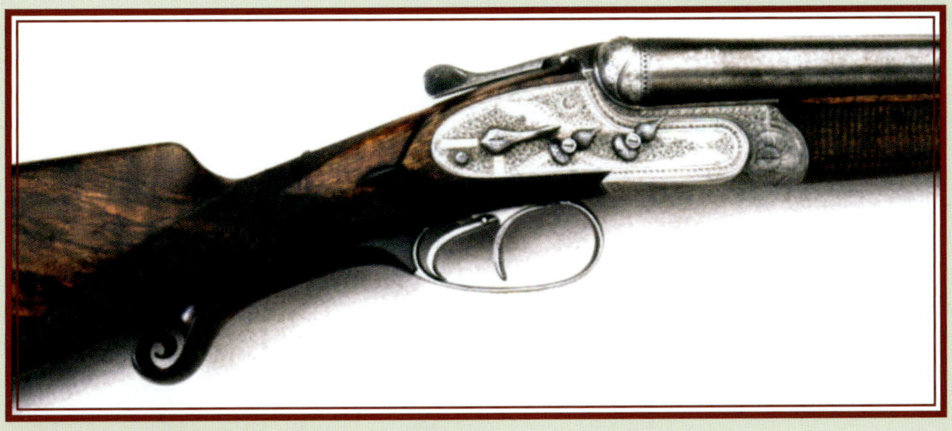

Mounted on the right sidelock plate of the same gun are the arrows for the rifle barrel and for the right shot barrel. The lever on the left of the two indicators is the barrel selector.

This is a Sauer & Sohn, Suhl, sidelock drilling with an indicator arrow for each shot barrel. The rifle-barrel lock is equipped with a hand-cocking lever on the left side of the wrist.

On other sporting arms, arrows or pointers of different shapes are incorporated into sidelocks or on the side of boxlock actions. Their disadvantage lay in the difficulty to see or feel their position in the dark. This also holds true for receivers with small windows cut into the side of the action to reveal the position of the strikers.

Signal pins extended horizontally through fences on French-made ideal hammerless guns and sporting arms made by the Berlin firm of Leue & Timpe. They indicated not whether the gun was cocked, but whether it was loaded.

Fences

Fences on Hammer Guns

Fences on hammer guns are the shell-shape depressions in the breechblock that contain the firing pins and retainers. They evolved from the high fences found on many percussion guns that protect the face of the shooter from sparks and pieces of exploding percussion caps. On self-cocking guns, fences are the protruding parts on both sides of the action behind the barrels. On German guns they are a half-round shape. Many Austrian and almost all English sporting arms have a flattened shape, called Holland & Holland fences. On crown guns they are called star fences *(Stern Muscheln).* Half and full fences are often found with wings of different dimensions on hammer guns.

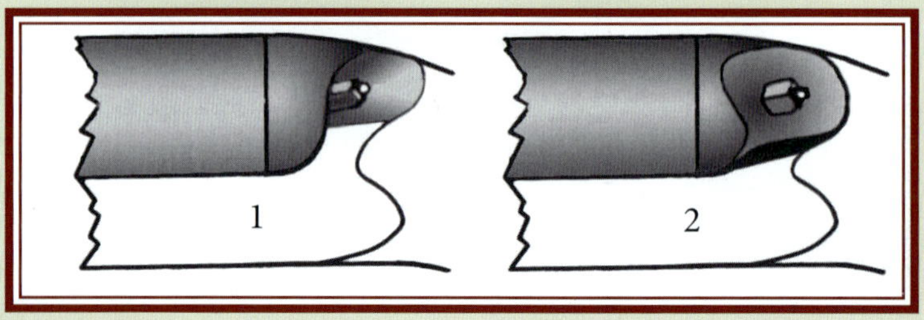

1. Half fences. *2. Full fences.*

High fences (left) on an Adam Kuchenreuter percussion double rifle, made circa 1850.

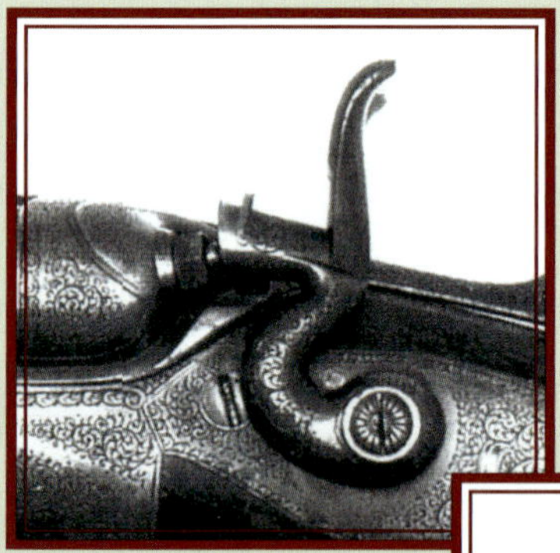

Full fences (left) on a double rifle by Johann Springer Erben, Vienna.

Half fences (right) on a stalking rifle by Ferdinand Fükert, Weipert.

Winged round fences (right) on a drilling by Thieme & Schlegelmilch, Suhl.

Winged round fences (left) on an O/U rifle/shotgun combination by Sauer and Sohn, Suhl.

Round fences (left) on a double by Anton Kuchenreuter, Cham.

FENCES ON HAMMERLESS GUNS

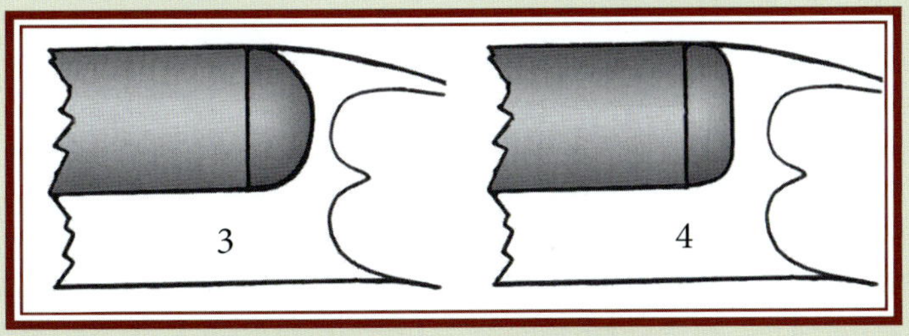

3. Round fences.

4. Holland & Holland fences.

Holland & Holland fences.

Round, side-clipped fences.

Contoured fence on a single-shot rifle.

Star fences.

Fences on O/U combination guns.

Triggers

On double shotguns and combination guns with two barrels, two triggers were and are standard. On a drilling or vierling the same trigger configuration, with the addition of a switch overlever or slide selector on the action, allows two triggers to service three or four locks. On a drilling, the forward trigger usually services the right shot barrel and rifle barrel; the rear trigger is used for the left shot tube. Brenneke, Fükert, Greifelt and several other gunmakers offered drillings with three triggers, one for each barrel.

The amount of pressure needed to release the sear and striker (trigger pull) was important. A soft trigger pull was desirable; it lessened the chance

Fükert drilling in caliber .25-35 Winchester, 20/20.

A Greifelt 12-gauge shotgun drilling.

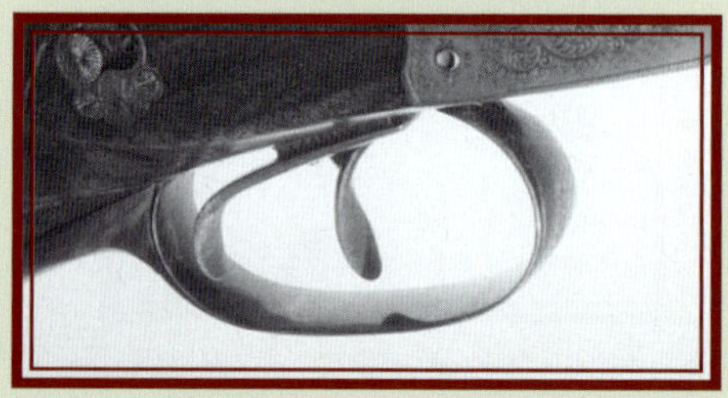

Angled triggers.

Heavy 12-bore double rifle made by Vienna gunmaker Franz Denk about 1880. The front stub trigger allowed for quick change from firing the right barrel to the left.

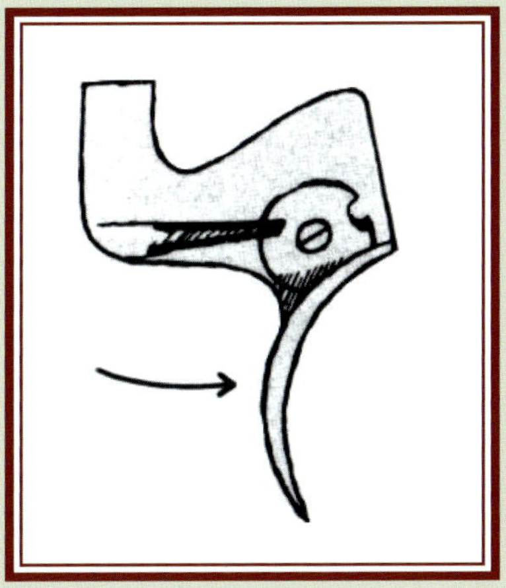

Several gunmakers engineered triggers to mitigate the effects of recoil by installing a hinged forward trigger blade called a *"folding" or "articulated" trigger* (Gelenkabzug). *This averted possible injury to the trigger (middle) finger of the shooter's right hand.*

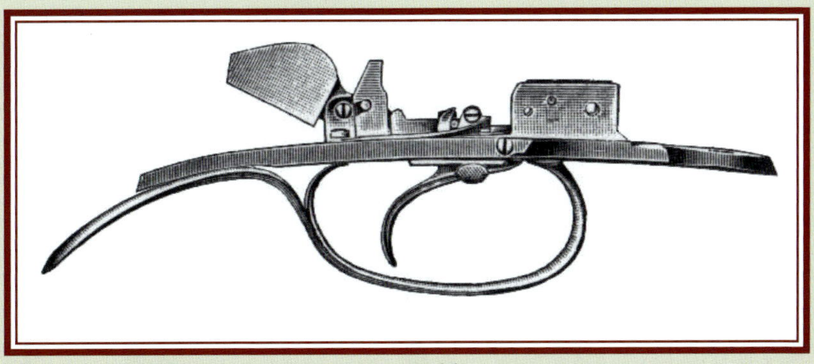

Single selective trigger by Franz Jäger, Suhl.

Single triggers (Einabzüge) *allowed for the discharge of two or three barrels with a single trigger assembly. Manufactured by several companies, single trigger devices were available on special order or for later installation.*

Opinions about the use of single triggers are divided. For special hunting situations, a single trigger permits the firing of two or more shots in rapid succession because the position of the shooter's right hand on the wrist of the gun does not have to change.

However, single trigger mechanisms are more complicated and prone to failure. There is also the danger of doubling if the trigger is not regulated precisely.

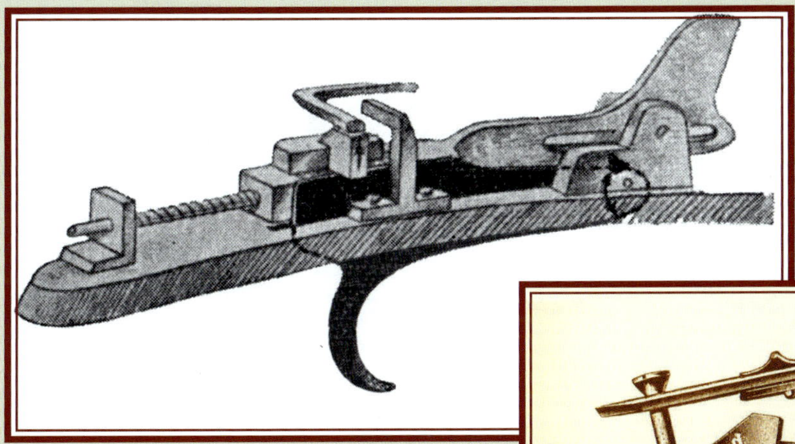

Left is a single trigger "Triumpf" by Siegfried Günther, Suhl, available in the right/left or the left/right sequence.

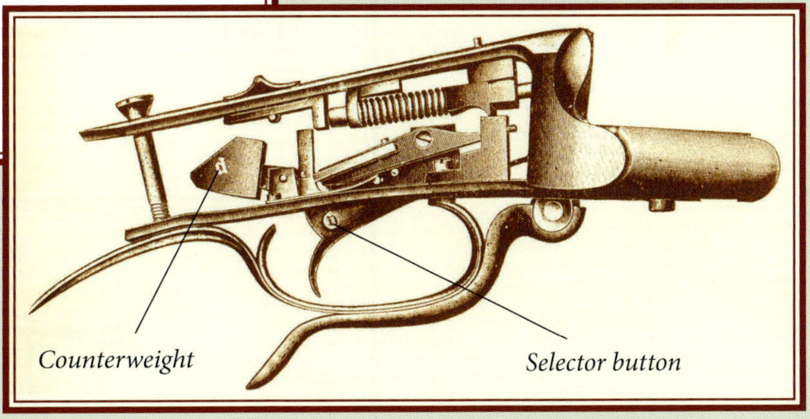

To selectively fire the left or right shot barrel on this drilling (right) sold by Venus Waffenwerke Oscar Will, a button had to be depressed on the trigger. To fire the rifle barrel, the trigger had to be pushed forward. The counterweight prevented doubling.

of a sudden jerk. If trigger adjustment screws were set too sensitively, it caused a second shot barrel or rifle barrel to discharge involuntarily. Good safety devices protecting unfired locks were essential.

Gunsmiths often angled the triggers on their double guns or they installed offset triggers. By slanting the blade surfaces with the finger position, the trigger pull was more comfortable, especially when shooting a long series of shots.

Collath

This single-shot, hammerless stalking rifle, made by gunmaker Collath, was cocked by a forward pressure on the trigger. To uncock the gun, the trigger had to be pulled while simultaneously holding the safety slide on the wrist with the right thumb. After trigger let-off, the slide was slowly pushed forward.

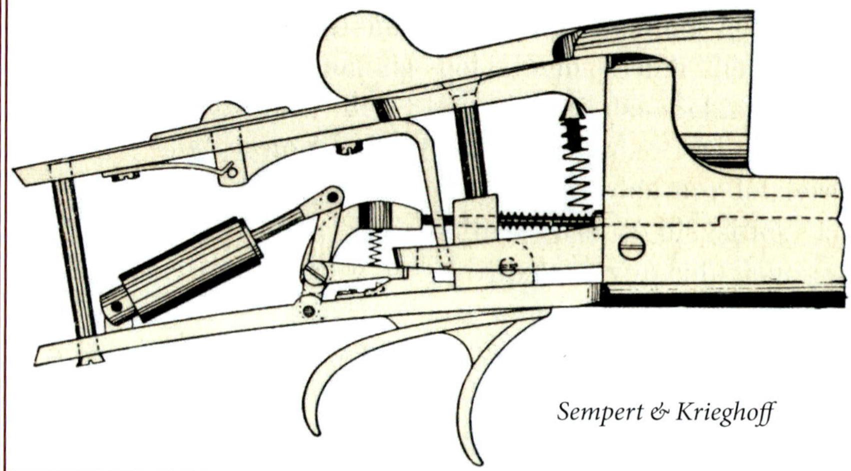

Sempert & Krieghoff

Gunmaker Sempert & Krieghoff offered a different trigger version that delayed the change-over from one lock to the other by a small pneumatic piston in the action.

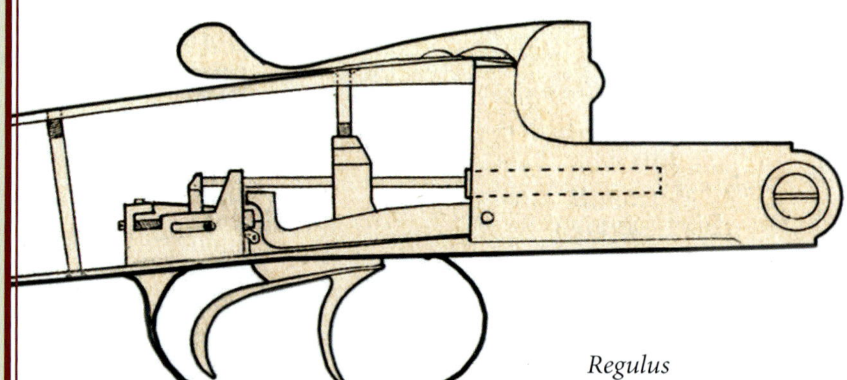

Regulus

A single trigger for doubles or drillings with the brand name "Regulus" was developed by Heinrich Scheid. It functioned as a single or double trigger. It was possible to discharge all barrels by pressing the forward trigger in rapid succession, or by using the two triggers in the conventional way.

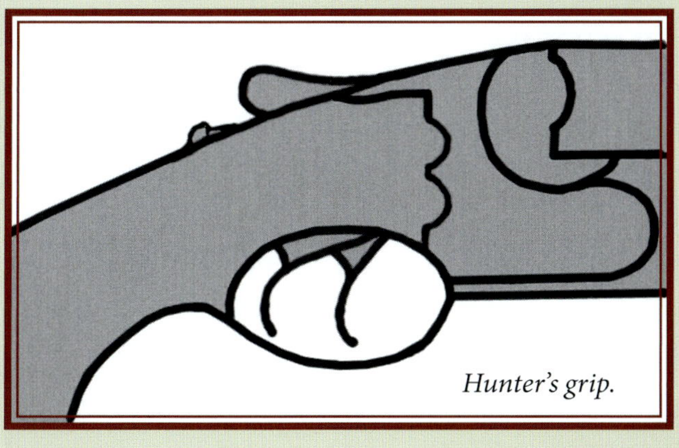

Hunter's grip.

Franz Jäger designed his O/U shotguns, side-by-side doubles, and dove guns (Taubenflinten) *with triggers and trigger guards moved well up into the underside of the action frame. Called the hunter's grip* (Jägergriff), *it permitted a natural and ergonomic handhold and prevented injury to the middle finger of the shooter when the gun recoiled.*

Gun manufacturer Pieper in Herstal, Belgium, a company known for its many innovations, experimented with combination guns built without conventional triggers underneath the action. Instead, the company fitted the trigger mechanism inside the stock, accessible by an opening in the right side of the wrist area.

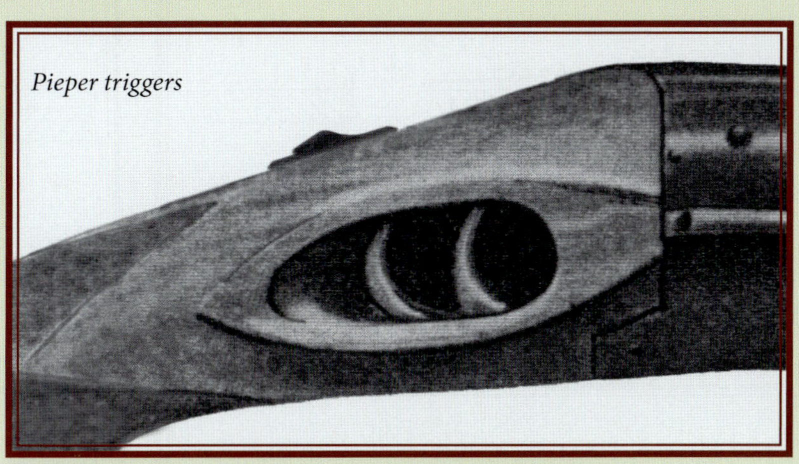

Pieper triggers

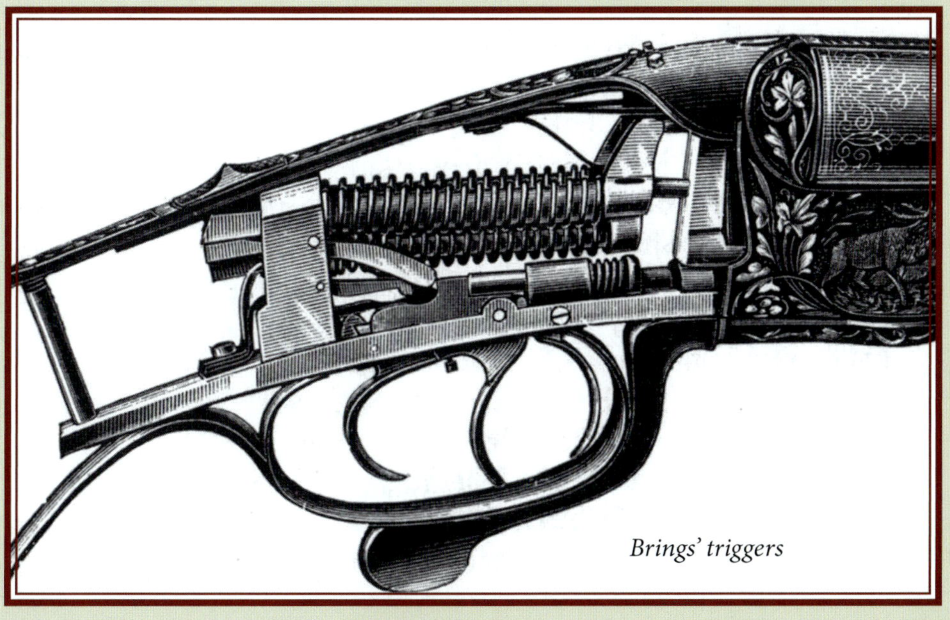

Brings' triggers

Hans Brings of Cologne built still another trigger arrangement into his drilling: a third trigger or lever hinged forward in front of the two conventional triggers. It followed the curvature of the front part of the trigger guard facing to the rear. When closing the action, all three locks were cocked and safe. By sliding the tang safety forward, both shot barrels fired like a shotgun. The lock for the rifle barrel was activated by slightly touching the rear-facing trigger with the index fingernail of the shooter's right hand before pulling the forward trigger. The very real danger of this arrangement lay in the accidental discharge of the rifle barrel caused by the recoil.

Set or Hair Triggers

The set trigger reduces the amount of energy necessary to pull the trigger and thereby increases accuracy. Most set triggers (*Stecher*) are adjustable with a small regulating screw behind the trigger blade. When turning this screw in a clockwise direction, the trigger becomes more sensitive. Because of the potential danger posed by hair triggers, they are not activated until immediately before a shot is fired. If the weapon is not discharged at that time, the hair trigger must be deactivated at once. If the trigger on a combination gun or double rifle is set too sensitively, doubling can occur, causing a second barrel to discharge simultaneously.

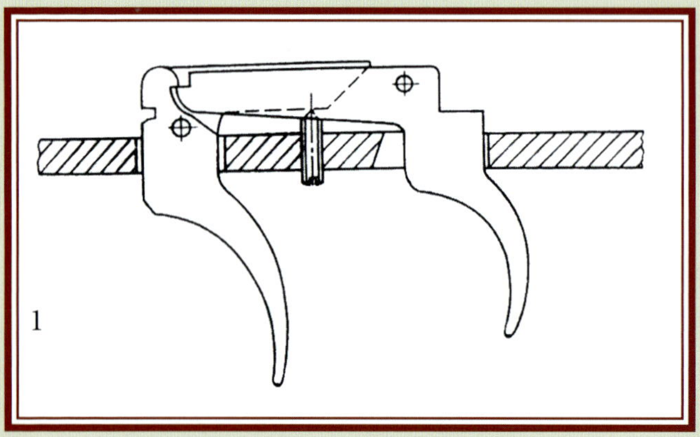

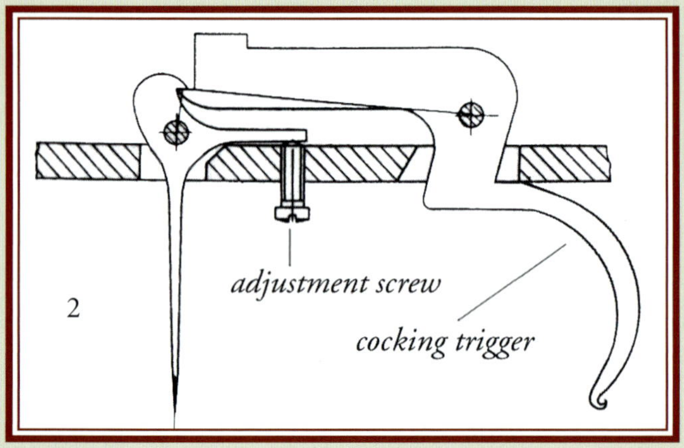

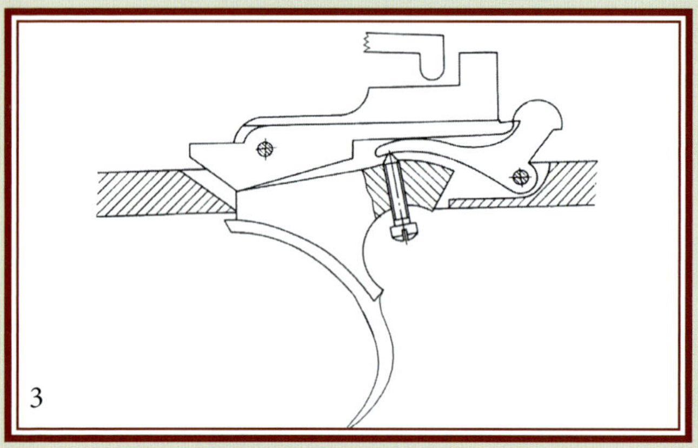

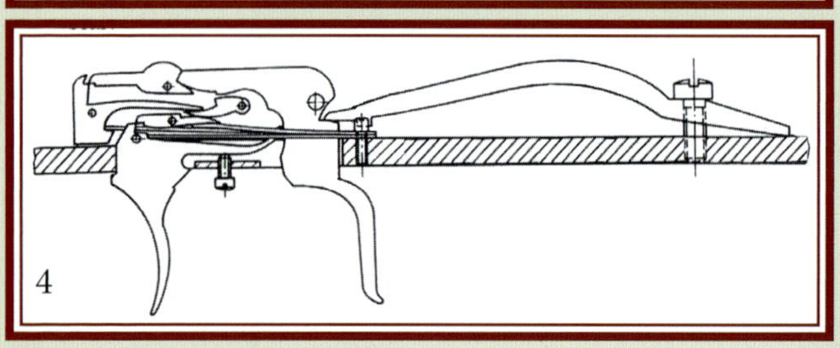

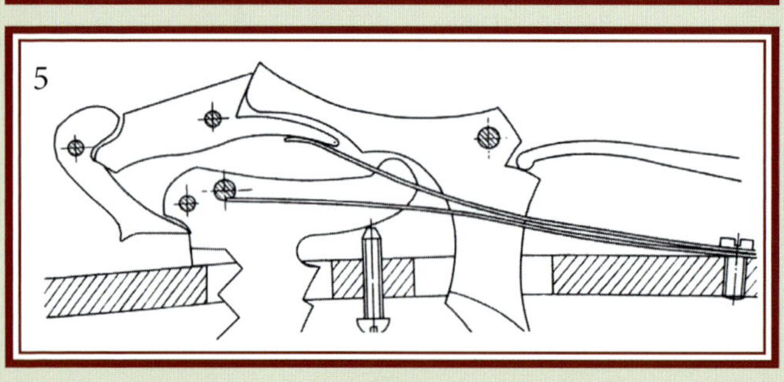

1. The double-set trigger (German trigger) is used on single-shot and target rifles. It consists of two trigger blades: The rear one cocks a spring-loaded mechanism, and the front one fires the shot. By pulling back on the rear trigger with the middle finger of the right hand and then slowly depressing the front trigger with the index finger, the set feature is deactivated.

2. The needle-set trigger (Nadelstecher) *functions similarly to the double set. This trigger is found on guns dating back to the sixteenth century.*

3. The single set or forward set, also called the French trigger (Rückstecher), *was first used on French dueling pistols. It was adapted to numerous drillings and combination guns because the other trigger(s) could be applied to other barrels. It is activated by pushing the front trigger forward until it is arrested by the sear with an audible click. On drillings, the front trigger fires the rifle barrel. On double rifles and combination guns with two different calibers* (Bergstutzen), *both triggers might have this feature. To deactivate this feature, the safety must be engaged and, preferably, the breech opened. The trigger is slowly moved backward with two fingers, one in front and one in back, to release it from the sear.*

4. & 5. Multiple set triggers are designed for target shooting, and depending on the design, this type of trigger utilizes up to seven transfer elements.

THE UNIQUE BUTTON TRIGGER

The button trigger was initially developed for the German emperor, Kaiser Wilhelm II, who was born with an underdeveloped left arm. He relied on custom-made shotguns with short, light forearms and reinforced pistol grips; he was able to shoot upland game for long periods using his right arm only. This photo shows Kaiser Wilhelm shooting single-handedly.

Triggers exposed.

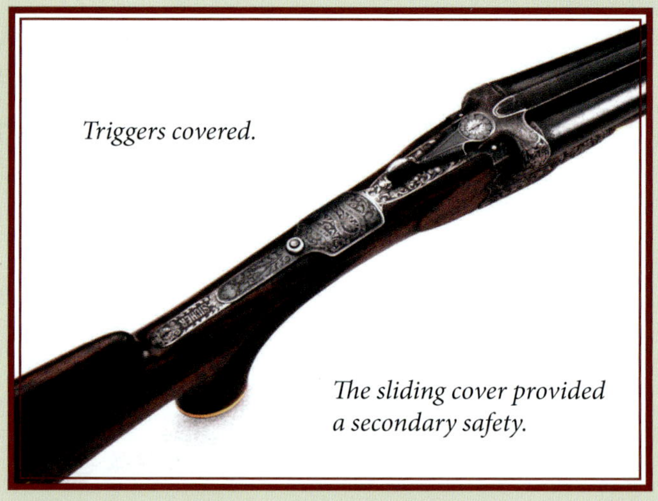

Triggers covered.

The sliding cover provided a secondary safety.

The German gunsmith Phillip Reeb of Bonn developed an unconventional way of firing a double-barrel shotgun: He omitted conventional triggers and the trigger guard, and the gun was fired by depressing one of two buttons recessed into the upper tang just behind the top lever. The buttons were protected by a sliding cover. An automatic safety prevented both barrels from being fired simultaneously.

A different model featured a sliding safety mounted on the left side lockplate. The button trigger arrangement, also called "thumb trigger," went through several stages of development and, in its final form, was patented as the Martin Button Trigger by the firm's successor, gunmaker Emil Robert Martin.

Sliding safety positioned on left sidelock.

An extended pistol grip with the lower tang terminating at the grip cap added strength to the wrist area of the gun.

SAFETIES

Gunmakers and their customers have always paid particular attention to the safeties of their firearms. The safety feature is an important part of the action, for it prevents injury to anyone handling a gun. Gun manufacturers also place great emphasis on the description of designs in their advertising brochures. In catalogs, safety functions are explained in detail and their superior engineering compared to lesser devices.

During the transition from percussion to breechloading firearms, various hammer and trigger safeties were adequate for the majority of guns with exposed hammers that could be lowered by hand into a safety rest. As more gun manufacturers began to build hammerless sporting arms, this was no longer possible. Newly developed safeties prevented movement of those parts that could cause a gun to fire accidentally. The hunting fraternity was

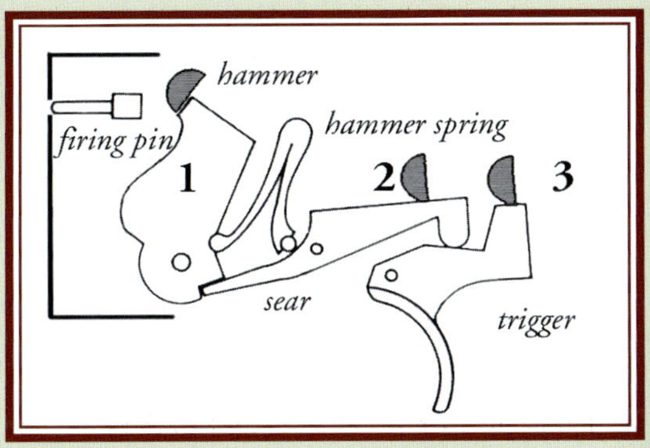

Possible safety systems: (1) hammer (2) sear (3) trigger safety (or a combination of them)

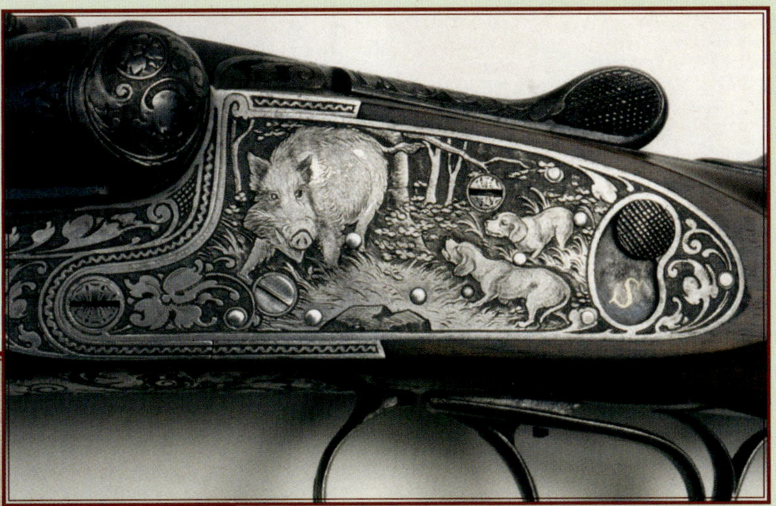

The Greener safety was incorporated into the left sidelock or situated on the left side behind the receiver above the triggers, and the triggers were blocked by a rotating shaft attached to a knurled lever. This system was widely adopted in one form or another by many gunmakers.

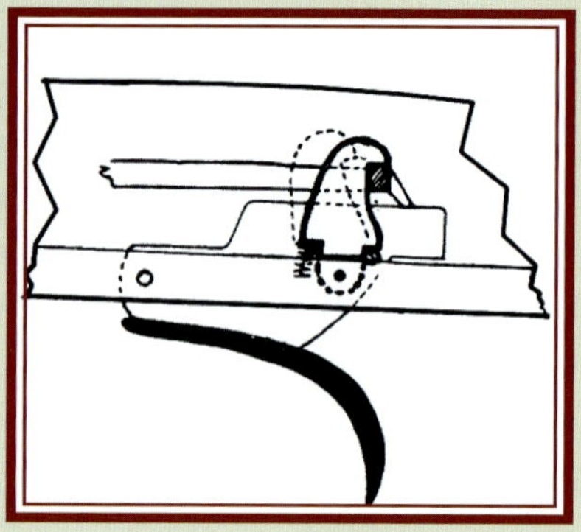

Automatic sear safety designed by Austrian gunmaker R. Mahrholdt of Innsbruck.

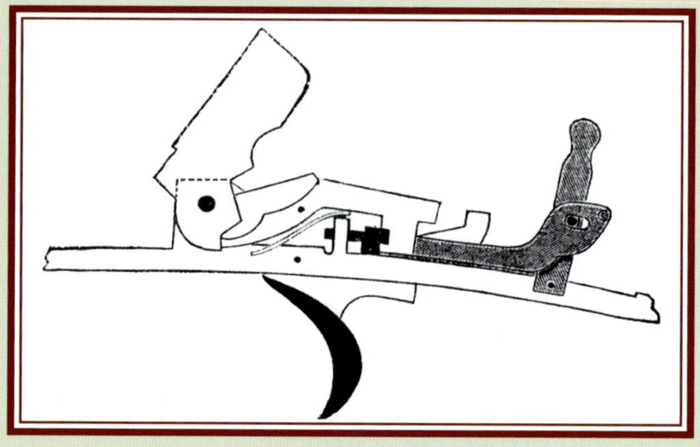

Automatic rifle lock safety on a Greifelt drilling.

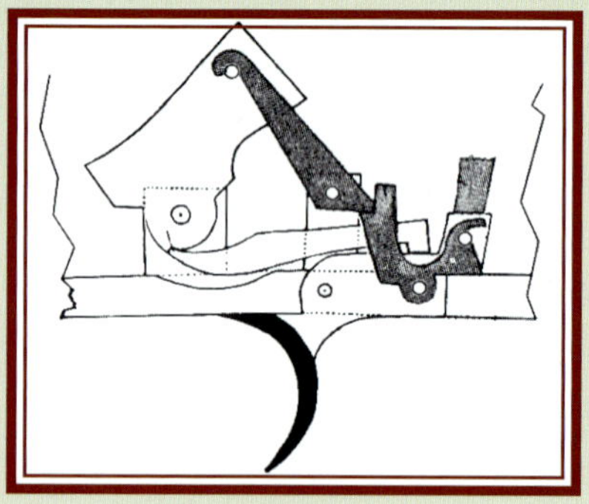

Automatic hammer safety by gunmaker A. W. Wolf of Suhl.

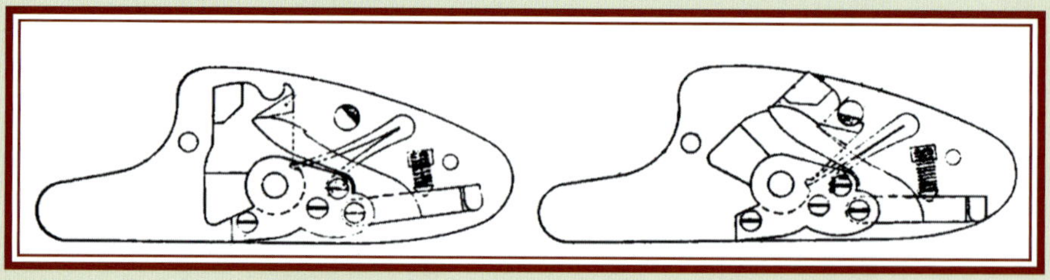

Sidelock hammer safety by gunmaker Friedrich Wilhelm Heym of Suhl.

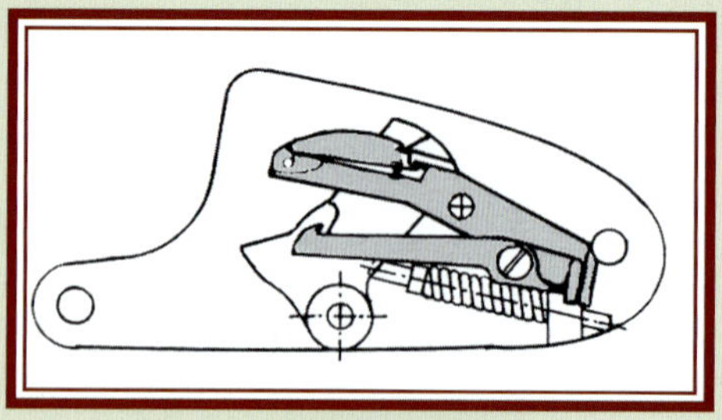

Overhanging sear safety (Fangstangen Sicherung) *on a sidelock by gunmaker Heinrich Krieghoff of Suhl.*

forced to change its habits and the way it handled sporting arms. On combination guns, additional safeties were more essential. They acted separately or simultaneously on the locks, selectively blocking a specific part of the action.

Used to the relative simplicity of a hammer gun, sportsmen initially were uneasy about hammerless safeties. Gunsmiths went to great lengths to allay this apprehension by incorporating multiple safeties into sporting arms, sometimes causing mechanisms to become unnecessarily complicated and prone to breakage. Over the years, hundreds of improvements and modifications were introduced, a process still continuing today.

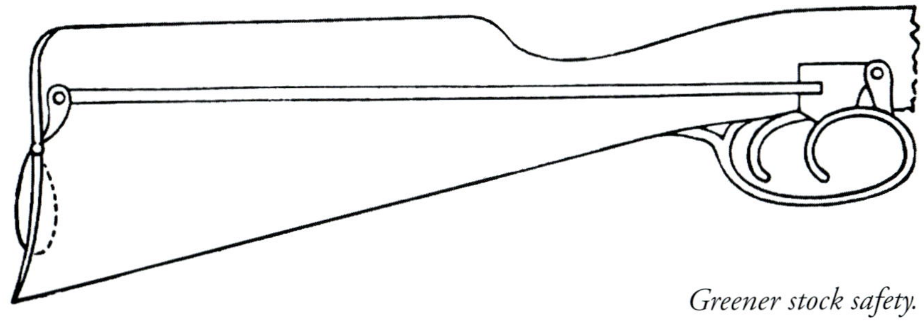

Greener stock safety.

Leberecht strap safety.

Sporting arms incorporating special safety features were advertised and sold as safety guns (Sicherheits Gewehre) *by Brenneke, Fükert, Kessler, Krieghoff, Haenel, Heym, Kuchenreuter, Schrader, Thieme & Schlegelmilch, and other gun manufacturers. Because of the complexity, necessary custom work, and hand fitting, these guns carried a higher price tag. Automatic safeties engaged when the weapon was loaded, the breech closed, or the action opened. They added protection but were a matter of preference with many shooters.*

Guns fitted with hand-cocking levers or slides (Handspanner) *were safer and increasingly in demand. Depending on the manufacturer, one or several barrels were equipped with this cocking mechanism. These guns were safe to carry loaded, easy to operate, and ready for a quick shot with a push of the thumb.*

A patented carrying strap safety by Leberecht of Amberg responded to a pull of the carrying sling or the stock safety by Greener. It proved to be impractical and was soon discontinued.

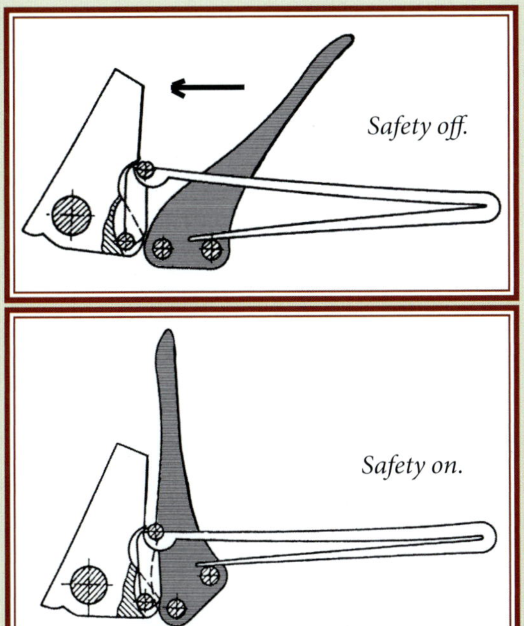

Safety off.

Safety on.

The Pieper Rationell safety employed a lever on the outside of the receiver, releasing the hammer spring.

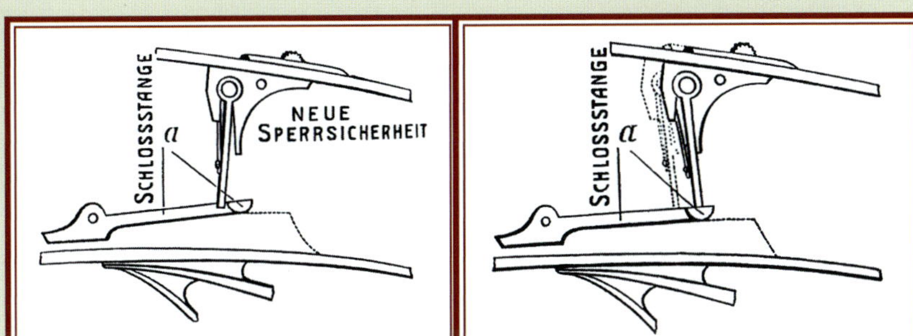

Fükert sear safety.

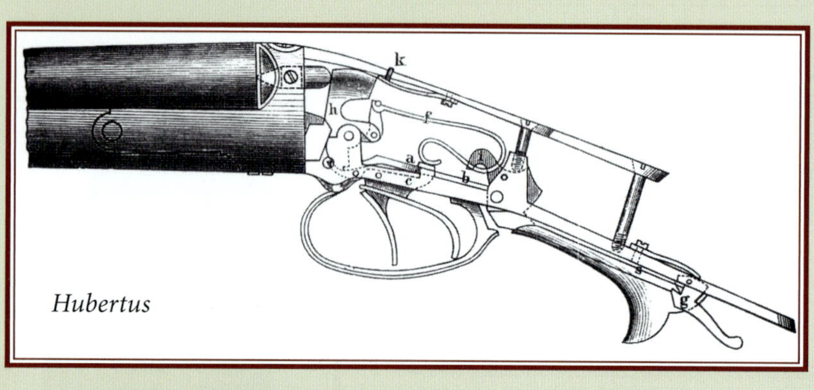

Hubertus

Prussian forester Feist developed a spring safety in 1879, calling his modified sporting arm the Hubertus gun (Hubertus Gewehr). This design was later marketed in cooperation with gunmaker Immanuel Meffert of Suhl under the "Hubertus" trademark and was patented by the firm.

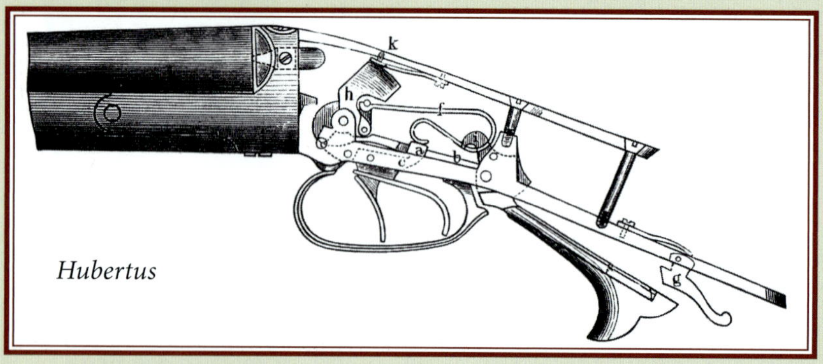

Hubertus

A spring-loaded horn lever behind the trigger guard functioned as a half-horn pistol grip and tensioned or completely released the hammer spring. The Hubertus safety was easy and reliable to operate, but its manufacture was so expensive that it was discontinued in the 1930s.

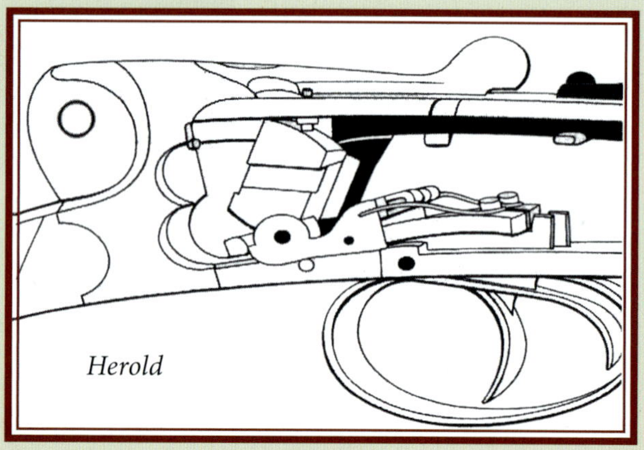

Herold

Gunmaker Franz Jäger invented a safety (Radial Sicherung) *that was engaged by a slide on the upper tang; the slide acted on the hammer spring.*

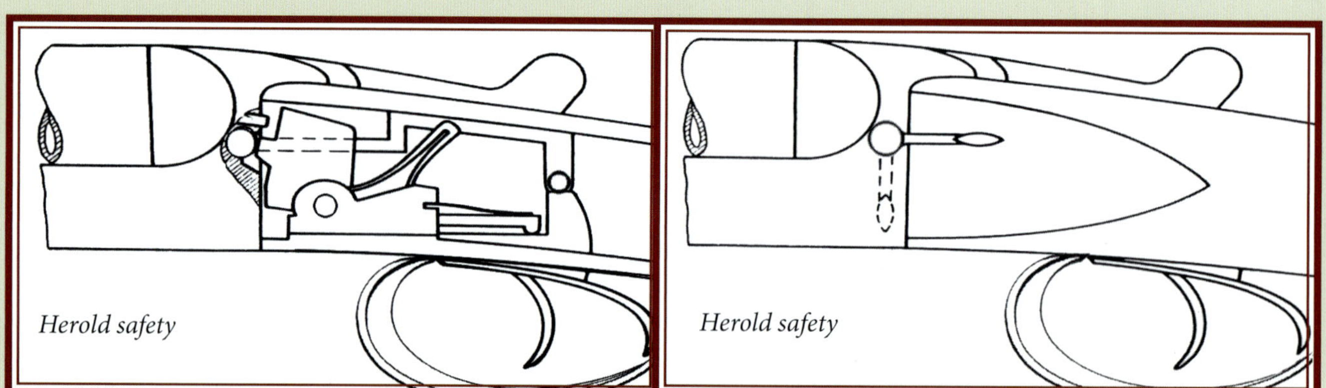

Herold safety

Herold safety

The Herold safety by the same company prevented the strikers from contacting the firing pins. The lever on the side of the action blocked the triggers at the same time.

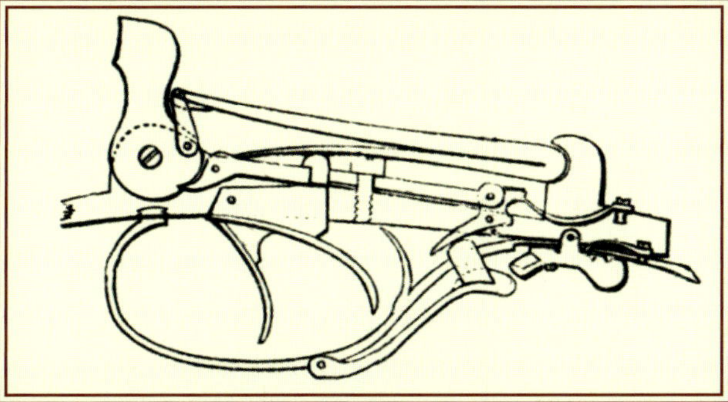

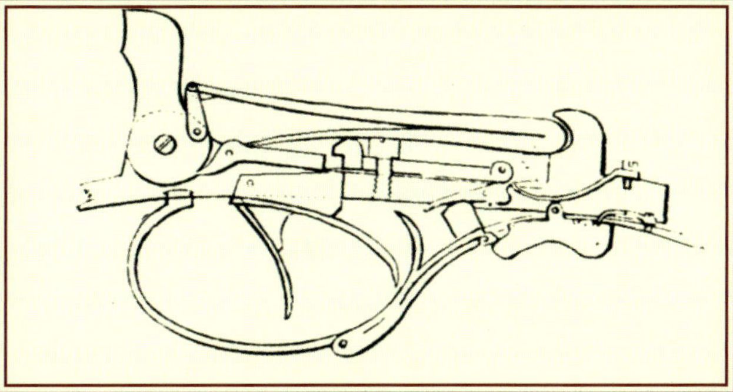

Timpe patented safety.

J. F. Timpe of Berlin patented a safety in 1884 that consisted of a combination trigger and sear system. It disengaged when the shooter gripped the wrist of the stock, thus depressing a hinged lever on the trigger guard.

English gunmaker Silver and German gunmakers Schlüter and Bornmann had developed similar earlier versions. A lever behind the trigger guard enabled the shooter to bypass this feature.

Timpe patented safety.

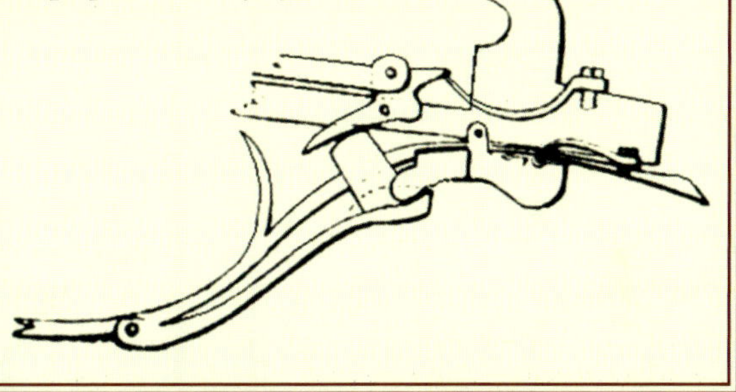

This photo illustrates the upper tang plates of five Collath drillings with butterfly or wing safety levers that block the internal hammers or strikers. The wing lever on the left is in the "safe" position; the others are in the "fire" position. Each of these extensively engraved plates has a different shape and each matches one of five guns. This necessitates a large amount of careful hand fitting.

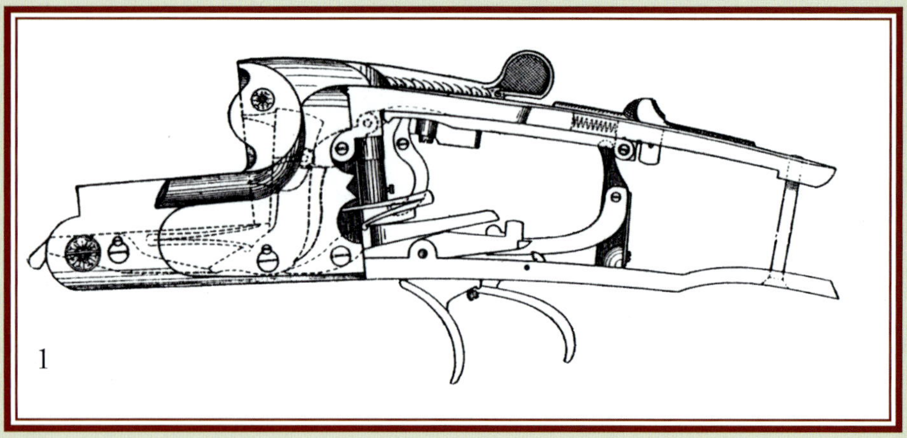

Trigger safeties on the various designs were actuated manually by a slide on the wrist behind the top lever, or they could be actuated automatically by opening the action, as shown in diagrams 1, 2, 3, & 4.

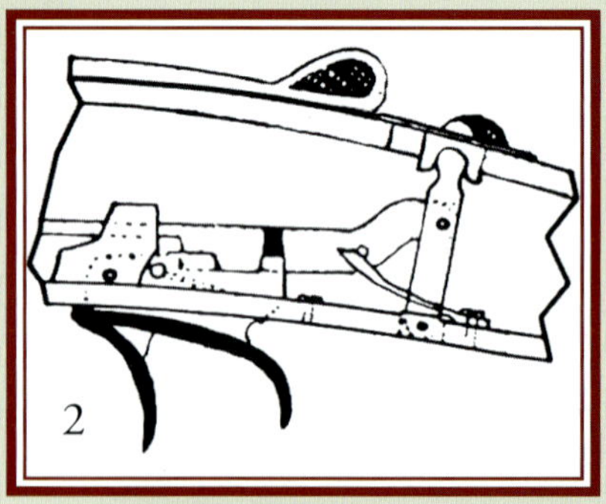

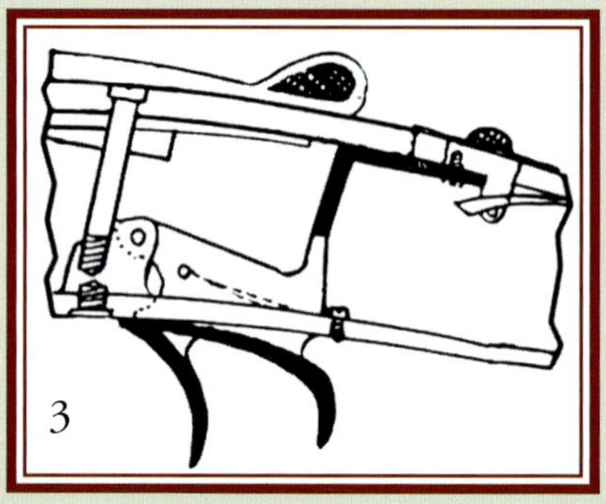

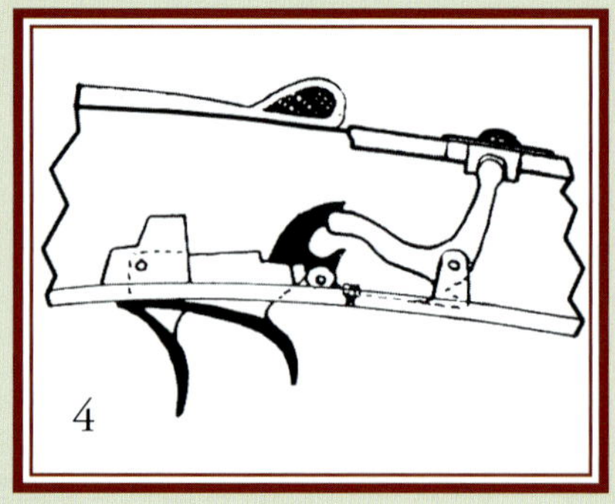

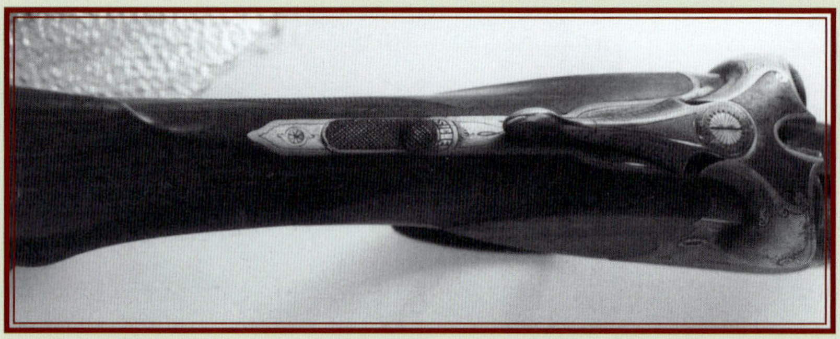

Safety slide on top tang.

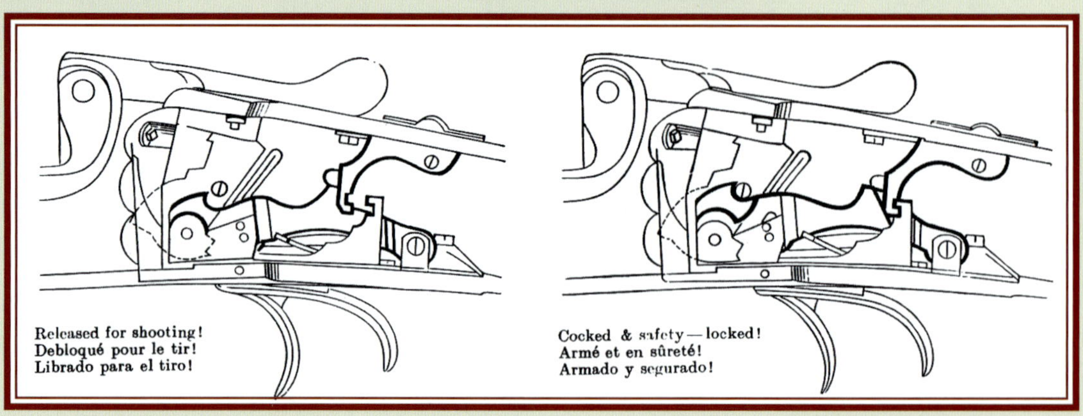

Released for shooting. *Cocked & safety in locked position.*

The safety for O/U combination guns designed by gunmaker Greifelt, Suhl, acted on hammers and triggers simultaneously.

HAMMERS

Early gunmakers profusely decorated and sculptured the hammer as an important and prominent part of any firearm. At times, dictated by the whim of craftsmen or by fashion, hammers took the shape of dragons, gargoyles, fish, or the heads of various animals. Since heavy hammers were no longer needed on modern breechloading arms, gunmakers reduced their size to lessen the danger associated with accidentally snagging the spur of the hammer during a fall. Hammers became lighter, smaller, and more elegant.

The development of new, hammerless guns with enclosed hammers (strikers) inside the action and sidelocks did not render all guns with exposed hammers obsolete. On the contrary, hammer guns remained popular. Today they are much sought-after and produced as custom-made guns on special order.

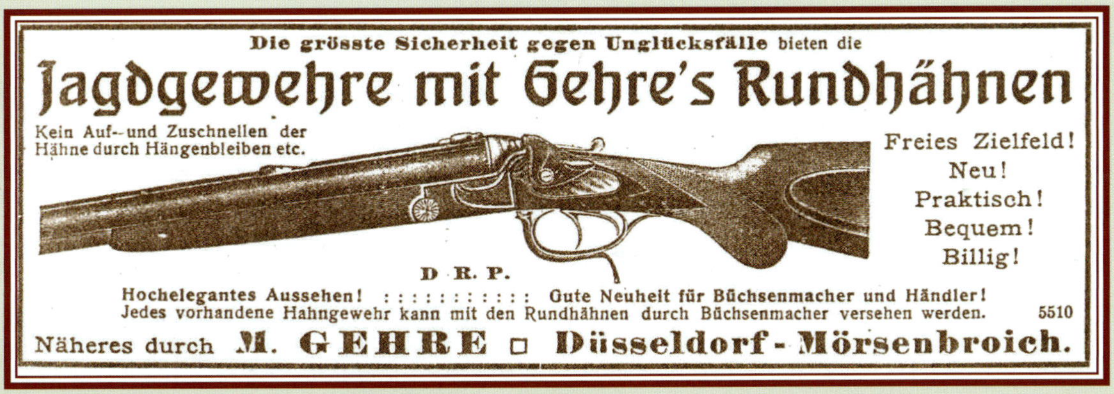

According to the ad above, the Gehre Company of Düsseldorf advertised "Round Hammers" this way: "The greatest safety in preventing accidents are guns equipped with 'Round Hammers' by M. Gehre. Unobstructed field of view; new, practical, inexpensive, convenient, elegant appearance; novelty for gunsmith and trader; and no unintentional cocking and falling of the hammers by catching (on branches). Every existing hammer gun can be fitted with 'Round Hammers' by your gunmaker."

(1) Small Ferlach-type hammer with small hammer spur. (2) Sculptured (fassioniert) *hammer. (3) Belgian hammer for inexpensive guns. (4) Early sculptured hammer. (5) Lever or pressure hammer. (Installed as a replacement, the lever hammer was meant to eliminate the possibility of a hang-up on branches and bushes.)*

At left, inside hammers (strikers) of a Collath shotgun showing firing pins and retainers (Schlagbolzen).

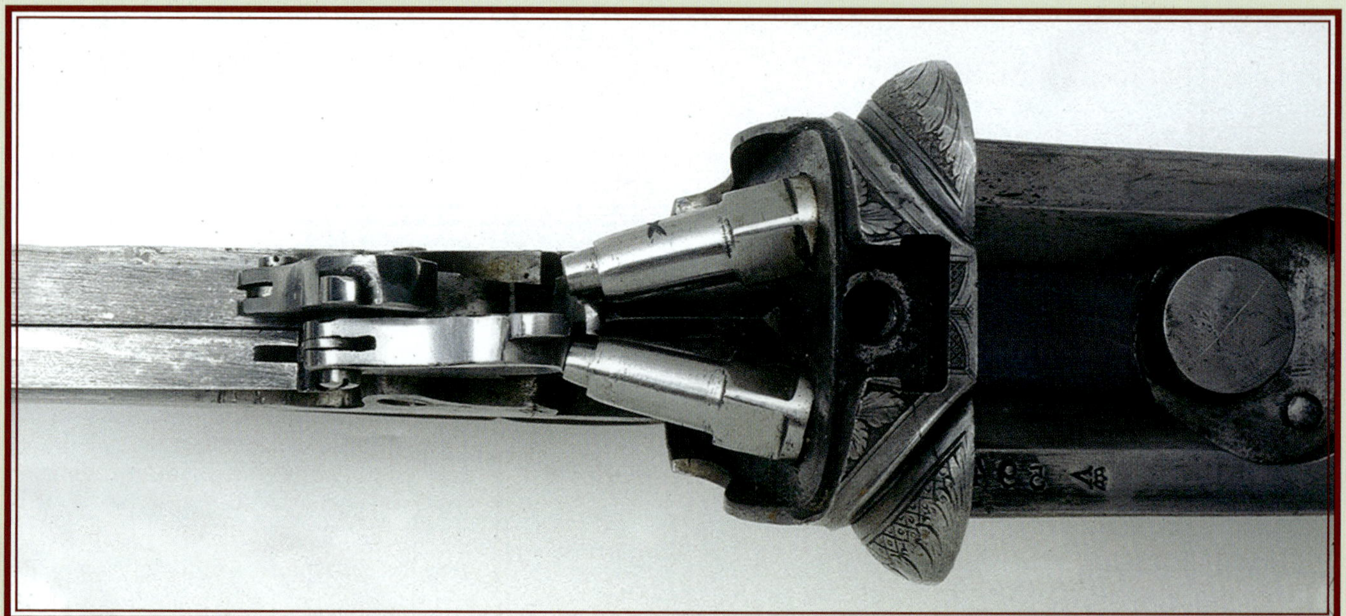

At right, an early Collath firearm with the firing pins connected directly to strikers (Schlagstücke); *on later models, retainers and pins could be unscrewed and replaced as a unit.*

On the left, a manual hammer mechanism for the rifle lock mounted on the trigger plate.

On the left and below, two half-hammer sidelocks with selective automatic or hand cocking.

Some sportsmen wanted the choice of cocking and decocking their firearms manually but also insisted on a self-cocking design when the breech was opened. Side-by-side shotguns, double rifles, and drillings of superb quality were available with this feature from several makers.

Half-hammer guns were promoted by makers W. Brenneke, Suhl, and G. Fükert, Weipert. They featured interior hammers with outside spurs that did not interfere with the shooter's line of sight.

Strikers on the trigger plate of a Blitz action vierling.

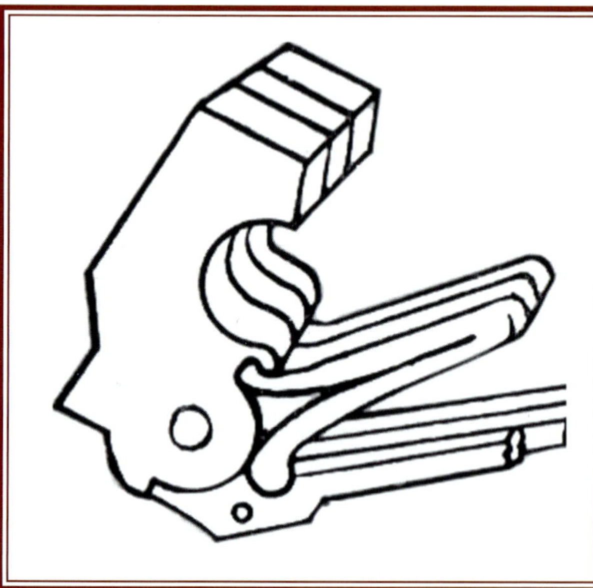

Blitz action striker arrangement on a Collath double-barrel shotgun.

At left, hammer leaf springs on a Stendebach shotgun with side-swinging barrels. The coil spring retracts the Roux underlever.

Stendebach system.

Note the two spring-loaded indicator pins extending through the top tang plate.

Selector Designs

Most hammer drillings with Jones underlever, sidelever, Roux, or locking levers under the fore-end featured a top lever to select either the shot barrels or the rifle barrel. The movement of the top lever to the left positioned a square transfer bar in front of the right hammer. The inside surface of the hammer was designed to fire the rifle barrel without the hammer face touching the shot barrel firing pin.

Top selector on Sauer sidelever drilling.

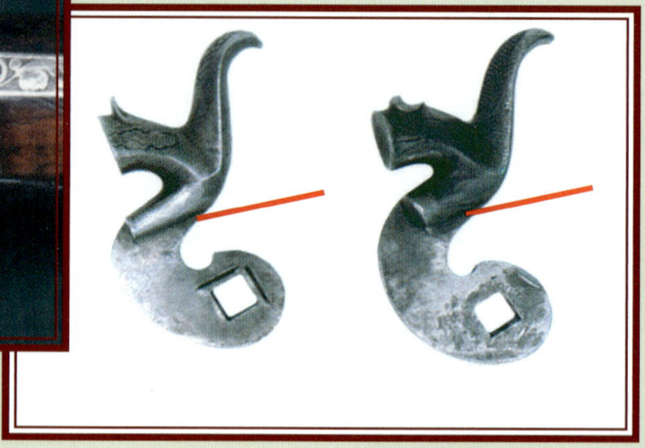

Inside bosses of right-hand drilling hammers.

At left is a G. L. Rasch drilling with a Roux lockup. The top lever is in line with the tang, and the left and right shot barrels are ready to fire.

At right, the top lever was moved to the left, and a transfer bar moves between the hammer and the firing pin of the rifle.

This shows a sliding selector on a Thieme & Schlegelmilch hammerless drilling. The front trigger on most drillings operates the rifle barrel or the right shot barrel; on some models the rear trigger is used to fire either barrel. By depressing the round knob on this model, the slide is arrested in either position to prevent unintentional movement.

This photo is of a Collath selector. Top lever hammerless drillings featured a sliding barrel selector on the tang; on some models this was combined with the safety. Other designs employed a top lever with dual functions: a move to the right opened the action and a move to the left actuated the rifle barrel. The selector fitted into the trigger guard on hammerless Collath drillings.

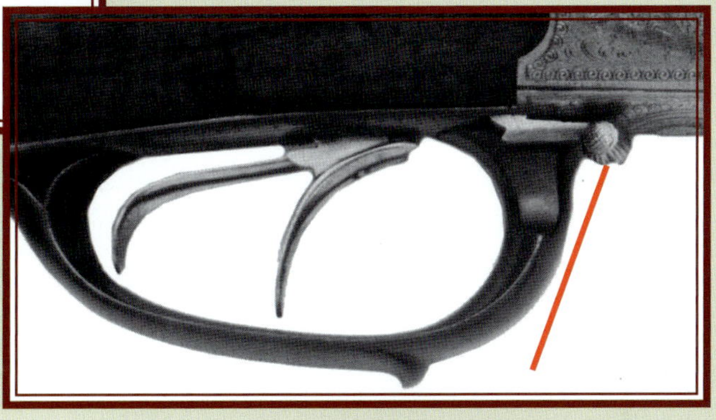

Ball or bullet (Kugel). *Some guns show the initial "K."*

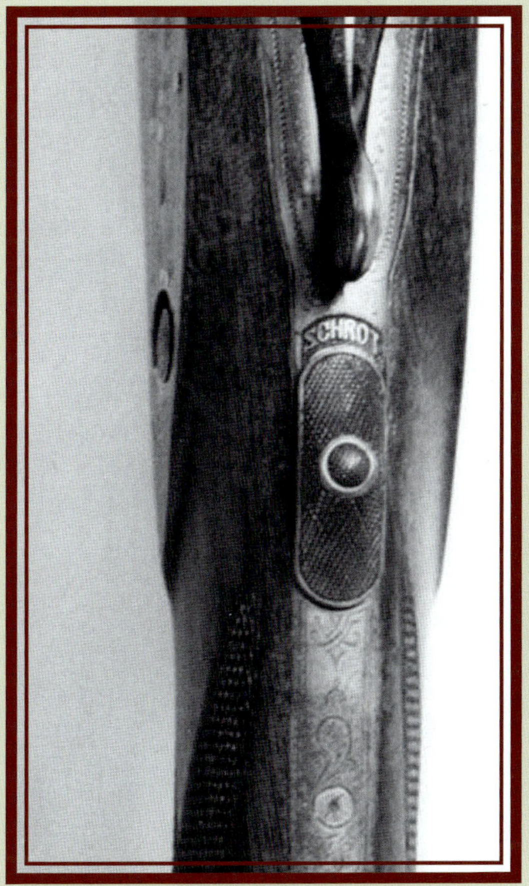

Shot (Schrot). *Some guns show the initial "S."*

Craftsmanship and Custom Work

The era when a firearm was made entirely by hand from start to finish has long since gone. In the past, the armorer or gunsmith in the employ of a sovereign was responsible for keeping the arsenal well stocked with edged weapons and firearms. He also had the important task of safekeeping military weapons, materiel, and gunpowder stored in an arsenal or magazine *(Zeughaus).* Leaving menial tasks to be performed by helpers, some armorers were able to concentrate on crafting hunting arms and armor for their masters. Months or even years spent on creating and embellishing a single weapon was not unusual.

When gunmaking established itself as a separate craft due to the increase in the use of firearms, gunsmiths attained more freedom to furnish hunting and sporting arms to a larger circle of aristocrats and citizens. The independent gunmaker initially made a gun by himself in its entirety but became conscious of the time and cost involved in building a firearm. He understood the need to delegate certain work to specific employees or to outside artisans, recognizing their special skill and ability to furnish quality parts within a specified time.

Many barrel makers, stockmakers, metal workers, and suppliers settled around gunmaking centers such

This photo shows Sauer employees blocking out, inletting, and finishing walnut in the stock-making shop in Suhl.

Gunmakers and facilities of large gun factories are occasionally shown in old manufacturers' catalogs, but photographs of small gun shops around the turn of the twentieth century are rare. Pictured above is the gun shop of Louis Knappworst in Braunschweig, circa 1908. He stands in the doorway, and to his right are his small son Georg and an employee.

This is the same shop, approximately ten years later with window displays of sporting arms, shells, and a variety of hunting accoutrements. Knappworst stands with his hunting dog Roland at his side. Also pictured is son, Georg, who had become a gunmaker's apprentice in his father's shop.

as Suhl in Germany, Ferlach in Austria, and Liege in Belgium. These areas also attracted silver- and goldsmiths, engravers, and any number of gun-related enterprises. Gunmakers and factories were supplied with parts and accessories by a number of producers and subcontractors—for example, certain companies specialized in importing, forming, and finishing buffalo horn for use as pistol grips, butt caps, trigger guards, and stock ornaments.

On break-open hunting arms, locks had to function flawlessly. The action had to be hand honed to such close tolerances that the breech closed with an audible sucking sound. Additional time and effort lavished on the smallest screw and bolt accounted for the higher price

Freehand Target Club "TELL," which was founded in 1885, is still in existence.

Paul Ernst Merkel at his workbench.

of these "fine guns." Custom work done by engravers, goldsmiths, and wood carvers often took months to design and complete, adding to the final cost.

The gunsmith's responsibility lay in the supervision of the final assembly of components into the finished product. To protect his name and reputation, each firearm was thoroughly tested and inspected before it left his shop. Although many operations became more and more automated, the fitting of parts and their interplay with each other were still a matter of handwork. Specialists with decades-long experience fine-tuned actions and systems, soldered barrels, and fitted claw mounts. Factories, which used any number of identical parts for their less-expensive models, also took orders requiring a large amount of hand fitting when a customer requested certain features on his gun.

In contrast to some larger gunmakers in the United States that sold relatively few models in large quantities and maintained custom shops for special orders, most small Continental gunmakers built or ordered arms according to their customers' requirements. These ranged from the selection of a specific caliber combination, shape of a stock, or the installation of any number of additional features.

Larger Continental manufacturers offered hundreds of varying features. A few arms dealers published catalogs emphasizing many different models. However, unless the gunsmith kept a specific model in stock, each arm was ordered and custom-built to the customer's specifications. Most medium-size gun manufacturers relied on outside suppliers to furnish barrels, locks, assemblies, and furniture.

The average regional gunsmith lived and worked in a small town or village, selling guns of his own design or guns offered by a larger manufacturer. He made repairs, installed scopes, altered stocks, and provided numerous other services. The regional gunmaker knew the needs of his neighbors and fellow hunters. He counseled them on the selection of a new or used drilling, shotgun, or stalking rifle and advised them on caliber questions. He might take customers out into the field to pattern a shotgun or sight-in a rifle if a shooting range was not available. Most *Büchsenmachers* were hunters themselves, active in the local gun or target club *(Schützen Verein)* or shooting associations.

In the gun shop of Waffen-Frankonia in Würzburg, a company founded in 1907, experts are at work building custom firearms or making necessary repairs.

Preparation of a set of O/U barrels prior to blueing.

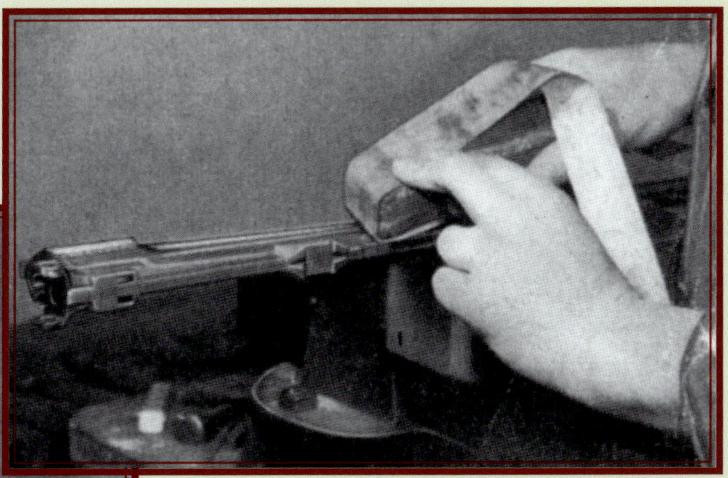

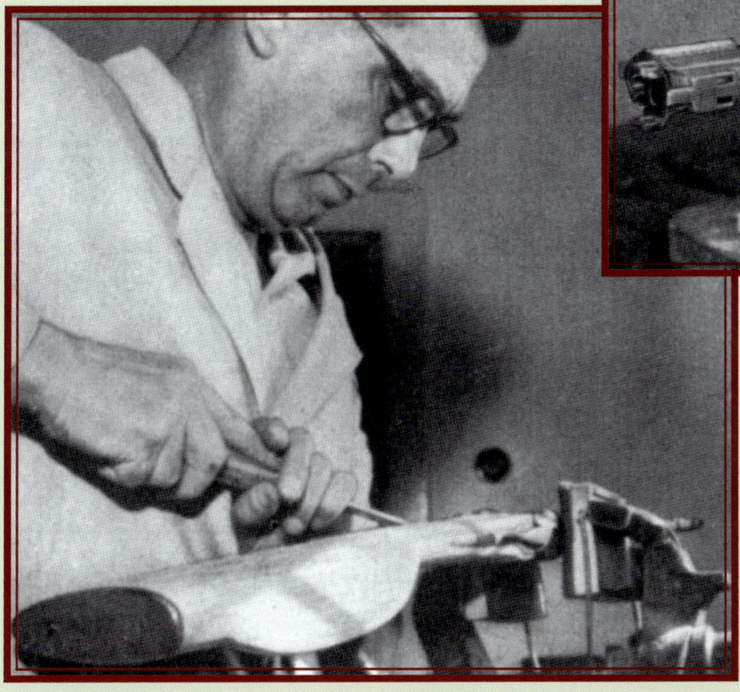

A craftsman is cutting and shaping the lockplate opening on a shell-shape stock (Muschel-schaft), *custom-made for a client with wide facial features.*

Waffen tips

Tools, typewriters, and bicycles were a few items that gunmakers produced during economic hard times.

The Importance of Testing Stations

In the latter part of the nineteenth century, there existed no established guidelines for gunmakers to adhere to when they advertised their products. The absence of any norms led to inflated, incorrect, or misleading claims by gun manufacturers about the performance of their products, and this lack of standards caused confusion among sportsmen and customers. In 1899, some two hundred hunters and sportsmen residing in or around Berlin founded an association whose aim was the establishment of a center where sporting arms could be performance tested. This new organization called *Deutsche Waffen Versuchsanstalt* (DEVA) (German Testing Facility) tested guns, related products, and accessories. In 1900, a similar nonprofit institute, the *Neumannswalder Waffen Versuchsstation* (Neumannswalder Testing Facility), was founded in Braunschweig by the publisher of the popular hunting periodical *Wild und Hund* (Game and Dog).

The newly founded centers or testing stations were extensively used by gunmakers and the public. They played an important role at a time of rapid improvements and innovations in gun technology. For a nominal fee hunters, shooters, dealers, gunmakers, or other interested parties could have their arms inspected for flaws, checked for wear, and tested for performance at these independently operated facilities. A record of the examination, entered into a small booklet complete with targets, accompanied each weapon when it was sold. The new owner had to scrutinize the overall condition of the gun, but the test assured him of its capability in the field.

Today these testing associations have reemerged and are active in providing answers for shooting and gun-related questions, analyzing newly developed ammunition and materials in test barrels, and providing an array of services to the hunter, sportsman, and gun enthusiast.

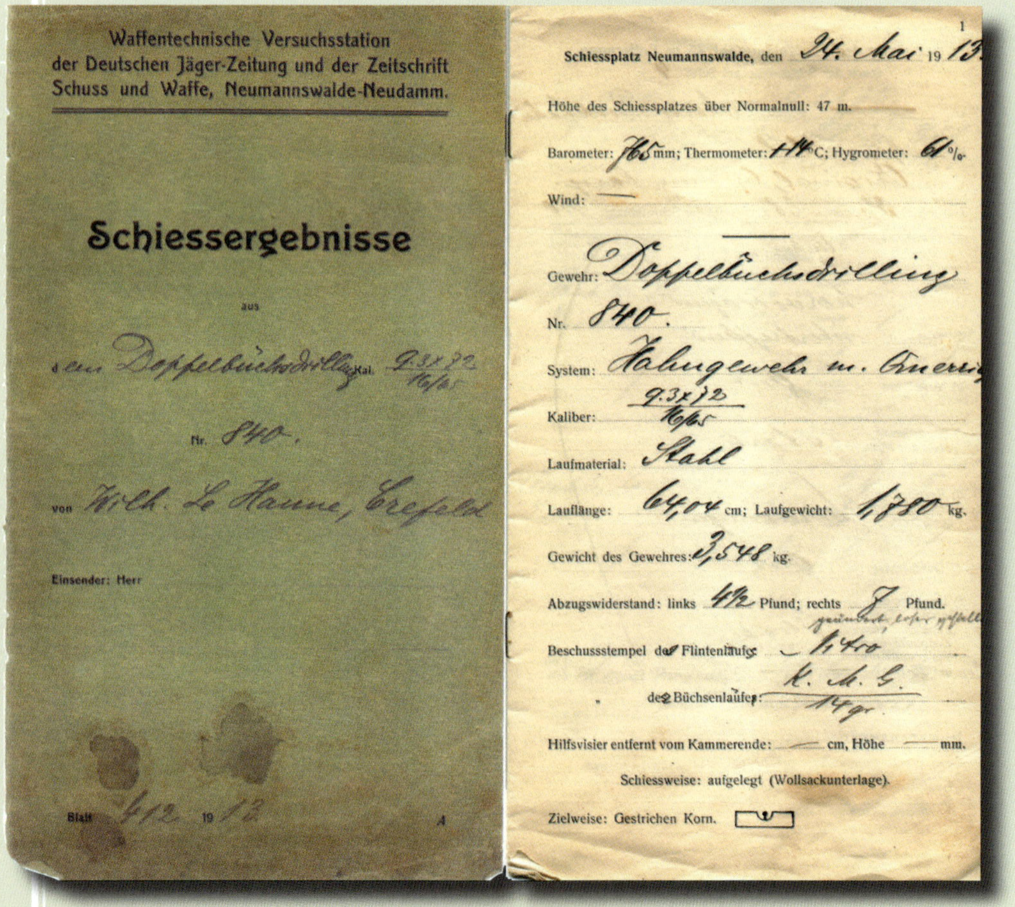

Results of a test on a double-rifle drilling (Waffenpass).

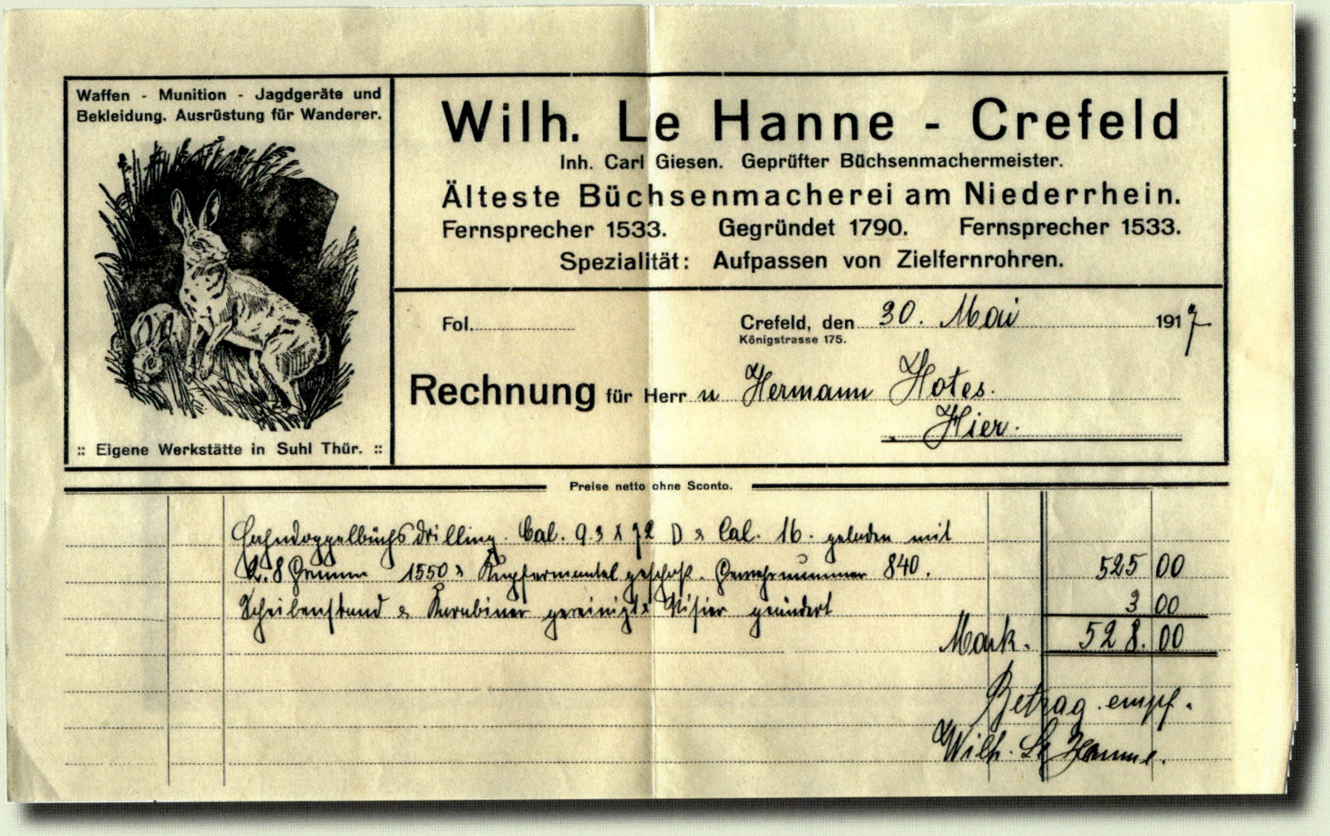
Waffen - Munition - Jagdgeräte und Bekleidung. Ausrüstung für Wanderer.

:: Eigene Werkstätte in Suhl Thür. ::

Wilh. Le Hanne - Crefeld

Inh. Carl Giesen. Geprüfter Büchsenmachermeister.

Älteste Büchsenmacherei am Niederrhein.

Fernsprecher 1533. Gegründet 1790. Fernsprecher 1533.

Spezialität: Aufpassen von Zielfernrohren.

Fol. Crefeld, den 30. Mai 1917

Königstrasse 175.

Rechnung für Herrn Hermann Hotes.

Hier.

Preise netto ohne Sconto.

...	525 00
...	3 00
Mark	528.00

Betrag empf.

Wilh. Le Hanne.

Bill of Sale

On 30 May 1917, the master gunmaker Carl Giesen, proprietor of the firm Wilhelm Le Hanne in Crefeld, sold a used double-rifle drilling to one Hermann Hotes, a resident of the same city. Including cleaning charges of 3 marks, the price for the gun came to 528 German marks or about the same sum in dollars at 1917 exchange rates.

The gun was accompanied by a performance test in the shape of a booklet, which included all pertinent data and the actual targets for all three barrels. This test was probably done at the request of the first owner four years prior in 1913. The accuracy of both rifle barrels out to 90 yards was a credit to the Garnierer, *the craftsman who "laid" and soldered the barrels.*

The performance test was performed 24 May 1913 at Neumannswalde, elevation above sea level 154 feet (47 meters). At the time of the test, the temperature was 58 degrees Fahrenheit (14 degrees Celsius), the atmospheric pressure was 765mm, humidity was 61 degrees, and wind speed was zero.

According to the above letterhead, this was the oldest gun shop in the lower Rhineland, founded in 1790. It had its own facilities in Suhl, and its specialty was the fitting of scopes.

Waffen tips

Ejectors for shot barrels on drillings were only available on special order.

PERFORMANCE TESTS

***Performance record**: double-rifle drilling* (Doppelbüchsdrilling)

Serial Number: 840 by Sauer and Sohn, Suhl

Cal: 9.3x72R, 9.3x72R – 16/65

Hammer gun with Greener crossbolt

Barrels: fluid steel

Barrel length: 25"(64.04 cm)

Barrel weight: 2 lbs, 15 oz (1,780 kg)

Gun weight: 3.55 kg

Trigger pull: left – 4½ lbs.

right – 7 lbs.

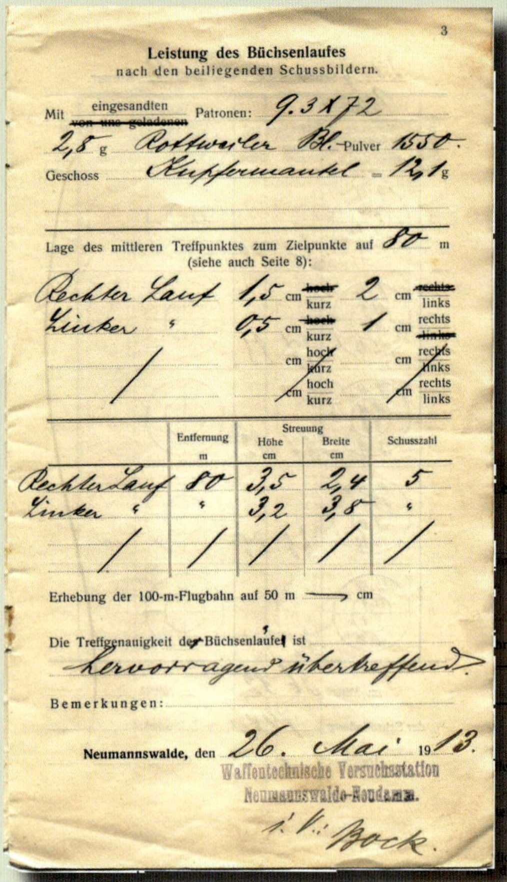

Leistung des Büchsenlaufes
nach den beiliegenden Schussbildern.

Mit eingesandten Patronen: 9.3x72
2,8 g Rottweiler Bl.-Pulver 1550.
Geschoss Kupfermantel – 12,1 g

Lage des mittleren Treffpunktes zum Zielpunkte auf 80 m (siehe auch Seite 8):

Rechter Lauf 1,5 cm kurz 2 cm links
Linker 0,5 cm kurz 1 cm rechts

	Entfernung m	Streuung Höhe cm	Streuung Breite cm	Schusszahl
Rechter Lauf	80	3,5	2,4	5
Linker	"	3,2	3,8	"

Erhebung der 100-m-Flugbahn auf 50 m —— cm

Die Treffgenauigkeit des Büchsenlaufes ist hervorragend überhoffend.

Bemerkungen:

Neumannswalde, den 26. Mai 1913.
Waffentechnische Versuchsstation Neumannswalde-Neudamm.
i. V.: Bock.

Performance of rifle barrels.

Apparently the 7-pound trigger pull had been changed according to the penciled notation on the weapon's performance record (Waffen Pass).

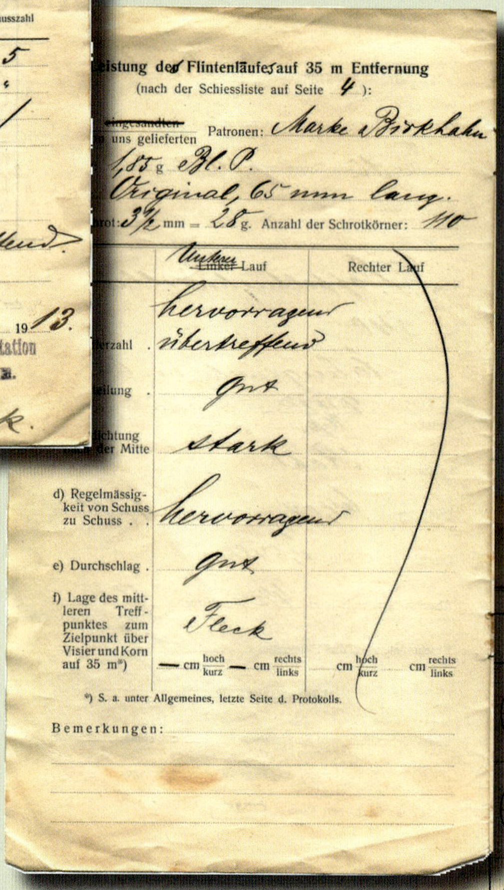

Leistung des Flintenlaufes auf 35 m Entfernung
(nach der Schiessliste auf Seite 4):

Patronen: Marke Birkhahn
1,85 g Bl. P.
Original, 65 mm lang.
Schrot: 3½ mm – 28 g. Anzahl der Schrotkörner: 110

	Linker Lauf	Rechter Lauf
	hervorragend	
...zahl	überhoffend	
...eilung	gut	
...ichtung der Mitte	stark	
d) Regelmässigkeit von Schuss zu Schuss	hervorragend	
e) Durchschlag	gut	
f) Lage des mittleren Treffpunktes zum Zielpunkt über Visier und Korn auf 35 m*)	Fleck	

*) S. a. unter Allgemeines, letzte Seite d. Protokolls.

Bemerkungen:

Performance of shot barrel.

Proof mark on shotgun barrel: Nitro

Proof marks on rifle barrels: KMG/14 grams (Kupfermantel Geschoss 14 grams—copper jacketed bullet/216 grains)

The gun was test shot with 187-grain (12.1 grams) bullets using 43.2 grains (2.8 grams) of Rottweil powder 1550 at 87 yards (80 meters) for the rifle barrels.

The results were excellent with 2-inch groups for both barrels. The shotgun barrel was patterned at 38 yards (35 meters) using Birkhahn shells with excellent results and good distribution, penetration, and strong density.

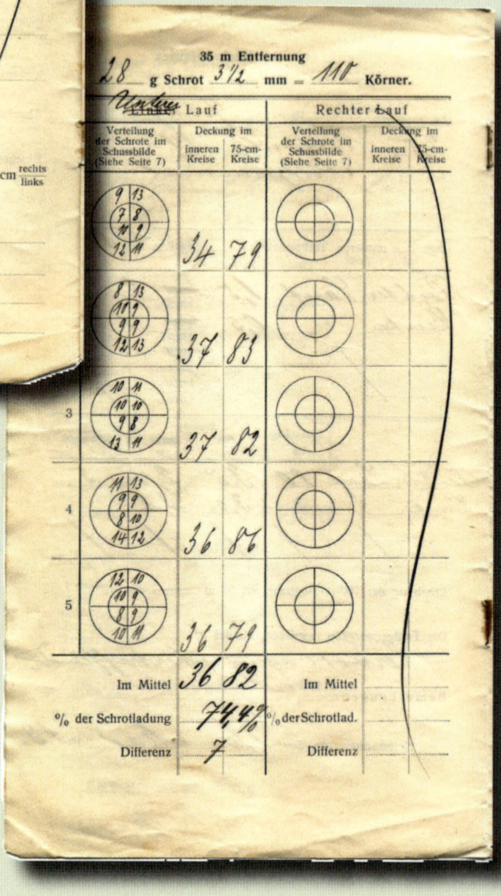

35 m Entfernung
28 g Schrot 3½ mm – 110 Körner.

	Linker Lauf Verteilung der Schrote im Schussbilde (Siehe Seite 7)	Deckung im inneren Kreise	Deckung im 75-cm-Kreise	Rechter Lauf Verteilung der Schrote im Schussbilde (Siehe Seite 7)	Deckung im inneren Kreise	Deckung im 75-cm-Kreise
		34	79			
		37	83			
3		37	82			
4		36	86			
5		36	79			
Im Mittel		36	82	Im Mittel		
% der Schrotladung		74,4%		% der Schrotlad.		
Differenz		7		Differenz		

Pattern of shot barrel.

Five rounds fired through left rifle barrel at 87 yards.

Five rounds fired through right rifle barrel at 87 yards (80m).

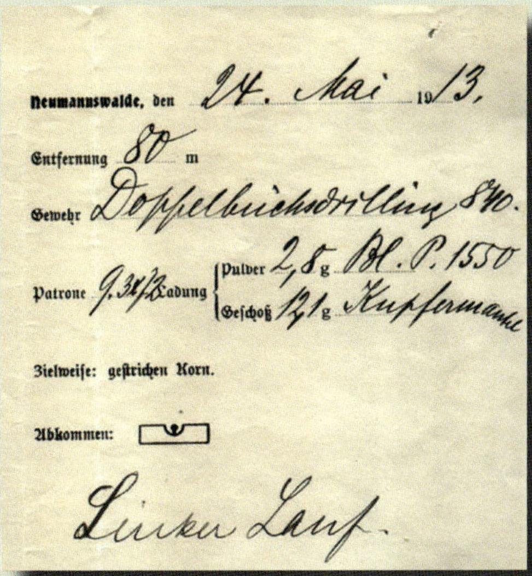

Neumannswalde, den 24. Mai 1913.

Entfernung 80 m

Gewehr Doppelbüchsdrilling 840.

Patrone 9,3x72 Ladung {Pulver 2,8 g Bl. P. 1550
Geschoß 12,1 g Kupfermantel

Zielweise: gestrichen Korn.

Abkommen:

Linker Lauf.

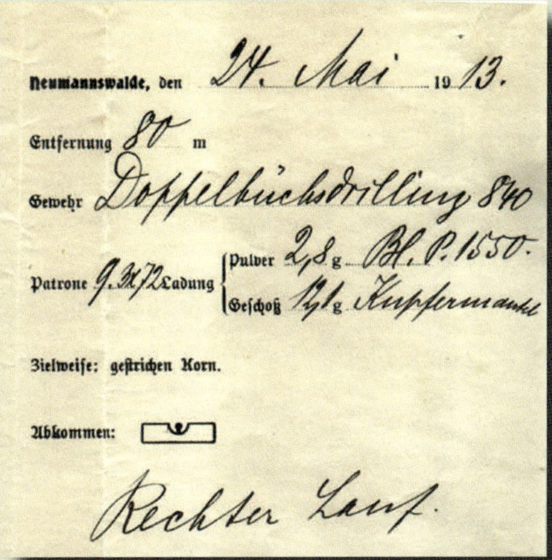

Neumannswalde, den 24. Mai 1913.

Entfernung 80 m

Gewehr Doppelbüchsdrilling 840

Patrone 9,3x72 Ladung {Pulver 2,8 g Bl. P. 1550.
Geschoß 12,1 g Kupfermantel

Zielweise: gestrichen Korn.

Abkommen:

Rechter Lauf.

Size of original paper targets was 18x18 inches. Size of black center was 6½ inches. Size of bull's-eye was 1½ inches.

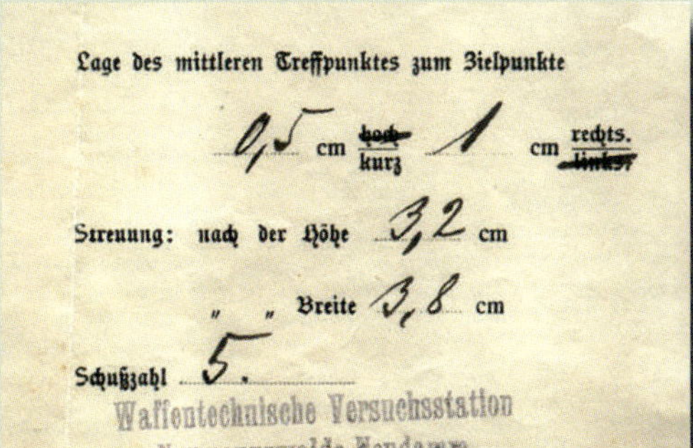

Lage des mittleren Treffpunktes zum Zielpunkte

0,5 cm ~~hoch~~ kurz 1 cm rechts. ~~links.~~

Streuung: nach der Höhe 3,2 cm

„ „ Breite 3,8 cm

Schußzahl 5.

Waffentechnische Versuchsstation
Neumannswalde-Neudamm.

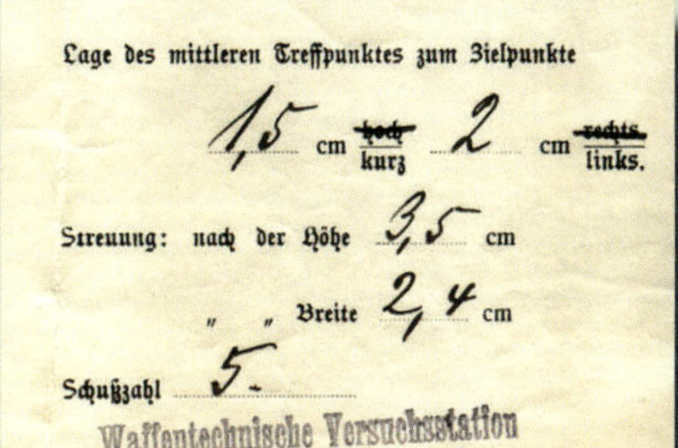

Lage des mittleren Treffpunktes zum Zielpunkte

1,5 cm ~~hoch~~ kurz 2 cm ~~rechts.~~ links.

Streuung: nach der Höhe 3,5 cm

„ „ Breite 2,4 cm

Schußzahl 5.

Waffentechnische Versuchsstation
Neumannswalde-Neudamm.

Gun Models

German and Austrian gunmakers borrowed names from mythology to identify makes or models, and to draw attention to particular features of their guns. Diana, the Roman goddess of the hunt, embodied the sportsman's ideal of hunting wild game and of protecting wild creatures and nature. Engraved scenes portraying Diana carrying a bow and arrows are found on many hunting arms. Several manufacturers used her name to designate their various models and accoutrements. Since 1890, the firm of Mayer & Grammelspacher offered its famous air rifles and target pistols under the Diana label.

Gunmakers also borrowed words from the German language. The word *Treff,* from *treffen* (to score) was given to many hunting and target rifles and accessories. In the Middle Ages, a herald (*Herold*) was an official or servant to a prince or sovereign. One of his duties was to announce the combatants at jousting tournaments for knights. "Herold" was the trademark of Suhl gunmaker Franz Jäger.

Suhl gunmaker Thieme & Schlegelmilch offered a Nimrod drilling that featured a special patented locking design. Nimrod, according to the Old Testament, was the son of Cush, known for his achievements as a "mighty hunter before the Lord." The term is generally used today to describe a dedicated, outstanding huntsman.

Waffen tips

Several regional gunsmiths developed ammunition for their own sporting arms and sold proprietary cartridges for these guns.

Jäger drilling, with Simson-Jäger lockup.

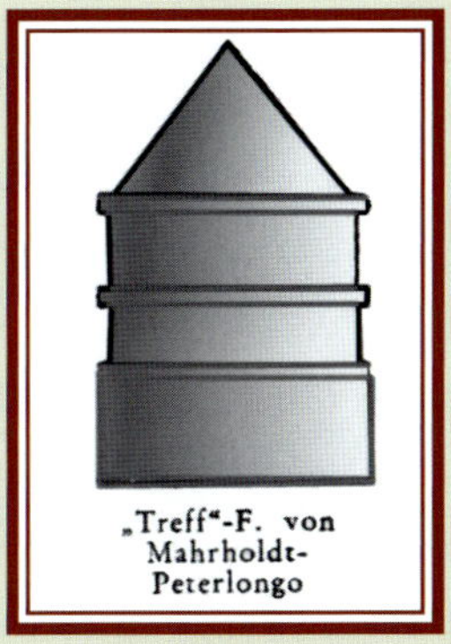

Shotgun slug designed by Austrian gunmaker Mahrholdt-Peterlongo, Model "Treff."

Drilling models were sold under various names by a number of gun manufacturers with logos such as: *"Perfekt,"* a safety drilling by R. Mahrholdt; *"Neptun"* and *"Triumpf"* by Sempert & Krieghoff; "Universal" by Franz Sodia; *"Imperator"* and *"Waidmannsfreund"* (hunter's friend) by H. Burgsmüller; *"Stresu"* by Franz Strempel; *"Waldläufer"* (woodsman) by Schmidt & Habermann; *"Krone"* (Crown) by Gustav Fükert; and *"Triumpf,"* "Venus," and "Sphinx" by gunmaker Oscar Will, Astoria.

Greif (griffin), *Herkules, Luchs* (Lynx), Ideal, Luna, Mars, Olympia, Original, Radial, *Rekord*, Tip-top, Venus, *Velo* (speed), *Zenit,* and a whole array of other labels and phrases were applied to air gun and air pistol models, target rifles, shotguns, and any number of accessories, actions, safeties, and scope designs to promote their sale. In the 1880 to 1930 time period, it was a common practice. In the succeeding years, numbers, letters, and more technical designations were preferred, as they are increasingly used today.

Trademarks

To prevent forgeries and to reassure their customers of a quality product, the German and Austrian steel factories of Krupp, Witten, Röchling, Poldi, and many others were required to emboss barrel blanks with their trademark. Imprinted "in the white" close to the chamber, these logos actually served as a legal document. Forgeries were treated as felonies. Over decades, signatures, etchings, stampings, and engravings on guns changed considerably due to changes in the artisans' or the public's taste, introduction of new materials, and the need of a manufacturer to keep records or symbols required by authorities. In addition to mandatory proof marks found on gun barrels and actions beginning in 1891, additional markings fell into separate categories:

1. Titles bestowed on makers by a sovereign
2. Identifying owners and companies
3. Production numbers and initials
4. Patent numbers and marks on barrels
5. Logos identifying a specific barrel steel
6. Inspection marks affixed by cities, states, and principalities *(Beschaumarken)*
7. Proof marks
8. Identifying signatures
9. Barrel and receiver marks
10. Signatures of makers and their hallmarks

The first part of this chapter deals with the above categories, and the end of the chapter shows the trademarks of various German and Austrian gun companies.

J. P. SAUER & SOHN / SUHL

MATERIALS FOR BARRELS.

The barrels of our guns are made exclusively of Krupp's fluid steel, Krupp's special gun barrel steel or Krupp's rustless "Nirosta steel."

The fluid steel barrels bear the inscription

"Fluss-Stahl Krupp, Essen,"

the special steel barrels bear the inscription

"Spezial-Gewehrlaufstahl" Fried. Krupp A.G., Essen

and the "Nirosta" steel barrels bear the inscription

FRIED.-KRUPP A.G. ESSEN

NIROSTA

Barrel logos in a J. P. Sauer & Sohn, Suhl, catalog.

TITLES BESTOWED ON GUNMAKERS BY A SOVEREIGN

Hofbüchsenmacher	Gunmaker to the court
Hofgewehrfabrik	Arms factory to the court
Hofgewehrlieferant	Arms purveyor to the court
Hoflieferant	Purveyor to the court
Königlicher Hofbüchsenmacher	Gunmaker to the king's court
K.u K. Kammerlieferant	Purveyor to the chamber of the royal courts of the Austrian empire and the Hungarian kingdom
K.u K. Hoflieferant	Purveyor to the court of the emperor and king *(Kaiserlich-Königlicher Hoflieferant)* of Austria
Hofbüchsenmacher se. Maj. d. Königs und Kaisers	Court gunmaker to his majesty, the king and emperor

IDENTIFYING OWNERS AND COMPANY DESIGNATIONS

The name of a gun manufacturer, gunsmith, or arms seller might include the word *Nachfolger* (successor), which indicated a change of ownership. After the death of a gunmaker, his widow sometimes continued the gun business to support her family and to provide for longtime employees. Taking advantage of the reputation of the original founder, current owners or proprietors retained the original firm name but added their name or standing to it.

Nachfolger	Successor
Witwe	Widow
Erben	Heirs
Gebrüder or Gebr.	Brothers
Sohn	Son
Söhne	Sons
Inhaber	Proprietor

Letters following company names designated their respective charter under German or Austrian laws. These letters were in reference to laws concerning liability, ownership, partnership, and stockholders.

A.G.	*Aktiengesellschaft*	Joint stock company
K.G.	*Kommanditgesellschaft*	Limited partnership
G.m.b.H.	*Gesellschaft mit beschränkter Haftung*	Limited partnership
Cie.	*Compagnie*	Company
Co.	*Company*	Company
O.H.G.	*Offene Handels Gesellchaft*	Company

PRODUCTION NUMBERS AND INITIALS

Barrel production numbers were stamped on the underside of barrels. On a drilling, they are found on rifle and shot barrels where they are covered by the forearm. One, two, or three initials of the barrel maker's name sometimes accompanied these numbers. Barrel table numbers are production numbers designating the caliber. They are at times mistaken for the proof date. The barrel number 11,8,35 does not mean the gun was proofed on 11 August 1935.

PATENT NUMBERS AND MARKS ON GUN BARRELS

Registered patent numbers preceded by the letters below can be found on the underside of frames, ahead or behind the trigger guard, or on barrel chambers. This was not a requirement by the state but gave notice that a patent had been issued for a specific gun action or feature. Gunmakers marked their firearms on the barrels or actions to show the patent numbers of several countries.

D.R.P.	*Deutsches Reichs Patent*	German patent (1871–1945)
D.R.G.M.	*Deutsches Reichs Gebrauchs Muster*	German utility or design patent (1871–1945)
Ges. gesch.	*Gesetzlich geschützt*	Design protected by law

INSPECTION MARKS

Prior to 1891, when proof marks became mandatory throughout the German empire, firearms were sometimes marked with a stamp required by one of the many independent states or municipalities in which the gun was made. Every gunsmith who lived and worked in the region or town had to have his guns examined and test fired by an inspector. This was required to assure the safety and quality of the arm and advance the reputation of the maker's locality.

Suhl 16th century

Suhl 17th to 18th century

Zella 18th century

Gotha 19th century

GERMAN PROOF MARKS

Decrees ordering the inspection of firearms by municipalities in central Europe date back to the fifteenth century. In 1891, Germany passed laws governing the uniform testing of all guns at government proof houses with increased powder loads. This was to protect users from cheaply made or faulty guns. Austria and Hungary passed similar laws the same year.

Barrels and actions were examined and measured during the test and, if passed, were stamped with proof marks. Foreign-made firearms fell under the same laws and were specially marked until 1914, when several European countries with similar test requirements agreed to honor each other's proof laws.

Germany maintained proof houses in Berlin, Suhl, Zella-Mehlis, Frankfurt a.d. O., and Oberndorf a. N. In Austria, different proof marks were in use for the gun manufacturing centers located in Ferlach, Vienna, Prague, Budapest, and Weipert.

1st proof mark—Prussian eagle for black powder

2nd proof mark—Prussian eagle and a U under a crown (Untersuchung *means examination)*

S — *Proof mark for shot barrels*

W — *Proof mark for choked shot barrels* (Würgebohrung)

G — *Proof mark for rifle barrels* (Gewehr)

E — *Proof mark for express rifles*

B — *Proof mark for finished guns* (Beschuss)

R — *Proof mark on barrels or actions after a repair*

S/W — *Proof mark for choked rifle barrels*

Nitro — *Proof mark for smokeless powder on shot barrel*

N — *Proof mark for smokeless powder on rifle barrel*

V — *Proof mark on guns that were in a dealer's inventory in 1891 when proof laws were first enacted* (Vorrat)

Stamping proof marks on barrels after test firing with increased loads.

PROOF MARKS OF THE AUSTRO-HUNGARIAN EMPIRE

Ferlach *Prague* *Budapest* *Weipert* *Vienna*

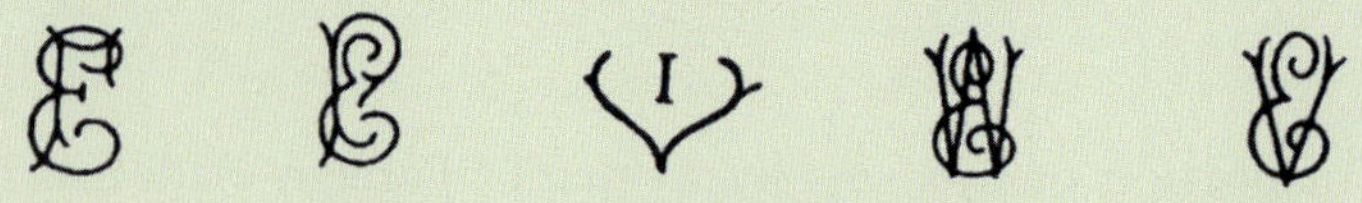

1st proof test

2nd proof test

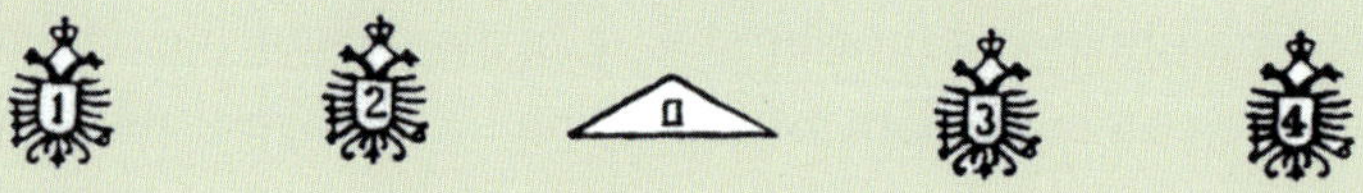

3rd and final proof test

Nitro proof

Proof for foreign-made firearms

Proof for increased load

Proof for firearms in dealers stock in 1892 (Vorrat)

BARREL ABBREVIATIONS

Kugel	Bullet
Nicht für Kugel	Not for bullet (rifle)
K. M. G. (KmG) Kupfermantel Geschoss	Copper-jacketed bullet
St.M.G. (StmG) Stahlmantel Geschoss	Steel-clad bullet
B. G. Bleigeschoss	Lead bullet

VARIOUS SMOKELESS (RAUCHSCHWACH) POWDERS USED FOR PROOF TESTING

SchP	*Schulze Pulver*	Smokeless powder
GP	*Gewehr Pulver*	Rifle powder
BP	*Büchsen Pulver*	Sporting rifle powder
BLP	*Blättchen Pulver*	Shaped nitro powder
RP	*Rottweil Pulver*	Rottweil powder
JB	*Jagdbüchsen Pulver*	Nitro powder for hunting arms

IDENTIFYING SIGNATURES AND GUILD GUNS

The custom of signing armor and arms by the majority of Continental metalsmiths and, later by gunmakers, goes back for centuries. A weapon could be either identified by the maker's hallmark, his initials in conjunction with his seal, or by his signature. On older guns, a barrel might be inscribed with the barrel-maker's name. On the same weapon, a gunmaker could sign his name on the lockplate, on the edge of the lock, or inside the lockplate.

Signatures included first names or initials in addition to the last name, and often the village, town, or city where the gun was made. In the case of identical place names, a region, river, or other geological feature was also included: "Frankfurt am Main" or "Frankfurt an der Oder." Place names that were preceded by the letter "A" or "An" (German for "at") as part of a signature on older gun barrels indicated that the gunsmith was not allowed residency in a given town or city. Because he was not granted citizenship, usually for religious reasons or guild restrictions, he had to work outside city limits in a suburb or village that was not well known. By substituting "An" for "In," he could still use the recognized city name to promote his business.

Inscriptions on barrels of most guns were read from the right, as is the case with most English sporting arms today. On German and Austrian firearms beginning in the late 1800s, signatures were positioned so they read from the left. Exceptions were the guns made by Kuchenreuter families. To this day, their barrel signatures are read from the right. Depending on the engraver, the script varied according to the maker's preference or fashion at the time. On more expensive firearms, the signatures were inlaid with platinum, gold, or silver. In some cases, it also included the title of the gunmaker bestowed on him by the reigning ruler.

With the onset of the industrial age, the practice of signing a firearm continued. The gunsmith, in most instances, no longer made the gun himself but ordered the sporting arm from a gun manufacturer. As the seller, he had his name engraved on the weapon and assumed responsibility for the arm, including making necessary alterations for his client and maintaining it after delivery.

Here we see a gold-washed master mark and silver inlaid script on the top flat of a single-shot rifle barrel by J. Christoph Kuchenreuter. This is either an early version of the Kuchenreuter name, or it was misspelled. Misspelled signatures and place names engraved on early firearms were common, depending on the knowledge or education of the craftsman or artist. With towns renamed and villages incorporated into larger cities over a span of decades, it is necessary to do research to determine the locality where the gunsmith once earned his livelihood.

This silver-inlaid signature is on the rib of a double rifle made by Bartholomeus Jos. Kuchenreuter, jun (junior) of Regensburg.

This gold-inlaid inscription is on the rib of a double rifle made by G. Leute of München (Munich).

This gold and silver inscription is on a double rifle by G. A. Klingenschmidt of Würzburg.

This is a 16-gauge shotgun by Immanuel Meffert of Suhl.

The engraved signature on the top barrel flat of this single-shot rifle is by maker Schmidt & Habermann, Suhl.

This drilling was made by Thieme & Schlegelmilch, Suhl. Starting in the 1890s, the law required every German gunmaker or gun trader who imported a firearm from a foreign country to have his name appear on the gun before it could be sold.

This drilling was made by Christoph Funk, Suhl.

Stamped signature identifies a J. P. Sauer drilling and is stamped with an early logo: Dreiläufer *system (three-barrel system)*

In the United States, German firearms without identifying marks or the maker's signature were referred to as "guild guns," a generic term for unmarked weapons. Since most gunmakers in Germany belonged to a guild or to a gunmakers' association, every unmarked firearm was a "guild" gun, for want of a better name.

In times of a temporary lull in business or declining orders, Continental gunmakers kept their experienced, highly specialized employees busy crafting unmarked sporting arms in popular configurations and calibers. These guns were produced in various price ranges, from the elaborate to the plain everyday weapon of the forester or farmer. The degree of finish depended on the clientele of a specific gunmaker.

When a new order was received, it was filled from stock on hand, sometimes with minor alterations. At that time a flat panel on the rib was engraved with the name of the maker or the name of the selling gunsmith, if requested. Because many customers were only interested in the performance of their newly acquired guns, they did not care if a signature was affixed to the firearm since they knew and trusted their gunsmith. After the weapon was handed down in the family and eventually sold and resold, the identity of the maker was often lost. Phrases like *Suhler Fabrikat* (of Suhl manufacture), *Ferlacher Fabrikat* (of Ferlach manufacture), or *Wiener Schule* (in the manner of Vienna gunmakers) were used to ascertain where a gun was made.

BARREL AND RECEIVER MARKS

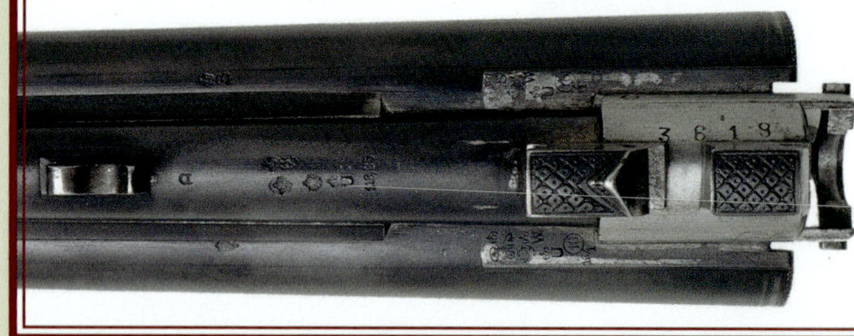

Sauer & Sohn Drilling

Serial number: 3619
Caliber: 9.3x72R, 16/16
W – choke bore
U – 2nd and final black-powder proof
118/85 – rifle barrel table (gauge) number
A – barrel maker's initial

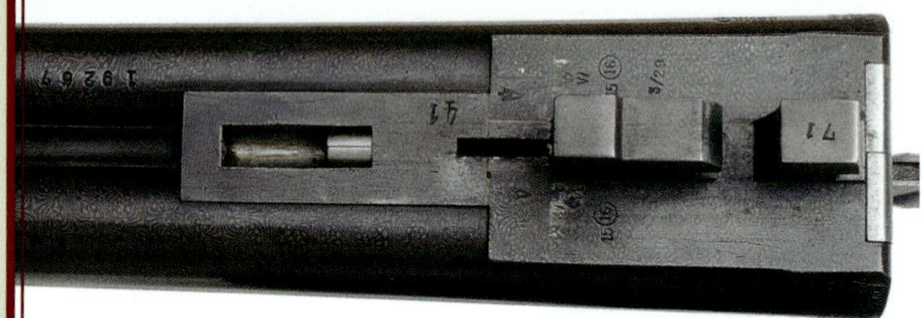

Meffert Side-by-Side Shotgun

Serial number: 19267
W – choke bore
16-gauge, nitro proofed Damascus steel
U – 2nd and final black-powder proof
R – repair, marked on top of barrels
V – the gun was made before 1891, but not proofed until March 1929, probably at the time of repair.

R and U were marked on the barrels after these Damascus barrels were reproofed. (Reparatur *means repair;* Untersuchung *means examination.)*

Barella Double Rifle

Caliber 9.3x74R, (8.9 bore)
U – 2nd and final proof
N – Nitro proof
Proof date: January 1925
St.m.G. 18 gr. – steel-jacketed bullet, 18 grams
(The early marking of 72½ for that caliber was restamped with 74 by the proof house.)

Cape Gun (unsigned)

Caliber: 9.3x72 R/20 (21-gauge)
8.8mm bore
U – 2nd and final proof
Nitro proofed

Collath Side-by-Side Shotgun, 16-gauge

Serial number: 4435
Production number: 5946
Cal. 3 – gunmaker Collath used his own shot caliber designations (caliber 3 corresponded to 16-gauge)
V – stamped on guns in 1891 that were inventoried prior to that year

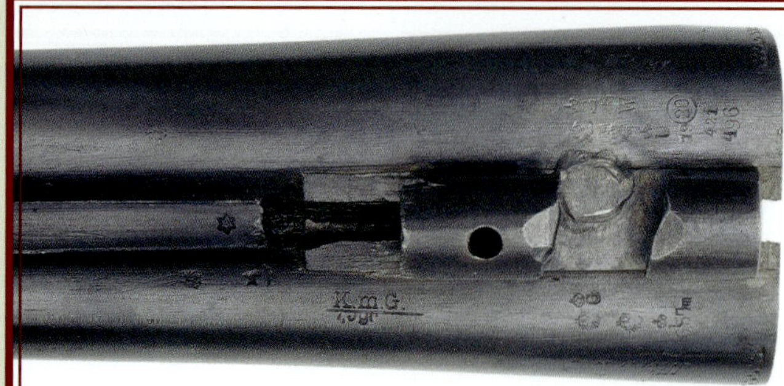

Geyger Caliber: 6.5 mm (6.5x52R – 25-35 W)

S – shot barrel caliber: 20 (19-gauge)
W – choke bore
G – rifled barrel
K.m.G. 7.0 gr. – 7-gram, copper-clad bullet

Collath Side by side Shotgun

Barrel number: 5946
N – Nitro proofed Krupp steel
S – barrel maker

Collath, O/U Rifle – Shotgun Combination

Caliber: C.16 – 8x58R (8x58$^{1}/_{2}$, old designation)
KMG 2 gr.: 1550 – 2 grams 1550 proof powder
St.m.G. – 12 g. – Steel-jacketed bullet 12 grams
Nitro proofed
TESCO – Collath trademark
P. S. – barrel maker's initials

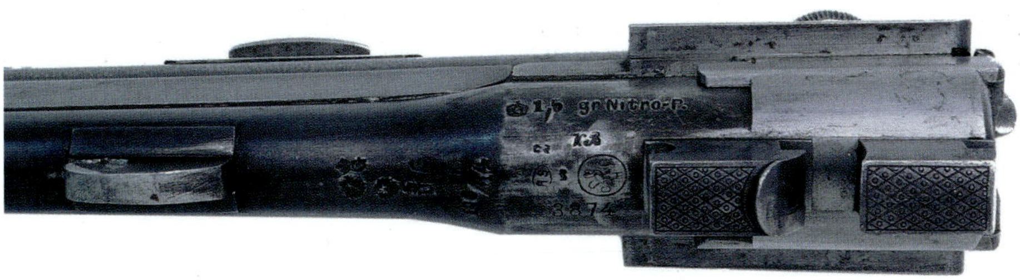

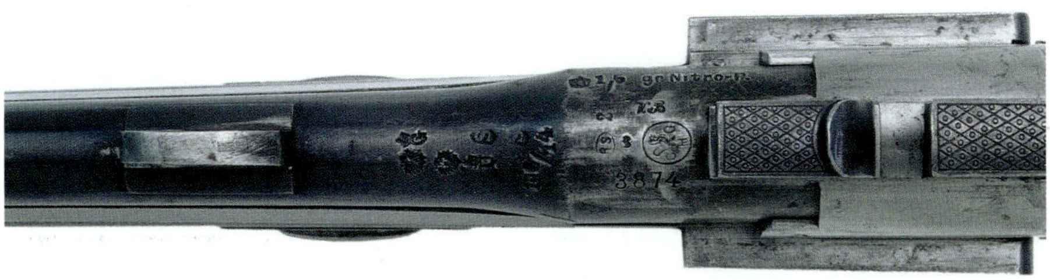

Geyger O/U Rifle/Shotgun Combination

Caliber: 8.15 x46R – (16/1)
Serial number: 3874
Nitro-proofed Damascus (1.5 gr. Nitro powder)
156/14 – barrel table (gauge) number
CGH – D. G. Haenel, Suhl, maker
G – rifle barrel proof

Sauer Rifle/Shotgun Combination

16-gauge	G – rifle-barrel proof
S – shot barrel proof	U – 2nd and final proof
W – choked barrel	N – Nitro proof
Cal: 9.3x72R – 16 (16/1 gauge)	118/35 – barrel table (gauge) number

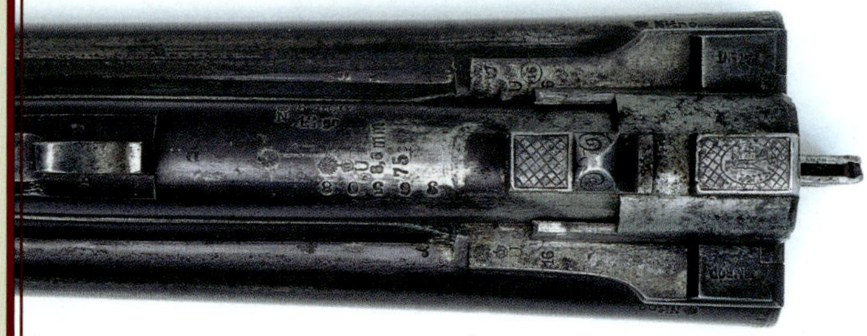

Thieme & Schlegelmilch Drilling

Caliber: 9.3 – 75R Nimrod (8.6mm/75) – 16/16
Serial number: 356508
Barrel serial number: 4803
J – barrel-maker's initial
W – choke bore
U – 2nd or final proof
NIMROD logo on underlug

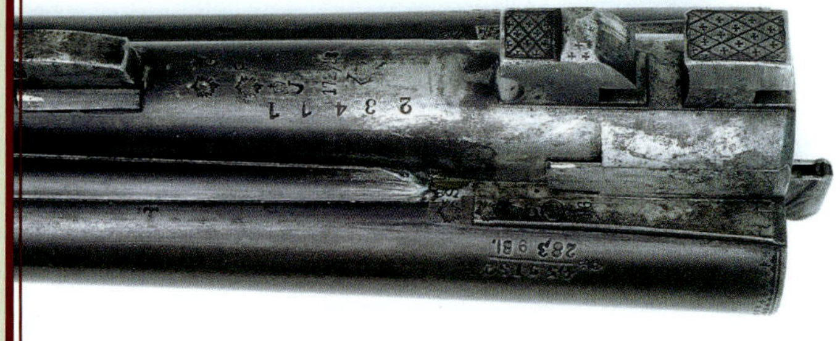

Thieme & Schlegelmilch Drilling

9.3x72R – 16/16
Serial number: 43411
Barrel number: 5258
172/28 – barrel table (bore) number
4.5 gr. TS 2 – 4.5 grams Troisdorf powder No. 2
28.3 gr.Gl. – lead shot

TRADEMARKS

Abesser & Merkel, Suhl, gunmaker

Adolph, Fred, Genoa, New York gunmaker ("If I rest, I rust")

Anschütz, JGA Zella-Mehlis, gunmaker

Anschütz, Udo, Zella-Mehlis, gunmaker

Becker & Holländer, Suhl

Behr's Waffenwerke GmbH, Suhl, gunmaker

Bergmann, Theodor, Gaggenau und Suhl

Berlin/Suhl Waffen-und Fahrzeugwerke, gunmaker

Bolte & Anschütz, Zella-Mehlis

Busch, Emil A.G., Berlin-Rathenau, optical manufacturer

Burgsmüller, Karl, Kreiensen, gunmaker

Burgsmüller & Söhne, Kreiensen am Harz (Harz mountains) gunmaker

Deutsche Versuchsanstalt für Handfeuerwaffen, Berlin, gun-testing institute

Deutsche Waffen und Munitionsfabriken A.G., Karlsruhe, ammunition maker

Deutsche Werke A.G., Erfurt

Dianawerk, Mayer & Gammelspacher, Rastatt

Eckholdt, Emil, Suhl, gunmaker

Franzoj, Johann, Ferlach, Austria, gunmaker

Funk, Christoph. Suhl, gunmaker

Gedaco, G. C. GmbH, Dornheim, ammunition maker

Geipel, B., GmbH, Erfurt, Saxony, gunmaker

Genschow, Gustav & Co., Berlin, gun and ammunition factory

Greifelt & Co., Suhl, gunmaker

Kennmarke :

Günther, Siegfried, Suhl, gunmaker

Haenel, C. G., Suhl, gunmaker

Hensold, H. & Söhne, optical manufacturer

Heym, Friedrich Wilhelm, Suhl, gunmaker

Hirtenberger Metallwaren A.G. Hirtenberg, Austria, ammunition maker

Jäger, Franz, Suhl, gunmaker, inventor

Kahles, Karl, Vienna, Austria, optical firm

Kerner, Ernst & Co., Suhl, gunmaker

Kiess, Fritz & Co., Suhl, gunmaker

Kommer, Theodor, Zella-Mehlis

Krausser, A., Zella-Mehlis, Waffenfabrik

Kriegeskorte & Co., GmbH, Stuttgart, gunmaker

Krieghoff, Heinrich, Suhl, gunmaker

Kuchenreuter, Michael, Cham, gunmaker

Langenhan, Fr., Zella-Mehlis, gunmaker

Mahrholdt, Richard, Innsbruck, Austria, gunmaker

Mauser Waffenfabrik, Oberndorf, gun factory

Menz, August, Suhl

ERMA – Erfurt

Gebrüder Merkel, Suhl, gunmaker

Moritz & Gerstenberger Waffenfabrik, Zella-Mehlis, gunmaker

Oigee Opt. Anstalt, GmbH, Berlin, scope manufacturer

Ortgies & Co., Erfurt

Paatz, Bernhard, Zella-Mehlis

Peterlongo, Johann, Innsbruck, Austria, gunmaker

Pickert, Friedrich, Zella-Mehlis, gunmaker

Gebrüder Rempt, (REMO) Suhl, gunmaker

Rheinische Metallwaren-und Maschienenfabrik, Sömmerda

Rheinisch-Westfälische Sprengstoff A.G., Nürnberg, ammunition maker

Röchlingstahl A.G., Völklingen, barrel maker

Römerwerk A.G., Suhl, gunmaker

Ruhrstahl, A G., Gusstahlwerk, Witten steel and barrel maker

Sauer, J. P. & Söhne, Suhl, gunmaker

Schilling, V. Charles, Hänel, C. G., Gaggenau-Suhl

Schmidt, E. & Habermann, Erfurt, gunmaker

Schmidt, Waffen-Schmidt, Suhl, gunmaker

Schüler, August, Suhl, gunmaker

Sempert & Krieghoff, Suhl, gunmaker

Simson & Co, Suhl, gunmaker

Sodia, Franz, Ferlach, Austria, gunmaker

Springer, Johann, Erben, Wien (Vienna), Austria, gunmaker

Stenda Werke, Suhl, Waffenfabrik

Steyr-Werke, A.G., Steyr, Austria, gunmaker

Teschner, G. & Co., Frankfurt/Oder, gunmaker

TirolerMaschienenbau und Holzindustrie, Kufstein, Austria

Venus Waffenwerk, O. Will, Zella-Mehlis, gunmaker

Vom Hofe, E. A., Berlin, inventor

Wienerwaffenfabrik, Vienna, Austria

Wahl, Albin, Zella-Mehlis

Walther, Carl, Zella-Mehlis, gunmaker

Weihrauch, Hermann, Zella-Mehlis, gunmaker

Westfälisch-Anhaltische Sprengstoff A.G., Berlin, ammunition maker

Zehner, Suhl

Zeiss, Carl, Jena, optical manufacturer

IN MEMORIAM

HANS E. PFINGSTEN (1937–2004)

Hans, in his all-too-short lifetime, was one who loved German guns and the traditions that accompanied them. Not only did he love them, he also studied them and shared what he learned with many others.

Hans was born in 1937, in Itzehoe, Germany, thirty-five miles north of Hamburg, the third child of Hans Leopold and Irmgard Pfingsten. World War II overshadowed his early years: the hardships a war brings, the firebombing of Hamburg, and the absence of his father, a captain in the German army. After the war in 1945, his father revitalized the family liquor business founded by Hans's great-grandfather in 1879.

Hans's interest in guns was nurtured in his childhood by hunting with his father and stories about his maternal grandfather, who held a high position in the forestry department under Kaiser Wilhelm II. When he was twelve, he found a discarded German machine gun buried in a ditch. He took it home and hid it in the attic. After cleaning it up and finding ammunition for it, he fired it into the attic floor for lack of a better place to shoot it. Although he tried to cover up the damage to the ceilings in the floors below, he did not get away with it. His father made him turn the gun in to the authorities.

At age seventeen, he began a four-year apprenticeship as an automobile mechanic and ended up working for Ford while restoring old cars on the side. In 1963, the twenty-six-year-old Hans came to the United States by ship; he brought only two suitcases with him. Although he had planned to stay for two years to learn English, the loss of his father shortly after his arrival and the great freedom he enjoyed in America changed his mind. He worked at different Volkswagen repair shops before opening his own in Garden Grove and later in Orange, California.

In 1969, Hans bought property in the high desert community of Morongo Valley, California, met and married his wife, Marcia, and began planting an oasis of trees. After weekending for nine years, the Pfingstens built a home and moved permanently to the desert with their two young sons. Within a couple of years, two daughters were added to the family. Hans worked with his father-in-law on mobile homes, and eventually he took over the business until his retirement in 2002.

Hans inherited his father's drilling and began collecting guns after arriving in the United States. He began buying and selling German and Austrian sporting arms in the 1980s and considered taking up gun engraving. Instead, he started writing about guns. In the 1990s, when he met his friend Bruce Hamilton, a graphic arts computer expert, he began writing in earnest. With Bruce's help, he put this volume together.

Hans Pfingsten died suddenly in 2004. This book was published posthumously through the effort of his wife, Marcia. His gunmaking friends Dietrich Apel, Larry Schuknecht, and Dick and Kathy Hummel kindly proofread and added valuable insights to the final copy.